Financing Politics

Financing Politics

Money, Elections, and Political Reform

Fourth Edition

Herbert E. Alexander
University of Southern California

A Division of Congressional Quarterly Inc.
1414 22nd Street, N.W., Washington, D.C. 20037

Printed in the United States of America

Library of Congress Cataloging-in-Publication Data

Alexander, Herbert E.
Financing politics : money, elections, and political reform / Herbert E. Alexander. -- 4th ed.
p. cm.
Includes bibliographical references and index.
ISBN 0-87187-691-4
1. Campaign funds--United States. 2. Campaign funds--Law and legislation--United States. I. Title.
JK1991.A6797 1992 91-46956
324.7'8'0973--dc20 CIP

Contents

Tables and Figures

Tables

Figures

Preface

Political money once again is being highlighted in the news. Not since the movement to reform campaign finance in the early 1970s has the role of money in politics commanded so much public attention. Journalists, political scientists, elected officials, and interested citizens are participating, perhaps as never before, in a lively exchange over the place and influence of money in election campaigns and legislative politics. This is a salutary development, for money serves as a tracer element in the study of political power. Whatever light can be shed upon transactions involving money illuminates the political processes, revealing important aspects of political behavior and improving understanding of the flow of influence and the use of power.

The fourth edition of *Financing Politics: Money, Elections, and Political Reform* provides the background and analyses needed for rational exchange and informed decision making. The book has been substantially rewritten and is not merely an update. Included are chapters on the 1988 presidential election and the 1988 and 1990 congressional elections. Discussed at length are new trends that generate publicity and controversy: the growth and influence of political action committees, the effects of independent expenditures, and the uses of "soft money." The evolution of the Federal Election Commission is examined and its impact analyzed, and recent developments in election campaign law and practice in individual states are described in detail. The text contains the latest information available and refers to the most significant recent studies of political finance.

Special thanks to Jennifer Knerr, senior editor of Westview Press, for permission to use materials, including tables, from *Financing the 1988 Election*. Some historical data are derived from my article "Financing Presidential Campaigns," in *History of American Presidential Elections, 1789-1968*, vol. 4, edited by Arthur M. Schlesinger, Jr., and Fred L. Israel. I appreciate the permission given by Chelsea House for use of materials from that article.

I especially thank Louis M. Peck, who was editorial consultant for this book. He conceptualized many of the changes and enthusiastically helped to implement them. Thanks also to Andra Armstrong and Suzanne

Holroyd. Gloria N. Cornette, assistant director of the Citizens' Research Foundation, always lightens my burdens and generously provides help and time in ways too numerous to list. She deserves special appreciation. None of those who were so helpful is responsible for errors of omission or commission; for them, as for interpretations, I bear sole responsibility.

Colleen McGuiness, project editor in the Congressional Quarterly Book Department, was especially helpful in her editorial suggestions and added immeasurably to the final product.

Without the contributions of numerous supporters of the Citizens' Research Foundation, this book would not have been possible. I appreciate the cooperation and encouragement received from officers and members of the board of trustees of the Citizens' Research Foundation, but the presentation does not necessarily reflect their views.

Financing Politics

1 Money and Elections

One of the more memorable phrases spoken in American politics during the past generation came from Jesse "Big Daddy" Unruh, the California kingmaker who served as speaker of the assembly and later as state treasurer. "Money," remarked Unruh, "is the mother's milk of politics."

More than twenty years have passed since Unruh said those words, and some think that the milk has soured. But the ensuing years have served to underscore, not diminish, Unruh's axiom. The issue of how American elections are financed is attracting more attention—and concern—today than at any time since the early 1970s, when the backwash of the Watergate scandal spurred reform at both the federal and state levels.

The disclosure requirements enacted in the wake of Watergate have forced campaigns to adopt detailed accounting practices, putting an end to the era when candidates receiving brown bags full of untraceable cash was common practice. Other Watergate-induced strictures, particularly contribution limits, have made it impossible for candidates to rely on a handful of "fat cats." This, in turn, has forced candidates to build broader fund-raising bases, reducing the potential leverage of any single contributor once a candidate has achieved office, but also taking more of the candidate's time.

What the post-Watergate reforms have not accomplished is to curtail the escalating amount of money cascading into American politics. In 1980, six years after the passage of the Federal Election Campaign Act (FECA) Amendments of 1974[1]—the most sweeping federal campaign finance law in U.S. history—total spending on campaigns at all levels had reached $1.2 billion. By 1988, that figure had more than doubled to $2.7 billion.[2]

In 1989-1990, spending in congressional elections was three and a half times as much as in 1975-1976, the first election cycle following the post-Watergate reforms. In some states, the increase has been even greater. In California, the nation's largest state, Democratic incumbent Alan Cranston and his Republican challenger spent a total of $23 million in a 1986 battle over a U.S. Senate seat—five times as much as what Cranston and the opposing candidate spent just six years earlier.[3]

Campaign finance reform has moved toward the top of the agenda in Congress and in many state legislatures not simply because of the sheer amounts being spent. Concerns also exist about the sources of this money. Reformers complain that the post-Watergate laws simply replaced large individual donors with new "special interest" contributors in the form of political action committees, or PACs. In addition, "soft money" entered the political lexicon in a big way during the 1980s, amidst charges that this practice is a circumvention of the law and an attempt by $100,000-plus donors to become once again players in the process. Soft money is raised and spent outside any contribution or expenditure limits of federal law but spent on state and local party activities intended in part to affect federal election outcomes.

Whatever the extent of actual corruption arising out of the current political finance system, a perception that the system is corrupt tends to undermine the confidence of rank-and-file citizens in the political process. In early 1990, a *Los Angeles Times* poll found that a majority of California voters believe the taking of bribes to be commonplace in the same state legislature where Jesse Unruh once held sway.[4]

In large part, this book will examine how political campaigns are financed, analyze the efforts that have been made to control abuses, and provide an outlook on future regulation. But this volume also will look beyond the current controversy to some of the basic underpinnings of the persistent debate over political money. Many implications arise from the ways in which American politics are financed, and they affect candidates from the White House to the courthouse—as well as the very nature of the two-party system that has evolved.

The vast amounts of money now being spent merely hint at the scope of the problem:

- What effect does money have on the ideal of equal opportunity to serve in public office? Or, put more bluntly, can candidates buy their way into office?
- Who contributes to political campaigns—and why?
- To what extent do actual or potential contributions influence the behavior of officeholders?
- What impact have the campaign finance reforms of recent years had on other aspects of the political system? Have they been desirable?
- What factors lie behind the skyrocketing costs of campaigns?
- Should—and can—the amount of money flowing through America's pluralistic democracy be limited?

Money is symbolic. The deeper competition is for power or prestige or other values. In this sense, money is instrumental, and its importance lies in how it is spent by people to gain influence, converted into other resources, or used in combination with those other resources to gain political power. Because of its universality, money also is a tracer element in the study of political power. Light thrown upon transactions involving money illuminates political processes and behavior and improves understanding of the flow of influence and power.

Splitting the Pie: The Distribution of Political Money

The $2.7 billion spent on elections in 1988—more than a third of which was expended by or on behalf of presidential and congressional candidates—is hardly small change. But is it excessive? When considered against the advertising budgets of the nation's largest consumer products manufacturers, or when balanced against how much is spent for chewing gum and cosmetics each year, the figure does not seem overwhelming. In a sense, it can be considered the cost of educating the American people on the issues confronting them. And given that hardly 50 percent of the eligible electorate bothered to go the polls in 1988, the case can be made that more, not less, needs to be spent on voter education.

The suggestion, however, is not that those concerned about the state of American political finance are alarmists. The problem is less one of the total amount of money being spent than how the money is raised and how the pie is distributed.

The American system is rooted in the assumption of political equality: "one person, one vote." But money, which candidates need to harvest votes, is not distributed equally. The substantial inequities of political financing have hindered the quest for political equality and have worried concerned Americans since the beginning of the twentieth century.

That worry has intensified as money has become indispensable to modern candidates—enabling them to buy advertising time, to pay pollsters and media consultants, and to perform the myriad other tasks involved in running for office in the 1990s. As the electorate expands but also becomes more dispersed, the development of communications media has made carrying on political campaigns easier. But it also has made them much more expensive than in the days of the Lincoln-Douglas debates or William McKinley's "front porch" campaign.

Skillful use of ideology, issues, and the perquisites or promises of office is what attracts financial support to political actors. Sometimes it comes in unethical or illegitimate forms, of which Watergate is the most notable example over the past generation. But most of the concern over today's campaign finance system involves contributions that are legal. The ever-broadening reach of government has given rise to a growing number of corporations, labor unions, and professional organizations that feel that a strong lobbying arm is the key to self-protection. In pressing their cases, they place further demands on the time of those who serve in Washington, D.C., and the state capitals. Consequently, these lobbies, with their political action committee arms, have been contributing heavily to incumbent legislators for "insurance" purposes—specifically, to guarantee that at least their phone calls are returned when a key issue is on the legislative agenda.

As lobbies and their political action committees have grown, a major shift has occurred in the ways in which money in the political system is distributed. According to the Federal Election Commission, incumbents outraised challengers by a ratio of about 2-to-1 in U.S. Senate races in 1989-1990; in House races, the margin was about 4-to-1. Part of the disparity can be attributed to PAC donation patterns: About 75 percent of PAC money given to congressional candidates goes to incumbents. But simply blaming the PACs is oversimplifying the problem.

With elections becoming more and more expensive, officeholders are raising money throughout their terms of office—not just in the election year. Former Senate majority leader Robert C. Byrd of West Virginia complained several years ago that the preoccupation with fund raising was interfering with the reason his colleagues were sent to Washington in the first place—to legislate. The result of incumbents hoarding money has been to put challengers, who often do not announce their candidacies until the year of the election, at a substantial disadvantage. But Byrd's complaint represents more: An institutional concern about the integrity of the U.S. Senate.

Leveling the Playing Field

The reform efforts of recent years, in addition to seeking to limit both real and perceived corruption, have attempted to smooth out the impact of political money—or, in current lingo, to "level the playing field." The basic concepts employed to put candidates on a more equal financial footing have included contribution limits, expenditure ceilings, and public financing. Some of the devices have worked well, some have brought unforeseen results, and others have run into constitutional problems.

The reform debate is hardly divorced from political self-interest. Just as money is not distributed equally in society, neither is power. Those in power—incumbents—have the ability to reform the political finance system. Power is a zero-sum game, and following naturally is that those who have power will be reluctant to enact changes that may force them to relinquish it. Throughout the late 1980s, Congress found itself in a stalemate over campaign reform largely because each major political party regarded the other's "reform" proposals to be little more than a self-interested attempt to protect or promote important sources of funding or spending. As Mitch McConnell of Kentucky, the Senate Republicans' point man on the issue, candidly observed: "Campaign finance is the rules of the game in our democracy, and either side would love to write the rules" in a way that benefits them to the detriment of the other side.[5]

In short, reform is not neutral. And when the rules of the game are revised, advantages shift and institutions change—sometimes in unforeseen ways. The rise of PACs at the federal level over the past generation can be traced directly to the changes made in the 1974 FECA amendments. Those changes were promoted by organized labor, which scarcely expected their archrivals in corporate America to benefit from the provisions to the extent they have.

The consensus among reformers and their supporters has been that democratic principles cannot be upheld in an atmosphere of unfettered campaign fund raising and spending. But before embracing the reform proposals put forth in recent years, several important questions must be put to their advocates:

- Will expenditure limits result in more or less communication between candidates and voters?
- Is voter turnout affected when expenditure limits reduce candidate opportunities to communicate with potential voters?
- Will government funding of campaigns be an opening wedge for control over various political activities?
- Do contribution limits and expenditure ceilings level the playing field or at least diminish incumbent advantage?

Does Money Win Elections?

Popular lore has it that the candidate who spends the most wins. On the surface, the record of recent elections seems to bear this out. On closer examination, the record is not so clear cut.

The concern over incumbents' lopsided fund-raising edge in congressional elections stems from the reelection rate in the U.S. House, which has been running at 96 to 98 percent in recent years. Some wags joke that unseating an incumbent member of Congress today is harder than ousting a member of the Supreme Soviet in the years before Mikhail Gorbachev took power. In state legislatures, where the incumbent fund-raising advantage may be even greater, reelection rates are regularly running at well over 90 percent. The advantages of incumbency, however, go beyond fund raising to increased visibility and taxpayer-supported staffs.

The presidential campaign also provides contradictory evidence on the relationship between money and victory. Because the presidential general election—in theory—is fully underwritten by public funds, Democrat Michael S. Dukakis and Republican George Bush had equal resources in 1988. But when soft money and other monies spent on behalf of the candidates are taken into consideration, more was spent by or on behalf of loser Dukakis than for winner Bush.

Money also can turn off voters. Frills, blitz campaigns, and wealthy candidates can create a backlash among the electorate. The record spending on the 1988 presidential races did not arrest the decreasing turnout of voters but produced the lowest in forty years.

Two recent Senate races, both involving very wealthy individuals, underscore this point. In 1988, in Wisconsin, multimillionaire Herbert Kohl, owner of the Milwaukee Bucks, outspent his Republican opponent by a ratio of better than 2.5-to-1. Four years earlier, Democrat John D. Rockefeller IV, scion of one of America's wealthiest families, outspent his West Virginia Senate opponent by a staggering 12-to-1 margin. Both Kohl and Rockefeller won, but narrowly, with 52 percent of the vote. In both races, the use of personal wealth to further their political careers became an issue.

Rockefeller's election, however, is an example of how, in a close race, money can make a difference. Rockefeller advertised heavily on Washington, D.C., and Pittsburgh television stations to reach voters in West Virginia's northern and eastern panhandles. The support he won in those areas may have saved him from political defeat.

While some historians doubt that the result of any twentieth century presidential race would have been changed had the loser spent more money, three contests during the past generation—Kennedy-Nixon in 1960, Nixon-Humphrey in 1968, and Carter-Ford in 1976—were decided by margins of 1 to 2 percent. Who is to say that an additional $200,000 here or $100,000 there would not have altered the outcome?

A number of factors can compensate for a shortage of cash. Low-budget candidates may be campaigning in areas predominantly favorable to their parties. They may be well-entrenched incumbents; Kohl's predecessor, William Proxmire, reported raising and spending precisely $0 in his 1982 reelection campaign and $697 in his 1976 reelection effort. Or candidates with few resources may be swept into office by a national trend or presidential landslide, although—with the exception of 1980—presidential winners have lacked coattails in recent years.

The candidate with more funding can find it all for naught if he or she makes some major mistakes and the opposing candidate is viable. The postmortems on the Bush-Dukakis campaign concluded that Dukakis was hurt badly by a failure to respond effectively to attacks by the Bush campaign. It was not that he could not afford to do so; he simply chose not to do so until it was too late.

Consider also the 1990 gubernatorial race in Texas in which millionaire Republican businessman Clayton Williams faced Democratic state treasurer Ann Richards. Williams was little known at the start. Like several other wealthy nonpoliticians in recent years, he raised his name identification and won his party's primary by spending heavily. But Williams, like others not accustomed to the political arena, had a proclivity for off-the-cuff remarks that offended significant groups of voters. While he started the general election as a heavy political favorite, and despite a $20 million campaign budget that far outdistanced Richards's spending, Williams came in second on election day.

The predispositions of voters, the issues of the moment, the support of various groups and the advantages of incumbency are all related to the final vote totals and often are more important than money. Independent decisions by the news media, particularly television, about what aspects of a campaign to cover can provide more exposure than advertising purchased by the candidates. Campaign schedules are now drawn up with a view to obtaining so-called "earned" media—in other words, free coverage on the national or local evening news programs.

But, if not decisive, money is at least capable of reducing handicaps for most candidates. No candidate can make much of an impression without it, especially a challenger who takes on an incumbent. Recent analyses of Senate campaigns have found that challengers do not need to equal or outraise incumbents to win. But they do need to reach a sufficient threshold of spending to be "financially competitive," allowing them to present their names, qualifications, and positions to the voters.

How Much Is Enough?

U.S. political costs tend to be higher than in some parliamentary democracies, where elections last for several weeks instead of several months or, as in presidential campaigns, several years. Moreover, unlike those countries where political parties receive free broadcast time on government-owned radio and television stations, the United States currently provides no certain free availabilities for its political candidates. Candidates and parties compete with each other not only for votes but also for the best time slots and space available to commercial advertisers—usually at a high price.

Cultural factors, however, do not begin to explain why even candidates with limited or nonexistent opposition feel compelled to accumulate huge campaign treasuries. To some extent, these activities are an effort to discourage potential opponents or to ensure preparedness should a well-heeled challenger suddenly emerge from the wings. Another reason candidates seem to raise and spend so lavishly is that little scientific evidence is available regarding the incremental value in votes of various levels of campaign spending. Perhaps half of all campaign spending is wasted. But no one knows which half.

Little research exists about the effectiveness of different kinds of campaign techniques. While few candidates are eager to pioneer with new techniques on their own initiative, they want to be prepared financially to follow suit if an opponent draws a new weapon in the arsenal. New variations of age-old techniques are constantly being developed. As an example, use of the print media has been enhanced by applications of computer technology, bringing increased use of direct mail that can be specially targeted to groups of potential voters and contributors. As opposed to the old days of envelope-licking volunteers, today's direct mail can be rapidly generated and addressed by computers. A quick response to events is possible from candidates whose districts do not conform neatly to local television markets. At the same time, these technologies and the consultants behind them drive up campaign costs.

Other new financial pressures are at work. Statutory spending limits in effect at the presidential level and in several states force campaigns to undertake vigorous cost-benefit budgeting of available resources. That may lead to the reduction or elimination of certain marginal activities, although no universal definition exists of what is marginal. This cost-benefit attitude also may explain the rise in so-called "comparative advertising," more commonly known as negative campaigning. A candidate often will receive more bang for the buck from a single critical ad that increases an opponent's "negatives" in public opinion polls than from a series of softer ads promoting his or her own virtues.

Finally, significant spending also stems from largely psychological motives. The candidate spends to quiet his or her anxieties (in most campaigns, plentiful), to stimulate workers, or to demonstrate viability to the media—which frequently handicaps races long before votes have been cast in primary and general election contests. Politicians often feel they must do something, anything, to keep the campaign going and morale high. The candidate's morale is bolstered by seeing his or her picture on billboards, posters, or television, and some campaign managers spend a considerable amount of money largely to keep a candidate from becoming overly anxious or discouraged.

Indeed, the costliest election is a lost one. But, to critics, the above-described factors have created the political equivalent of an arms race out of control. While straining the metaphor a bit, the blue-ribbon California Commission on Campaign Financing was largely on target in 1985 when it wrote:

> Candidates fear that opponents will outspend them, that first strikes will overwhelm them, that last-minute attacks will unseat them, and that innovations will make their contemporary weapons and defenses obsolete. Candidates turn to deterrence, the massive buildup of money and arms, for security.[6]

So many candidates these days are professional politicians—with no other assured livelihood—that their quest for job security may become paramount.

2 Pre-1972 Campaign Money

Significant restrictions on the raising and spending of campaign funds are a relatively new development in the two-hundred-year life of the American Republic. For the first half of that period, legal restraints on federal campaign finance were nonexistent. For most of the latter portion, the laws that were placed on the books were ignored or successfully circumvented. Finally, Congress enacted meaningful reforms in four laws in the 1970s. Prompted in part by the Watergate affair, the laws were not as successful in curbing campaign excesses as their sponsors had hoped. Nonetheless, those statutes put an end to a colorful—albeit often unscrupulous—era of political finance.

The Early Years

For the first several decades following George Washington's inauguration in 1789, the Federalists and the Jeffersonian Republicans were less political parties than factions; their members were in large measure landowners and merchants who considered politics an avocation rather than a career. Consequently, the presidential candidates themselves underwrote most of the costs of the campaigns, aided by assessments placed on officeholders or government employees.

But the system that evolved proved costly even for men of means, and only a few could afford to run. The presidency provided a low salary that did not begin to make up for the cost of seeking the office, and entertaining and other office-related expenses further taxed the chief executive's personal funds. Thomas Jefferson, scion of a Virginia family with extensive landholdings, found himself almost insolvent at the end of his second term as president in 1809.[1]

Andrew Jackson's legacy, in addition to democratizing the makeup of political parties and diluting the power of Congress through creation of the nominating convention, includes the "spoils system." Those who supported the new president were rewarded with government jobs and contracts. By the 1830s—when Jackson and Martin Van Buren were molding the modern political party—Democrats were levying regular assessments on government employees in the New York Customs House. Both parties relied on this practice, which lasted into the twentieth century and became a target for early civil service and campaign finance reformers.[2]

Twenty years later, the Democratic National Committee (DNC) was set up to raise funds for the party's 1852 presidential candidate, Franklin Pierce. The man behind the DNC's creation was financier August Belmont, an American who represented France's powerful House of Rothschild. Belmont's solicitations on behalf of Pierce apparently fell short of expectations, for reportedly "at the opportune moment Belmont stepped in and contributed a large sum to the national committee. Thus the matter of funds was taken care of." [3]

Belmont would not be the last party chairman with strong ties to a major business interest. Nor would he be the last to employ his wealth for the benefit of the party.

The Gilded Age and the Rise of Corporate Money

With the end of the Civil War, individuals who had amassed fortunes from the Industrial Revolution—along with the great corporations these men had spawned—began to pay a major share of presidential campaign costs. Republican Ulysses S. Grant, the hero of the Union cause in the Civil War, is said to have assumed the presidency in 1869 more heavily mortgaged to wealthy contributors than any candidate before him.[4]

Grant's $150,000 campaign was largely financed by such tycoons as Jay Cooke, Cornelius Vanderbilt, and members of the Astor family.[5] They represented the railroad and land interests that, along with major industrial corporations, supplied most of the Republicans' money. Throughout the 1860s and 1870s, Cooke held intimate fund-raising dinners in Washington, D.C., for the benefit of the Republican party.[6]

Although most captains of industry perceived the Republicans as the party of their interests, the Democrats were not deterred from also seeking corporate largesse. Besides Belmont, the Democrats could count on such individuals as Cyrus H. McCormick (whose invention of the mechanical reaper revolutionized American agriculture) and Samuel J. Tilden, a wealthy Albany, New York, lawyer. In 1868, when New York governor Horatio Seymour was the party's presidential nominee, eight Democrats including Belmont, still chairman of the DNC, signed a contract with the party's treasurer in which each pledged $10,000 "to defray the just and lawful expenses of circulating documents and newspapers, perfecting organizations, etc., to promote the election of Seymour and Blair." [7]

In contrast with the latter part of the twentieth century, when the public financing of presidential campaigns drove much of the "special interest" money into congressional races, the corporate executives of one hundred years earlier were able to minimize their spending on legislative contests.

"Until Amendment XVII to the Constitution [ratified in 1913] required popular election, United States senators were chosen by state legislatures, and it was much cheaper to 'buy' members than to have to cultivate the entire electorate," writes Samuel Eliot Morison. "Consequently, few reached the Senate without financial support from one or more of the leading 'interests,' such as railroading, oil, textiles, iron and steel, mining and sugar refining. . . . All became very rich, some were gentlemen, some were not."[8]

Of the wealthy politicians of the Gilded Age, Tilden reputedly was among the honest ones. In 1876, having reached the governorship of New York, he was nominated for president by the Democrats. The party was hoping to take advantage of the Credit Mobilier scandal, in which several promoters of the Union Pacific—hoping to divert profits from railroad construction to their own enrichment—sought to head off congressional interference by placing large blocks of Union Pacific stock in the hands of Vice President Schuyler Colfax and several Republican senators.

Tilden was worth as much as $10 million,[9] and Thomas Nast, the leading cartoonist of the day, caricatured him as supporting the Democratic campaign chest out of his own "barrel."[10] In fact, Tilden was notoriously tightfisted, and that may have contributed to his defeat by Republican Rutherford B. Hayes. Although Tilden won the popular vote, Hayes triumphed in the electoral college, in part because Tilden was unwilling to spend the money to woo electoral votes.

Self-financed candidates and wealthy contributors were not the only source of funding for campaigns in the latter part of the 1800s. In the presidential election of 1880, Republican James A. Garfield appealed to his managers to assess government employees for campaign contributions. This practice was circumscribed by reform legislation several years later, as the Progressive Era dawned.[11]

The Progressive Era

The rise of the reform movement at the end of the nineteenth century posed a major challenge to the large industrial corporations that had emerged in the post-Civil War era. In response, owners and operators of big businesses—long a financial mainstay for presidential candidates—expanded their activities into other areas of campaign finance.

> Such magnates as John McCall of New York Life Insurance, Henry H. Rogers of Standard Oil and [railroad magnate] Edward Harriman began both to contribute more consistently and to grant funds to a party rather than a man. They were attempting . . . to incline all important party members in their favor instead of stringing a few as company puppets. The more extensive the magnate's political concern, the more important

> it was to condition countless, unknown officials in all parts of government to respond appropriately whenever his interests came under consideration.
>
> The managers of the Republican Party, which was almost the exclusive beneficiary, were naturally delighted. Businessmen's detached representatives had only weakened party discipline. Discretionary funds now brought prestige and control back into the hands of such men as Mark Hanna, George Cortelyou, and Nelson Aldrich, and regular donations allowed them to plan campaigns rather than approach each election hat in hand.[12]

Hanna was the leading political kingmaker of the era. A wholesale grocer from Cleveland, he rose to become a maker of presidents because of his ability to raise funds for the Republican party. In 1888, when the party's presidential nominee, Benjamin Harrison, succeeded in ousting incumbent Democrat Grover Cleveland, Hanna raised so much money that the Republican National Committee (RNC) was unable to spend it all. Hanna returned the excess to donors on a pro-rata basis.[13]

While the term "fat cat" was not popularized until 1928 (by Frank Kent of the *Baltimore Sun*), its derivation goes back to the first Harrison-Cleveland race. As William Safire notes: "High-pressure fund-raising was called 'fat-frying' in the campaign of 1888. Publisher Henry L. Stoddard wrote historian Mark Sullivan: '[Mark] Hanna was *a* fat-fryer. *The* fat-fryer was John P. Forster, president of the League of Young Republican Clubs. It was in 1888 that he wrote a letter suggesting "to fry the fat out of the manufacturers." ' "[14]

In Hanna's view, few things could not be bought. His battle to secure the Republican presidential nomination for fellow Ohioan William McKinley in 1896 reportedly cost $100,000.[15] Hanna was named chairman of the RNC that year. After McKinley became the party's nominee, Hanna organized a presidential campaign on a financial scale never before seen. Hanna set contribution quotas on many large businesses: Banks, for example, were assessed at one-quarter of 1 percent of their capital. Hanna "introduced some semblance of business method into a system of campaign contributions which at its worst had fluctuated between the extremes of blackmail and bribery."[16]

If Hanna felt most things were for sale, he occasionally sent signals that McKinley was not. In 1900, when McKinley successfully sought reelection to a second term, Hanna returned a $10,000 donation from a Wall Street brokerage firm that he believed was making a specific policy demand.[17] New York business interests furnished nearly 90 percent of Republican presidential campaign funds in 1896 and 1900.[18]

Large business interests felt they could not afford to ignore the Republicans given the alternatives—the Democratic party, William Jennings Bryan, and free silver. The McKinley-Bryan campaigns of 1896 and

1900 pitted rich against poor and Eastern establishment against Western farmers. In the free silver policies advocated by Bryan, big businessmen saw a major threat to the existing economic order from which they had so handsomely profited.

Consequently, Bryan's campaigns were handicapped by a shortage of funds. In 1896, he managed to raise about $675,000, less than 20 percent of the $3.5 million raised by the Republicans. About $3 million of the GOP take was said to come from New York City—the nation's financial capital—and Chicago, its transportation hub.[19] Bryan's donations were limited largely to a group of wealthy silver mine owners.[20] Harold L. Ickes, a leading progressive Republican who went on to serve as secretary of interior during the Franklin D. Roosevelt (FDR) administration in the 1930s, worked in that election for McKinley. He later wrote: "I never doubted that if the Democrats had been able to raise enough money, even for legitimate purposes, Bryan would have been elected."[21]

If Hanna sought to make clear that no favors would be done in return for contributions, Theodore Roosevelt all but bit "the hand that fed him." He readily assaulted the industrial trusts and the men behind them—many of whom provided the money that helped to elect him to a full term in 1904. Placed on the Republican ticket in 1900 as the vice presidential nominee, Roosevelt succeeded to the presidency in 1901 following McKinley's assassination. Looking ahead to the 1904 campaign, Roosevelt turned down the suggestion of muckraking journalist Lincoln Steffens that he rely on small donations in the $1 to $5 vicinity.[22] Instead, he solicited funds from two of the country's wealthiest men: Harriman and steel magnate Henry C. Frick, a partner of Andrew Carnegie. "He got down on his knees to us. We bought the son of a bitch and he did not stay bought," Frick later reported bitterly.[23]

When William Howard Taft, Roosevelt's secretary of war and a member of a wealthy Cincinnati family, was tapped to run for the Republican nomination in 1908, his brother, Charles P. Taft, sought to avoid such problems. Charles Taft contributed a total of $250,000 to his brother's campaign in 1908 and his unsuccessful reelection bid in 1912 because he did not want William Howard Taft to have to go hat in hand to large corporations—or to be under obligation to them as president.[24]

But legislative efforts during the Progressive Era to bar political contributions from corporations did little to slow down their financial participation in politics in the coming years.

The New Deal

The 1936 presidential election—in which Theodore Roosevelt's distant cousin, Democrat Franklin D. Roosevelt, sought a second term—was to be one of the most expensive on record. Total expenditures in that contest were not exceeded until almost a quarter of a century later in the John F. Kennedy-Richard Nixon race of 1960.

The 1936 election was notable for a couple of new fund-raising techniques that enabled the Democrats to tap into corporate coffers and wealthy individual contributors. It also marked the first time that organized labor played a significant financial role in national politics.

The Democrats found a way around the ban on direct corporate contributions by producing a book at their national nominating convention. It contained pictures of party leaders and articles about various aspects of government authored by party figures. Advertising space was sold to national corporations, and the book was sold in various editions—ranging from a $2.50 bargain copy to a $100 leather-bound version autographed by FDR.

The success of the book (it resulted in $250,000 in advertising and sales revenues) made such publications a staple of succeeding political conventions—both Democratic and Republican—through 1972.[25] After 1936, the money raised at the national level by this means was used to cover convention expenses instead of general campaign costs. At the local level, however, program books often helped to fund party organizations.

Not to be outdone by corporate America, United Mine Workers president John L. Lewis wanted to show up at the White House during the 1936 campaign with a check for $250,000—and offered to bring along a photographer to ensure wide exposure for the event. But Roosevelt vetoed the idea.[26] In the early part of the twentieth century, the fledgling union movement had not been a major political contributor; unions funds were used for postage, leaflets, and union speakers addressing members instead of for direct donations to candidates. But, in 1936, organized labor contributed an estimated $770,000 to Roosevelt's reelection, with Lewis's United Mine Workers providing $469,000 of that.[27]

Meanwhile, a Philadelphia contractor named Matthew McCloskey had a more affluent constituency in mind. McCloskey, who later served as treasurer and finance chairman of the DNC, is credited with creating a major fund-raising method that year: the $100-a-plate dinner. McCloskey arranged a dinner at the time of FDR's inauguration to raise money for the Democrats.[28] The idea spread rapidly, and soon $100-a-plate dinners, luncheons, breakfasts, and brunches became commonplace at all levels of the political system. As time progressed, the affluence of the donors and the needs of the parties—to say nothing of plain old inflation—gave rise to $500- and $1,000-a-plate affairs for more select groups.

Fat Cats, Corporations, and Labor Unions

Big contributors continued to play a major role in the campaigns of the 1940s, 1950s, and 1960s. In 1948, for example, approximately seven of every ten dollars (69 percent) contributed to the Democrats' national party committees were from donations of $500 or more. This proportion held steady into the 1960s; for example, it was 69 percent in 1964, and 61 percent in 1968.

The Republicans of that era were even more dependent on the large donor. In 1956, almost three-quarters of national GOP funds (74 percent) was derived from $500-plus donors. While the inflation of the late 1960s and 1970s makes $500 seem a less than overwhelming amount, in the early 1960s certain models of automobiles could be bought for little more than twice that amount.

And those $500 gifts were a mere pittance when measured against some of the contributions in the 1968 presidential campaign. Republican Richard Nixon and Democrats Eugene McCarthy and Robert F. Kennedy are believed to have had at least one $500,000 donor each in bids for their respective party nominations. Stewart R. Mott, an heir to the General Motors fortune, gave $200,000 to McCarthy after spending $100,000 trying to persuade New York governor Nelson Rockefeller, a Republican, to run as an anti-Vietnam War candidate.

When Rockefeller finally decided to run, he benefited from a contribution of almost $1.5 million from his stepmother, Mrs. John D. Rockefeller, Jr. At the time, federal law did not require reporting of campaign funds during the prenomination period. Most presidential campaign committees were legally established in states (such as Delaware) that had no disclosure laws, thereby providing anonymity to donors. But, for unknown reasons, one major Rockefeller committee was established in New York, which did have a disclosure law.

The result was that Mrs. Rockefeller's donation of $1,482,625 came to light. She was subsequently required to pay gift taxes of $854,483, making her donation one of the more unusual in the recent annals of American politics. Because gift taxes applied only to contributions in excess of $3,000, large donors generally managed to avoid taxes by splitting up their gifts into smaller denominations that were made to a large number of committees—most of which existed only on paper.

But even the Rockefeller largesse paled before that of W. Clement Stone, chairman of the Combined Insurance Company of America. Stone gave more than $2.8 million to the Republicans, all but $39,000 of which went to Nixon's 1968 prenomination and general election efforts.

The Nixon campaign also brought fund raising into the electronic age. One fund-raising dinner was held in which twenty-two cities were linked by closed-circuit television. That event alone grossed $6 million and netted $4.6 million, which was one-fifth of the total cost of Nixon's 1968 campaign. He managed to outspend his Democratic opponent, Hubert H. Humphrey, by a ratio better than 2-to-1.

Notwithstanding this financial firepower, Nixon was almost overtaken by Humphrey in the closing weeks of the campaign largely because of a different kind of political financing: in-kind contributions from labor. Then, as now, many political observers contended that labor's strength lay not in its campaign chests but in the volunteers it could muster to register voters and ensure they reached the polls on election day. In 1968, the unions registered 4.6 million voters and distributed more than 100 million pamphlets and leaflets from Washington, D.C. At the local level, labor deployed 100,000 telephone callers and house-to-house canvassers to remind sympathetic supporters to turn out. On election day, almost ninety-five thousand union volunteers were put to work as poll watchers, telephone callers, and drivers to make sure "their people" voted.[29]

Like corporations, unions also learned ways to get around federal prohibitions against direct contributions. They formed political auxiliaries, notably the AFL-CIO's Committee on Political Education (COPE), to collect voluntary contributions from union members for donations to candidates. The first such committee was formed in 1944, the last time that Franklin Roosevelt sought reelection. That was the year in which the Republicans charged that everything the Democrats did had to be "cleared with Sidney"—a reference to Sidney Hillman, chief of the Congress of Industrial Organizations (CIO) prior to its merger with the American Federation of Labor (AFL).[30]

Not to be outdone, corporations increasingly looked for ways throughout the middle part of the twentieth century to get around the ban on direct contributions. They often provided complimentary use of company goods and services, ranging from furniture and typewriters to office suites and storefronts. Many firms provided free air travel to politicians even when no campaign was taking place. Corporations frequently kept executives on the payroll when they were working full time for a campaign.

At times, corporate America stepped over the line in its effort to help favored candidates. In 1968-1969—the last year of the Johnson administration and the first year of the Nixon administration—the Justice Department obtained fifteen federal indictments against corporations, many of them located in southern California, for deducting as legitimate business expenses payments that were effectively contributions. All but one of the indicted firms were convicted for such abuses as attempting to disguise political donations as "business as usual" payments to law, public relations, and advertising firms.

But national parties remained eager for the assistance provided by corporations in financing national nominating conventions. Continuing the tradition of FDR, the Republicans and Democrats published quadrennial convention books, with advertising selling at about $5,000 a page. In 1964, the Democrats upped the ante: They published their convention book as a memorial to President Kennedy, sold advertising for $15,000 a page, and cleared a profit of an estimated $1 million.

The Republicans, out of power in both the executive and legislative branches, responded a year later with a program called "Congress: The Heartbeat of Government" for which they charged $10,000 per advertising page and raised about $250,000. That prompted the Democrats to produce yet another book in late 1965 entitled "Toward an Age of Greatness." Prepared for distribution at fund-raising movie premieres by Democratic congressional candidates during the 1966 campaign, it again charged $15,000 per advertising page and earned at least $600,000.

This escalating duel for corporate advertising dollars was slowed when both Congress and the press reacted with criticism. In 1966, legislation was adopted that barred corporate tax deductions for advertisements in political program books. But the convention books were back in business in 1968, when Congress modified the law to allow tax deductions only for ads in programs printed in connection with the nominating conventions.

Many businesses also helped host cities to shoulder the costs incurred by a national political convention. For many years, hotels, restaurants, and transportation companies servicing the host city made donations—which were considered legitimate business expenses—to nonpartisan committees that guaranteed the financial bids needed to attract a convention to a particular city. These funds were used to help the city pay for the additional services required by such a tremendous gathering.

One of the most controversial examples of this practice was ITT's reported pledge of $100,000 or more to help San Diego finance the 1972 Republican convention. The subsequent uproar, which caused the Republicans to relocate the convention, was concerned not so much with the propriety of the pledge itself as allegations that the pledge was connected to a government settlement of an antitrust suit against ITT.

ITT was but one of a score of major American corporations that was to find themselves under public scrutiny as a result of the 1972 election. Advertising in convention books was prohibited for 1976 and subsequently, and public funds were provided to help cover the costs.

Watergate

In many respects, the 1972 presidential election was a throwback to the no-holds-barred days of the late nineteenth century, when national elections were largely the province of wealthy individuals and giant corporations. According to testimony before the Senate Select Committee on Presidential Campaign Activities (known as the Watergate Committee), officials of Richard Nixon's campaign—the Committee to Re-elect the President—suggested to corporate executives that a "quota" of $100,000 was expected from large companies, evoking memories of Mark Hanna.

The Watergate scandal—which drew its name from the June 1972 bungled burglary at DNC headquarters, located in Washington, D.C.'s Watergate complex—encompassed a wide range of illegal acts and "dirty tricks." Officials of the Nixon reelection committee broke the law not only in some of the ways in which they spent the money but also in some of the ways in which they collected it.

Corporations as Defendants

In the years prior to Watergate, it had been widely suspected that some businesses regularly ignored the ban on direct corporate contributions. Given the infrequent federal prosecutions of corporations for illegal political practices, many business executives had little fear of being caught.

However, what was particularly startling about the roster of illegal corporate contributions in the 1972 campaign was its "blue chip" quality and the amounts of money involved. The picture that unfolded in congressional hearings and judicial proceedings between 1973 and 1975 suggested corporate giving on a scale unlike anything previously imagined. Moreover, these disclosures cast light on a multitude of unethical practices by American industry, both within the country and abroad.

In the wake of the 1972 election, twenty-one companies pleaded guilty to charges—brought against them by Watergate special prosecutor Archibald Cox—of making illegal corporate contributions totaling $968,000. About $125,000 of this largesse was divided among five Democrats who sought their party's nomination in 1972: Sen. George McGovern of South Dakota, the eventual nominee; Sens. Hubert H. Humphrey of Minnesota, Edmund S. Muskie of Maine, and Henry M. Jackson of Washington; and Rep. Wilbur D. Mills of Arkansas. But most of the money—$842,500—went to the Nixon campaign.

Beginning in the fall of 1973, the special prosecutor brought charges against such household corporate names as American Airlines, Goodyear Tire and Rubber Company, and the Minnesota Mining and Manufacturing Company (widely known as 3M). They were later joined by other well-known firms, including Braniff Airways, Gulf Oil Corporation, and Ashland Oil Company.

In addition, a *New York Times* survey disclosed that most prime defense contractors were solicited by fund raisers from the Finance Committee for the Re-election of the President. The survey uncovered a distinct pattern of high-pressure solicitation. The customary $100,000 quota for large corporations was scaled down somewhat when smaller companies were approached.[31]

Several large companies—American Motors Corporation,[32] Union Oil Company, and Allied Chemical Corporation[33]—refused when solicited for large amounts. Officials of the corporations that donated claimed they did so not to obtain favors, but to avoid possible retaliation by the Nixon administration. Many of these officials said they had felt pressured to give because they had been approached by high government officials—such as Secretary of Commerce Maurice Stans, who went on to serve as finance chairman of the Nixon reelection effort—or persons close to Nixon, such as Herbert Kalmbach, the president's personal attorney. Gulf Oil's Claude Wild said he decided to arrange the contribution so that his company "would not be on a blacklist or at the bottom of the totem pole" when it came time for someone in Washington to return his phone calls.[34]

As reports of the pressures put on potential corporate contributors were published, the conventional image of the greedy business executive as the corrupter—seeking to buy favors from politicians—underwent a change. The businesses were seen as the victims, not the perpetrators, of what some saw as extortion. George Spater, chief executive officer of American Airlines, told the Senate Watergate Committee that he was motivated by "fear of the unknown," likening his state of mind to "those medieval maps that show the known world and then around it, Terra Incognita, with fierce animals."

The Finance Committee for the Re-election of the President maintained that it never solicited corporate contributions. It said that committee solicitors merely asked corporate executives to raise money from their colleagues. The committee admitted that target amounts had been proposed, but that no quotas were set.

But the targets—by their very nature—suggested quotas that, if unmet, would pose problems for those not complying. And a pattern of pressure was reported by so many corporate executives that the abuses could not be attributed simply to a few overzealous fund raisers invoking the implied power of an incumbent. Indeed, the Senate Watergate Committee found that those soliciting corporations on behalf of the Nixon campaign made little effort to see that the law was upheld. "There is no evidence that any fund-raiser who was involved in these contributions sought or obtained assurances that the contribution was legal at the time it was obtained," the committee said.[35]

Whatever the amount of duress involved, the corporations that gave did their best to hide the fact that the contributions had originated in their corporate treasuries. Thus did the term "money laundering" enter the

American political lexicon. American Airlines, for example, sent money from a U.S. bank to an agent in Lebanon—supposedly for the purchase of aircraft. The money came back to a second U.S. bank and was then forwarded to the Finance Committee for the Re-election of the President. Other firms drew on secret slush funds, sold bogus airline tickets, or created fictitious bonus schemes for employees. The latter device was employed at the Cleveland-based American Shipbuilding Company, where eight company employees received "bonuses" and were then ordered to contribute a total of $25,000 to the Nixon campaign. The man behind the scheme: company chairman George Steinbrenner III, then—and later—principal owner of the New York Yankees. Steinbrenner was found guilty and fined for his role by the courts. As a consequence, the baseball commissioner barred him from active involvement with the Yankees for two years.

The discovery of such practices led to a widening circle of investigations that, by mid-1975, were being pursued by four government agencies and one Senate subcommittee. The focus shifted from the relatively limited issue of illegal contributions to U.S. politicians to the question of multimillion dollar expenditures by corporations seeking contracts or influence abroad. Put in perspective, $100,000 to a presidential campaign was not much compared with the millions of dollars known to have been given to politicians in Italy, Korea, and other countries by certain American multinational corporations. Among such companies, this practice was regarded as a necessary evil if they were to catch up and compete with their foreign counterparts.

Some foreign companies showed little hesitancy to use money to advance their business interests in the United States. Watergate investigators uncovered several sizable gifts to the Nixon campaign from foreign nationals associated with interests that stood to benefit from favorable U.S. policy decisions. These included $25,000 from a representative for Philippine sugar interests[36] and $27,500 from the head of a Greek company chosen to supply fuel to the U.S. Sixth Fleet.[37] Under federal law at the time, soliciting, accepting, or receiving a political contribution from a "foreign principal" or his or her agent was a felony.[38] However, a direct contribution from a foreign national with no connection to a foreign principal was considered legal, even though it provided a loophole through which individuals who neither resided in the United States nor had the right to vote in U.S. elections could contribute generously.

A New Generation of Fat Cats

The 1972 campaign was the high watermark for large donors. Because of the several Watergate investigations, more information is available about 1972 elections than any before or since. Some 1,254 individuals contributed a total of $51.3 million[39]—an average of more than $40,900 per individual. Unlike the corporate contributions described above, these sizable gifts by individuals were legal under statutes in force at the time. However, in the debate that followed Watergate, the propriety of such large donations generated tremendous controversy.

The three largest contributors in 1972 accounted for donations of $4 million. As in 1968, the most generous donor was W. Clement Stone, who gave $2,141,656—all but $90,000 of which went to the Nixon reelection campaign. In second place was Richard Mellon Scaife, heir to the Mellon family's oil, aluminum, and banking fortune (including Gulf Oil and Alcoa). He gave $1,068,000 to the Republicans, with $1 million of that going to Nixon.

General Motors heir Stewart Mott was the Democrats' largest financial angel. He gave $822,592 (not including some $25,200 in investment-loss deductions) to liberal candidates and causes in 1972, particularly those opposed to Nixon's policies in Vietnam. About $400,000 of Mott's money went to Democratic presidential nominee McGovern.

With the exception of Scaife, the "old money" of American politics—derived from the fortunes of such families as the Fords, the Rockefellers, the Whitneys, and the Astors—was conspicuously absent from the 1972 campaign. They were displaced by nouveau riche donors who, besides Stone, included names such as John A. Mulcahy, Anthony Rossi, and Abe Plough.

The latter three, who contributed to Nixon, all could boast of Horatio Alger success stories. Mulcahy, who gave Nixon $625,000, was an Irish immigrant who rose to the presidency of a steel industry equipment supplier and later became a major stockholder in Pfizer, a major pharmaceuticals manufacturer. Sicilian-born Rossi, a one-time bricklayer and tomato farmer, built Tropicana into a major company, while Plough began as a door-to-door medicine oil salesman and rose to become chairman of Schering-Plough—makers of St. Joseph's aspirin.

Just as George McGovern won the Democratic nomination over the opposition of the party establishment in 1972, such old-line Democratic contributors as the Harrimans and the Lehmans were replaced by upstarts. McGovern's biggest contributors included Max Palevsky, at one time the largest stockholder in Xerox Corporation; Harvard Professor Martin Peretz (now owner of the *New Republic* magazine) whose wife, Anne, was a Singer Company heiress; and Uruguayan-born Alejandro Zaffaroni, president of Alza, a California drug research firm.

Several of the largest contributors that year gave to some of McGovern's opponents in the Democratic primaries and then switched to Nixon in the general election. Another Horatio Alger story, Meshulem Riklis—chairman of the board of the Rapid-American Corporation—gave $125,000 to Hubert Humphrey and lent him another $550,000, most of which was never repaid. Riklis also gave $100,000 to Henry Jackson before contributing $188,000 to Nixon. Leon Hess, chairman of the Amerada-Hess Oil Company, gave $225,000 to Jackson and $250,000 to Nixon.

The sheer size of these sums, to say nothing of their potential for influencing the federal officeholders who received them, prompted Congress in 1974 to limit individual contributions to $1,000 per candidate per election. It was only one element of what was to be the most sweeping campaign reform law in the nation's history.

3 The Drive for Reform

The drive for campaign finance reform is more than a century old. At times, the main concern has been to hold down the size of campaign contributions to prevent the wealth of a powerful few from corrupting the system. On other occasions, the debate has focused on restraining campaign spending to ensure that those of modest means were not priced out of the elective office market. To date, legislative remedies have been applied to both of these policy concerns but success has remained elusive.

Recognizing the need to avoid obligations to special interests was a long time coming, although, in an 1873 speech at the University of Wisconsin, Chief Justice Edward G. Ryan of the Wisconsin Supreme Court declared: "The question will arise . . . which shall rule—wealth or man; which shall lead—money or intellect; who shall fill public station—educated and patriotic free men, or the feudal serfs of corporate capital"? [1] Nonetheless, in the decades that followed, few in power took Ryan's question seriously. Major proposals for reform were met with apathy in the nation's capital. From the early twentieth century (when President Theodore Roosevelt proposed disclosure laws, a prohibition on corporate giving, and government subsidies for candidates) until John F. Kennedy took office in 1961, several presidents went on record in favor of reform. But none took vigorous action.[2]

Kennedy's appointment of a bipartisan Commission on Campaign Costs started the modern reform era, but another decade would pass before Congress enacted major legislation: the Federal Election Campaign Act of 1971, or FECA,[3] which replaced the half-century-old Federal Corrupt Practices Act. Three years later, in 1974, the Watergate scandal yielded a series of sweeping amendments to FECA that shaped how campaigns are conducted today. Further amendments to the FECA were enacted in 1976 and 1979. And the Revenue Act of 1971 also played an important role.

However, as restrictive laws have been enacted during the past century, campaign professionals and election lawyers invariably have found ways to circumvent them. When Congress would act to cut off one source of campaign contributions, another would emerge to keep the money pump primed. Efforts to put a cap on campaign spending also have yielded a variety of innovative techniques to skirt the limits. Concern about such unforeseen consequences continues to pervade congressional efforts to make further changes in the campaign finance system.

Early Efforts at Regulation

The first campaign finance reform law was the Civil Service Reform Act of 1883, which barred federal employees from being assessed or solicited for campaign contributions. The legislation was pushed through Congress by President Chester A. Arthur, an unlikely candidate for the role of reformer.

Arthur was part of the New York Republican machine headed by Roscoe Conkling. In the late 1870s, Arthur served as collector of the Port of New York until he was fired for corruption by President Rutherford B. Hayes. But Arthur was placed in the number two spot on the Republican ticket in 1880 largely to appease Conkling and the so-called "Stalwart" wing of the GOP. When the assassination of James A. Garfield elevated Arthur to the presidency in late 1881, he surprised just about everyone by running a scandal-free, reform-minded administration. His backing of civil service reform so angered Republican party bosses that he was denied renomination in 1884—the last sitting president to be cast aside by his own party. The excesses of bosses such as Conkling during the Gilded Age produced an outcry for reform during the first decade of the twentieth century as the Progressive Era dawned.

Late in 1905 a New York state legislative committee investigating the insurance business discovered that several of the nation's largest insurance companies secretly had contributed to the 1896, 1900, and 1904 Republican presidential campaigns. The immediate response to this revelation was the introduction in Congress of a bill to prohibit corporate contributions. The bill was written by Republican reformer William E. Chandler, who had been senator from New Hampshire from 1887 to 1901 and had served in the Lincoln, Johnson, and Arthur administrations. He was unable to persuade any Republican senator to cosponsor his bill, so he went to South Carolina Democrat Benjamin Tillman. Congress passed the bill in 1907, and it remains essentially in force today, although somewhat revised. The ban on corporate and bank contributions later was extended temporarily to labor unions in the Smith-Connally Act of 1943—when public resentment of wartime strikes was running high—and then made permanent by the Taft-Hartley Act of 1947. None of these laws, however, stopped corporations and unions from donating a variety of goods and services in lieu of cash.

The 1907 act was followed in 1910 by the Publicity Act, the first federal campaign disclosure law. The bill was written by the National Publicity Bill Organization, a reform group founded in response to the 1905 insurance investigation, which included such diverse political figures as Charles Evans Hughes (who was later to become a Republican presidential candidate and chief justice of the United States), populist Democratic presidential aspirant William Jennings Bryan, Harvard University president Charles William Eliot, and American Federation of Labor president Samuel Gompers. The 1910 Publicity Act required post-election disclosure by House members and by political committees operating in two or more states, which included national party and presidential campaign committees. Amendments passed in 1911 extended the law to cover Senate campaigns and require preelection disclosure. It also limited Senate and House campaign expenditures to $10,000 and $5,000, respectively.[4]

These limits were challenged in a case that came before the Supreme Court in 1921. Truman Newberry, who had defeated Henry Ford (of automobile fame) for the Republican nomination for U.S. senator from Michigan in 1918, was subsequently convicted of excessive campaign spending.[5] But the Supreme Court ruled that congressional authority to regulate elections did not extend to primaries and nominating conventions, and—because much of Newberry's spending preceded the primary—the Court overturned his conviction. This narrow interpretation of congressional authority was rejected in a 1941 Supreme Court decision relating to federal-state powers.[6] But Congress did not reassert its prerogative to require disclosure of campaign funds in prenomination campaigns until the early 1970s.

In keeping with the *Newberry* decision, the Federal Corrupt Practices Act of 1925 repealed disclosure requirements for primary elections, while raising the spending ceiling to $25,000 for Senate races in some high-population states. In general, however, the Corrupt Practices Act codified existing law without substantial change. It required disclosure of general election receipts and expenditures by candidates for House and Senate (although not for president and vice president) and by political committees that sought to influence federal elections in two or more states. Like the Watergate-induced campaign reforms that were to come fifty years later, the Corrupt Practices Act was a legislative response to a scandal—Teapot Dome, in which President Warren G. Harding's secretary of the interior had accepted kickbacks for turning government oil reserves over to private companies.

In 1940, the Corrupt Practices Act was supplemented by a provision of the Hatch Act that barred an individual from contributing more than $5,000 per year to a federal candidate or campaign committee. But neither the strictures of the Corrupt Practices Act nor the Hatch Act proved to be particularly effective.

The Corrupt Practices Act required candidates to report spending made with their "knowledge or consent." Most candidates interpreted this clause to mean personal expenditures only, and consequently many of them disclosed only those and not their supporting committee costs. They also circumvented the admittedly out-of-date spending limits by establishing several different campaign committees.

Those contributing to campaigns used a similar maneuver: They donated the $5,000 maximum allowed by law to each of a multitude of committees. This made gifts of $100,000 or more from one individual to one candidate legally possible, and the political species commonly known as the "fat cat" continued to thrive.

The Corrupt Practices Act provided for fines up to $10,000 or two years in jail or both for willful violations. But no record exists of anyone ever being prosecuted under the law.

In a 1963 letter to Congressional Quarterly (which had inquired about the failure to prosecute more than fifty House candidates who did not file required reports for the 1962 election), the Justice Department said its policy was "not to institute investigations into possible violations . . . in the absence of a request from the Clerk of the House of Representatives or the Secretary of the Senate."[7] Not surprisingly, neither of those officials—both of whom owed their patronage jobs to members of the Senate and House—ever made such a request.

A New Frontier for Reform

The ease with which candidates and contributors evaded the provisions of the Corrupt Practices Act increased pressure for stronger campaign finance laws in the years following World War II. Presidents Harry S. Truman and Dwight D. Eisenhower both expressed concern about the methods used to raise money for political campaigns. In Congress, reform-minded legislators proposed tying an increase in the Corrupt Practices Act's spending limits—considered unrealistically low given postwar prices—to tighter disclosure requirements.

"Clean elections" bills did pass the Senate in both 1960 and 1961, only to die in the House. Then, as now, the House contained a large number of members from "safe" districts who had little desire to alter the rules of play that helped to keep them employed.

But, with the coming of John F. Kennedy's "New Frontier," campaign reform took on a much higher profile. Kennedy, just forty-three when he was elected, was both aware of the advantages enjoyed by a wealthy candidate and sensitive to charges his father's personal fortune had helped to buy him the Democratic nomination over several more senior politicians. (Kennedy employed his trademark humor in an effort to defuse the controversy surrounding the role of his father, former U.S. ambassador to Great Britain Joseph P. Kennedy. Reminding campaign audiences that he had announced that donations would not be the governing factor in determining ambassadorial appointments, he would grin and add: "Since then, I have not received one single cent from my father.")

Even before he was inaugurated in January 1961, Kennedy set in motion the events that led to the creation of the Commission on Campaign Costs. It was chaired by Alexander Heard, then of the University of North Carolina, who a year earlier had published a highly regarded book on the subject entitled *The Costs of Democracy.* The commission's report, released in 1962, presented a comprehensive program for reforming political finance at the state as well as federal level.[8] One idea presented for the first time was providing public "matching" funds, or incentives, to presidential candidates.

While public financing of presidential campaigns was to become law just over a decade later, the commission's recommendations were received without enthusiasm on Capitol Hill. Certain members of Congress were distrustful of a presidential initiative in an area traditionally regarded as legislative turf. And Lyndon Johnson also evidenced little interest in the issue when he ascended to the presidency following Kennedy's assassination in November 1963.

But Johnson's attitude changed markedly a couple of years later. "We have laws dealing with campaign financing. But they have failed," Johnson said in a May 1966 letter to congressional leaders. "They are more loophole than law. They invite evasion and circumvention. They must be revised." Johnson proposed changes designed to bring about meaningful disclosure by all campaign committees and to end the practice of evading the $5,000 contribution limit by giving to many different committees.

By all indications, Johnson's embrace of campaign finance reform was a pragmatic one. House minority leader Gerald R. Ford and other Republican leaders were questioning the relationships between the $1,000-a-year "President's Club" and the award of federal construction contracts, and Johnson hoped to defuse GOP criticism by offering an election reform program. In one instance, Republicans sought to link $23,000 in contributions from the chairman of Houston-based Brown and Root to the decision to award the firm a share of an $800 million construction contract in South Vietnam. After Johnson's death, biographer Robert Caro was to detail the degree to which the founders of Brown and Root, Herman and George Brown, had bankrolled Johnson's early political career in Texas.[9]

Forerunners to FECA

Johnson's 1966 reform package was transmitted to Capitol Hill late in the Eighty-ninth Congress and was never reported out of Senate committee. But Congress was becoming more receptive to changes in campaign finance laws. The controversy that year surrounding personal use of political funds by Sen. Thomas Dodd, D-Conn.—for which Dodd was ultimately censured by the Senate—helped to spark new interest in reform. So did the rapidly rising costs faced by congressional candidates because of the increasing importance of television advertising in politics. Television costs, which stood at only $6.6 million in the 1956 general election, were to more than quadruple to $27.1 million by the 1968 general election.[10]

Two pieces of legislation considered by Congress in 1966 helped to pave the way for election reform measures that later became law. One, a comprehensive proposal sponsored by Reps. Robert Ashmore, D-S.C., and Charles Goodell, R-N.Y., provided for creation of an independent Federal Election Commission (FEC) to analyze, audit, and publicize reports submitted by federal candidates and campaign committees involved in federal elections. The other, authored by Sen. Russell Long, D-La., advocated public financing of presidential campaigns.

The Ashmore-Goodell bill ran into problems because of pressure on House liberals from organized labor, which feared that the proposal would curtail practices used to evade the law against direct political contributions by unions. A weakened version of the proposal, which eliminated the proposed commission as sole repository of campaign reports, did pass the Senate in 1967 by a surprising 87-0 vote. But the House failed to act.

The public financing initiative fared better. Like Johnson, Long was an unlikely reformer; both were products of oil-rich states with traditions of rough-and-tumble politics. But Long outmaneuvered Johnson, whose election reform plan featured a relatively modest proposal for tax deductions of up to $100 on political contributions. Caught off guard, the White House decided late in the 1966 congressional session to support Long's more ambitious plan.

Long's bill, attached as an amendment to unrelated legislation, initially called for direct federal appropriations to political parties based on their presidential candidates' performances in the previous election. During Senate debate, it was revised to require that funding come from a $1 checkoff on tax returns. Despite a lack of visible support in the House, by the public or the press, the bill was passed on the second-to-last day of the Eighty-ninth Congress and signed into law by Johnson.

The measure, the first time that federal financing of an election campaign had been enacted, would have provided about $30 million to each political party in 1968. But the new law soon met with a negative response, and in the spring of 1967 Congress voted, in effect, to suspend the law until guidelines were adopted on how to distribute the money.

Most Republicans, whose party had an advantage over the Democrats in the raising of private contributions, had little incentive to support public financing. Some Democrats, while favoring the concept, wanted the law scrapped because it permitted commingling of public and private funds and failed to address congressional campaigns. One of the leaders of the fight to roll back the law, Sen. Robert F. Kennedy, D-N.Y., expressed concern that national party chairmen would use the money as both a carrot and stick to cajole large states to support the nomination of a particular candidate. A year later, Kennedy challenged Johnson for renomination.

Landmark Legislation of 1971

The Ashmore-Goodell legislation and the Long Act might be termed the parents of two 1971 laws that marked a major turning point in the history of campaign finance reform. Ashmore-Goodell was the forerunner of the Federal Election Campaign Act of 1971, which replaced the loophole-ridden Federal Corrupt Practices Act of 1925. Meanwhile, the public financing of presidential elections first proposed in the Long Act was finally allowed to take effect in different form under the Revenue Act of 1971.

Federal Election Campaign Act

President Richard Nixon signed FECA on February 7, 1972. Ironically, the law—which required fuller disclosure of political contributions and expenditures than ever before—was to play a key role in the Watergate affair that led to Nixon's resignation two and a half years later.[11]

The general format for disclosure imposed on candidates by FECA remains in force. Political committees with $1,000 or more in receipts or expenditures were required to file regular reports (the current threshold, contained in 1979 revisions to FECA, is $5,000). Expenditures and donations of more than $100 to candidates and political committees had to be disclosed, including the contributor's name, address, occupation, and principal place of business. (Again, the 1979 FECA amendments raised the threshold to contributions of more than $200.)

Under the Senate-passed version of FECA, an independent Federal Election Commission was to collect and monitor this information. But House Administration Committee chairman Wayne L. Hays, D-Ohio, who was to be a constant irritant to reformers during the early 1970s, managed to kill that provision on the House floor. In the final legislation, the clerk of the House was given jurisdiction over disclosure for House candidates, while the secretary of the Senate received similar responsibilities with regard to Senate candidates. The General Accounting Office, a part of the legislative branch trusted by Congress, was to be the repository for reports by presidential candidates and miscellaneous committees.

FECA was intended to be more than just a disclosure law. Enacted at a time when campaign expenditures were rising rapidly, it also was designed to curtail the costs of campaigns and the advantages enjoyed by wealthy candidates. (A survey by the National Committee for an Effective Congress found that, in the seven largest states where Senate elections were held in 1970, eleven of fifteen candidates were millionaires.)

But FECA as passed in 1971 was to have little impact on either of these problems. The provision limiting federal candidates to spending 10 cents per voter on "communications media" was replaced by a more comprehensive series of limits in 1974, which, in turn, were declared unconstitutional by the Supreme Court in 1976.[12] FECA's contribution limits on candidates and their immediate families ($50,000 for president or vice president; $35,000 for senator; and $25,000 for House member) also were tossed out by the Supreme Court in 1976. Only the presidential limits remain in effect, and they apply only to candidates who agree voluntarily to abide by them in return for public financing.

Revenue Act of 1971

President Nixon signed the Revenue Act of 1971 after exacting a concession from Congress that public financing of presidential elections would be postponed until after the 1972 election. This saved Nixon, then seeking his second and final term, from having to compete under a system of public financing.

The measure reflected the 1966 Long Act in that it provided for creation of a Presidential Election Campaign Fund, with the money collected from an income tax checkoff. But the Revenue Act revised Long's original proposal so that the funding went directly to presidential candidates instead of being funneled through political parties.

As a result of the Revenue Act of 1971, the checkoff has been a fixture on federal income tax returns since 1973. Anyone with income tax liability is permitted to designate $1 in tax money ($2 on joint returns) to the Presidential Election Campaign Fund. In recent years, however, participation in the checkoff has dropped, raising the possibility that the fund will run out of money by the mid-1990s.

The Revenue Act of 1971 also provided for a tax credit and tax deduction to encourage political contributions. Taxpayers could claim a credit against their income tax liability for 50 percent of their contributions up to a maximum of $12.50 ($25 on joint returns). Alternately, taxpayers could claim a deduction for the full amount of a contribution up to a ceiling of $50 ($100 on joint returns).

In contrast to the controversy surrounding the checkoff, the tax credits and deductions had an easy passage. The $50 deduction was raised to $100 ($200 when filing jointly) in 1974 but was then repealed by the Revenue

Act of 1978.[13] Meanwhile, the $12.50 tax credit was increased to $25 ($50 on a joint return) in 1974 and then to $50 ($100 on a joint return) in 1978—to counterbalance repeal of the deduction. However, the credit was then withdrawn when Congress overhauled the income tax system in 1986, on grounds of revenue loss and uncertainty as to their effectiveness as an incentive to giving. Numerous calls have since been made to reinstate tax credits as a means of encouraging small donations from individual contributors.

The Impact of Reform: The 1972 Campaign

The immediate result of FECA was that an unprecedented amount of information about the sources of campaign money and how it was being spent came to light during the 1972 presidential election. Unlike the Corrupt Practices Act, the new law's disclosure requirements covered prenomination campaigns as well as the general election. FECA also closed the longstanding loophole in the Corrupt Practices Act that required financial reporting only by multistate committees. This had allowed political committees operating in just one state to avoid disclosing their contributions and finances.

The new law took effect April 7, 1972, sixty days after Nixon signed the legislation. By the end of the year, it had yielded more than a quarter of a million pages of financial data from candidates. In turn, this treasure trove of information enabled journalists and academics to report campaign practices in greater detail and with greater certainty than ever before.

A half dozen of the 1972 presidential contenders, all but one of them Democrats, sought to enhance their "good government" credentials by voluntarily disclosing some or all of the contributions received prior to April 7. But the Nixon campaign declined to do so. Common Cause, the Washington-based self-styled citizens lobby, filed suit to force disclosure of the pre-April 7 receipts and expenditures of the Nixon campaign.

The legal action produced an agreement by which the Nixon organization disclosed part of the information sought just prior to the November 1972 election. Full disclosure by the Nixon campaign was agreed upon and complied with in September 1973. The disclosures revealed that, during the period between March 10, 1972—the last filing required under the Corrupt Practices Act—and April 7, 1972, Nixon campaign committees raised $11.4 million. Almost half of that amount was received within the forty-eight hours immediately prior to the effective date of FECA.

Congress did not stipulate whether contributions made between the last filing under the Corrupt Practices Act and the effective date of FECA were subject to disclosure. The Committee for the Re-election of the President clearly sought to exploit that uncertainty. The result of the court action was to upset this fund-raising strategy, albeit not until long after the election returns were in. Thus the 1972 Nixon campaign—perhaps best known to posterity for its secret funds, undercover operations, and "dirty tricks"—became the first presidential campaign in history required to make a full disclosure of its finances.

The Aftermath of Watergate: The 1974 FECA Amendments

Much as the Tillman Act of 1907 and the Corrupt Practices Act of 1925 were born as a reaction to excesses within the political finance system, the Watergate scandal brought new pressures for reform. The result was the Federal Election Campaign Act Amendments of 1974, the most sweeping change imposed upon the interaction between money and politics since the creation of the American Republic. The 1974 law continues to have a profound impact on the way in which campaigns are conducted.

Despite the impetus of the Watergate affair, acceptance of reform by members of Congress did not come easily. In July 1973, the Senate passed a reform bill that put a ceiling on campaign spending, limited individual contributions, and created an independent Federal Election Commission. But the measure stalled in the House, with Wayne Hays once again a major stumbling block.

Meanwhile, Nixon, seeking to contain the damages of the Watergate affair enveloping his presidency, sent his own campaign reform proposals to Congress. Nixon combined a call for creation of another commission on the subject with several proposals that had little chance of passage. Consequently, his initiative pleased almost no one. One idea he clearly did not like was public funding of elections. Nixon, who had successfully exempted himself two years earlier from having to run under a system of public financing, derided it as "taxation without representation." [14]

In the spring of 1974, after shutting off a filibuster by Southern Democrats and conservative Republicans, the Senate passed a second reform bill that combined its 1973 measure with a call for public funding of both presidential and congressional primary and general election campaigns. Finally, just hours before Nixon announced his resignation from the presidency on August 8, 1974, the House passed a campaign reform bill by an overwhelming margin of 355-48. But it differed markedly from the Senate bill in that it provided public financing only for presidential elections.

After an often bitter standoff between House and Senate negotiators that lasted for weeks, the Senate conceded on public financing of congressional elections, and the final bill signed by President Gerald R. Ford on October 15, 1974, contained public funding only for presidential elections. This included matching funds to private donations of $250 or less raised during the prenomination campaigns, flat grants to political parties for their national nominating conventions, and large grants to major party nominees to provide full public financing of general election campaigns.

President Ford, a longtime opponent of public financing, expressed reservations about some sections of the law. But he went along, saying that "the times demand this legislation."[15]

The presidential financing structure is one of three major provisions of the FECA amendments of 1974 that remain in force. The independent oversight agency proposed in the Ashmore-Goodell legislation almost a decade earlier was created in the form of the Federal Election Commission.

Finally, and perhaps most significantly, the law sharply curtailed the role of that long-time fixture of American politics: the fat cat. In contrast to the millions of dollars contributed by men such as W. Clement Stone and the hundreds of thousands of dollars by Stewart Mott during the 1972 campaigns, individuals were barred from giving a federal candidate more than $1,000 per election. They also were not permitted to exceed an aggregate annual ceiling of $25,000 for contributions to all candidates and federal party committees and federally registered political action committees.

The bill also created a series of mandatory spending limits on congressional races. House candidates were given a ceiling of $140,000 ($70,000 each for the primary and the general election). Senate candidates were restricted by a population-based formula that permitted a certain amount of spending per voter; the limit was $250,000 in the smallest states.

But these congressional limits never took effect. They were to be wiped out little more than a year later by a landmark Supreme Court ruling—*Buckley v. Valeo*.

A Constitutional Challenge

An unusual provision of the FECA amendments of 1974 authorized any eligible voter to challenge the constitutionality of the law and—to expedite the proceedings—required the case to be referred directly to the U.S. Court of Appeals. The provision had been sponsored by Sen. James L. Buckley, a New York Republican who had won election in 1970 running on the Conservative party line. Buckley immediately took advantage of his legislative handiwork and brought suit in January 1975, contending that the new law violated several First Amendment rights.

Buckley became the lead plaintiff in an ideologically diverse group that included former Minnesota senator Eugene J. McCarthy, who had run for the 1968 Democratic presidential nomination on an anti-Vietnam War platform, and General Motors heir Mott, who contributed heavily to McCarthy as well as to Democratic presidential nominee George McGovern in 1972. The lead defendant was Secretary of the Senate Francis R. Valeo, followed by the clerk of the House, the U.S. attorney general, the FEC, and three reform groups—Common Cause, the Center for Public Financing of Elections, and the League of Women Voters.

On January 30, 1976, a little more than a year after the case was first filed, the Supreme Court reversed the Court of Appeals ruling and found several major sections of the FECA amendments of 1974 to be unconstitutional.[16] The decision was to have a significant impact on the regulation not only of federal elections but also of state and local elections.

In *Buckley v. Valeo,* the Court faced the difficult judicial task of balancing the First Amendment rights of free speech and free association with the power of the legislature to enact laws to protect the integrity of the electoral system against Watergate-style abuses. The central question was posed by Justice Potter Stewart during oral arguments: Is money speech and speech money? Or, stated differently, is an expenditure for free speech the same thing as speech itself, given the expenditures necessary to buy broadcast time or newspaper space to reach large audiences?

A majority of the Court answered the latter question in the affirmative, ruling expenditure limits to be a "substantial" restraint on free speech that could prevent a candidate from making "significant use of the most effective modes of communication." The decision asserted the broadest protection to First Amendment rights to assure the unrestrained interchange of ideas for bringing about popular political and social change. Consequently, the Supreme Court rejected as unconstitutional the mandatory spending limits placed on federal campaigns by the 1974 FECA amendments, along with the restrictions on the amount a candidate could spend using personal resources.

However, the Court made a significant exception to this finding: If a candidate voluntarily accepted public financing, the government could require that campaign expenditure limits be abided by as a condition of that acceptance. The impact of this was to preserve the presidential financing structure outlined in the 1974 FECA amendments. During the last four presidential campaigns, all but one nationally known candidate has taken public funding and adhered to prescribed limits. But the *Buckley* decision invalidated the spending ceilings for congressional races, because the 1974 law did not provide public financing as a means of giving incentives to legislative candidates to comply voluntarily with expenditure limits.

What the Court said in effect was that public financing must be offered as an option that the candidate can accept or reject. If accepted, conditions can be laid down for eligibility, and one of the conditions can be that the candidate voluntarily agree not to spend in excess of a given amount.

While eliminating mandatory spending limits, the justices ruled the other major underpinning of the 1974 law—contribution limits—to be constitutional. The Court asserted that these represented only a marginal restriction on a contributor's First Amendment rights because "the quantity of communication by the contributor does not increase perceptibly with the size of his contribution." In this instance, the Court said that First Amendment considerations were outweighed by the possible influence of large contributors on a candidate's positions, which, in turn, could lead to real or perceived corruption once the candidate took office.

The Court also sustained the disclosure requirements of FECA and made clear that "independent expenditures" by individuals or groups were a constitutionally protected form of free speech only if the spending was truly independent. Consequently, independent expenditures could not be coordinated with candidates or their organizations, or consented to by candidates or their agents.

Finally, the Supreme Court, while upholding the concept of a bipartisan regulatory commission to administer campaign finance laws, ruled the structure of the new Federal Election Commission to be unconstitutional on separation-of-powers grounds. The 1974 FECA amendments had provided that four of the six commission members be appointed by Congress, but the Court said this represented an attempt by the legislative branch to exercise powers reserved to the executive branch.

The ruling was an appropriate ending to a rocky first year for the fledgling FEC.

Early Days—and Problems—at the FEC

The FEC, formally organized in April 1975, was created to centralize the administrative and enforcement functions that had been divided between the General Accounting Office, the secretary of the Senate, and the clerk of the House in the original 1971 FECA legislation.[17]

To achieve credibility, the FEC clearly needed to be independent from Congress, which the FEC was established to regulate. But, from the outset, a potential conflict was apparent between the new commissioners' ties to Capitol Hill and their responsibility for impartial handling of campaign finance issues involving campaigns for Congress. It hardly helped that four of the first six appointments to the commission were former U.S. House members.

By the same token, some members of Congress did not want the FEC to exercise a lot of independence when it came to congressional elections. Wayne Hays had reluctantly gone along with creation of the FEC in the 1974 law and had sought to retain congressional control of the six-member commission by having two members, each of different parties, appointed by the House Speaker and two, each of different parties, by the president pro tempore of the Senate (usually the senior senator of the party in power).

In addition, the 1974 FECA amendments provided that any regulation promulgated by the FEC could be nullified if one house of Congress vetoed the proposal within thirty days. This was a variation of the so-called "legislative veto" that Congress applied to a number of regulatory agencies throughout the 1970s. In the early 1980s, the Supreme Court was to wipe out this practice on the grounds that it violated the separation of powers outlined in the Constitution.[18] In the interim, however, the practice threatened the ability of the FEC as well as other regulatory agencies to act in a truly independent manner.

Congress rejected the first two regulations proposed by the FEC. One sought to treat donations used by members of Congress to supplement their office accounts as political instead of legislative funding, thereby making them subject to the same limits and disclosure requirements as campaign contributions. The Senate, many of whose members at the time relied heavily on such donations to supplement their office expense accounts, vetoed the proposal in late 1975.

The second proposed FEC regulation would have required that all candidate and political committee reports be filed first with the FEC, which would then provide microfilm copies to the clerk of the House and secretary of the Senate. But this move, designed to provide quicker publication of the reports at a central location, was rejected by the House. Many House members were concerned that they could not expect the same deference from the FEC as they received from the clerk of the House; that is, the ability to have their disclosure filings checked before submitting official reports, thereby avoiding possible violations of the law.

Congressional hearings on the proposed regulations, as well the FEC's budget, produced several well-publicized shouting matches between Hays and the commission's first chairman, former representative Thomas Curtis, R-Mo. When the FEC was reconstituted in the spring of 1976 to resolve the constitutional issues voiced in *Buckley v. Valeo*, Curtis paid a political price. The House included an amendment prohibiting commission members from engaging in outside business activities. The move was aimed at Curtis, who served on the commission part time while maintaining a law practice in St. Louis. When that provision became law, Curtis asked President Ford not to reappoint him to the FEC.

The Rise of PACs

The reforms enacted in the 1970s provide a prime example of the law of unforeseen consequences: Efforts to solve one set of problems almost invariably give rise to another set of problems. While the FECA of 1971 and the 1974 FECA amendments sought to restrict the influence of the wealthy individual donor by means of contribution limits and disclosure requirements, they also sanctioned the widespread establishment of political action committees, or PACs. These groups have increased the role of special interests in the political process and have become as controversial as the traditional fat cats of yesterday.

During the debates of the early 1970s, organized labor pushed strongly for PACs. The irony is that the resulting legislation triggered the creation of many corporate and trade association PACs that came to rival labor PACs in political influence.

Prior to the enactment of the reform legislation of the 1970s, labor unions already were experienced in the formation of political action committees. While federal law had long barred use of union dues to support federal candidates, labor PACs found a way around this by soliciting voluntary contributions from union members. Corporate PACs also were legal as "separate segregated funds" without money commingled with corporate treasury funds, but the use of corporate money to support them was not. That served to stymie their growth.

While labor could not use union dues to make contributions to candidates, it did utilize this source of funding to defray the cost of administering PACs. A Supreme Court decision brought the practice into question in the early 1970s, and—at the time Congress was debating FECA in 1971—labor was looking for a way to head off a Justice Department challenge to its use of dues for PAC administrative expenses. In appealing to Congress, labor included concessions to corporations in its proposed legislation as a means of gaining Republican support.

As signed into law, FECA did not change the longstanding—and heretofore poorly enforced—prohibition against using corporate or union funds for contributions to candidates. However, it did formally sanction the use of corporate funds and union dues to set up and administer PACs. It also permitted taking advantage of such funds to finance partisan communications with either stockholders or union members and their families, as well as for nonpartisan voter registration and get-out-the-vote drives aimed at these groups.

Despite the new law, labor officials discounted the possibility of major growth among corporate PACs. FECA maintained the prohibition against federal contractors contributing "directly or indirectly" to a campaign (which had been adopted as part of the Hatch Act of 1940). Because most of the nation's largest corporations had federal contracts, and because use of corporate funds to administer a PAC could be considered an indirect contribution, labor reasoned that few corporations would find it legally possible to establish PACs.

It was to be one of the several miscalculations labor would make during the PAC debate of the early 1970s. Even with the restrictions on federal contractors, almost ninety corporate-related PACs were in existence during the 1972 campaign, with many of them springing up after the 1971 law.

The SunPAC Advisory

The blossoming of the corporate PAC can be traced to the 1974 FECA amendments, when Congress decided to repeal the Hatch Act provision barring corporations and unions holding federal contracts from forming PACs. Again, labor had taken the lead: Several unions with government contracts to train workers were concerned that they would have to get rid of either their PACs or their contracts unless the law was changed.

While the repeal protected those unions, the far more significant impact of the change was to allow many large corporations with defense contracts to establish PACs. Many of the largest companies in the United States have since taken advantage of the opportunity to do so. (The 1974 law also set a limit of $5,000 per election on the amount a PAC could give to an individual candidate.)

Actually, it was not until the FEC's "SunPAC" advisory opinion (AO) in November 1975 that many companies decided to jump on the PAC bandwagon. In a 4-2 decision, the FEC ruled that SunPAC, Sun Oil's political action committee, could use corporate funds to solicit voluntary political contributions from employees and stockholders. The commission cautioned that a potential for coercion existed in soliciting employees and thus issued guidelines.

Reassured by the FEC about the legal validity of corporate PACs, the business community soon recognized its potential as a means of competing with labor unions for political influence. Consequently, in the six months following the SunPAC decision, the number of corporate PACs more than doubled.

The 1976 FECA Amendments

The *Buckley* decision, which gave Congress thirty days to reconstitute the Federal Election Commission as a body entirely appointed by the president, prompted the third debate over FECA in less than five years. President Ford wanted legislation that would simply remedy the FEC's constitutional flaws and argued against Congress revisiting the whole range of controversial issues that fell under the umbrella of campaign finance reform.

He did not get his wish. Congress decided to make significant revisions dealing with the FEC's compliance and enforcement procedures and the issuing of advisory opinions. And a highly partisan clash over PACs ensued as labor, alarmed by the growth of corporate PACs, sought to limit the fund-raising ability of PACs.

By the time the FECA amendments of 1976 were signed into law in May, the initiative in campaign finance regulation clearly had passed from reformers and their allies in the media to those directly affected by the new rules of the game: incumbent legislators, political parties, and major interest groups.

The PAC Debate

Labor's effort to curtail business PACs led to a standoff during the Senate debate over the 1976 amendments. Angered by the FEC's SunPAC advisory opinion permitting corporations to solicit all employees, stockholders, and their families for contributions, labor lined up behind a Democratic-sponsored proposal that would allow companies to solicit only stockholders and "executive or administrative personnel."

But the Republicans, who saw in corporate PACs a major new ideological and financial ally, rushed to their defense, arguing that the proposal would tip the "partisan advantage" toward labor. And the Ford White House hinted at a veto if the restrictions on corporate PACs remained in the bill.

The impasse gave way to compromise after several days. The Democratic proposal limiting corporate PAC solicitations to stockholders, executives, and their families was adopted. Likewise, union PACs were restricted to soliciting members and their families. However, the compromise also permitted corporate PACs to seek contributions from all employees, by mail, twice a year. In addition, trade association PACs were given permission to solicit stockholders and executives of any member corporation once a year.

The Republicans, who were a minority in both houses of Congress and consequently had limited leverage, were less than thrilled with the arrangement; the business community also was generally unhappy. But, in the long run, the restrictions in the 1976 amendments did little to impede the growth of corporate and trade association PACs. The number of corporate PACs, which stood at just under 300 when Ford signed the FECA amendments of 1976 in May, more than tripled to 950 by the end of the decade.

The 1976 PAC debate also provided another application of the law of unforeseen consequences. While the Republicans viewed corporate and trade association PACs as their natural allies, many of these PACs turned out to be far more pragmatic than ideological in their financial choices. A substantial portion of their donations went to Democrats. This increasingly angered the Republicans, and little more than a decade after the 1976 FECA amendments were enacted, a Republican president and GOP congressional leaders were advocating an outright abolition of PACs.

Reconstituting the FEC

To meet the separation-of-powers objections raised by the Supreme Court, the 1976 FECA amendments reconstituted the FEC as a six-member body appointed by the president and subject to confirmation by the Senate. (The secretary of the Senate and the clerk of the House, or their respective representatives, were made ex-officio, nonvoting members.) And, following the clashes between the FEC and Capitol Hill during the agency's first year of existence, Congress took the opportunity to place the FEC on an even tighter leash:

- A vote of four members of the commission was required to issue regulations and advisory opinions, as well as to initiate civil actions and investigations. On a commission that, under law, could contain no more than three members of the same political party, the effect of this provision was to give either the Democrats or the Republicans effective veto power over the commission's actions.
- The commission was allowed to issue advisory opinions only in response to specific situations of fact, not to spell out commission policy. In other words, such opinions were not to be regarded as precedents unless the activity covered by the advisory opinion was "indistinguishable in all its material aspects" from an activity already covered by an AO. The FEC could initiate an investigation only after receiving a properly verified complaint or had reason to believe, based on information received in the normal course of its duties, that a violation had occurred. It was barred from action on the basis of anonymous tips or complaints.

The FEC, however, was granted exclusive authority to prosecute civil violations of campaign finance law and was given jurisdiction over violations formerly covered only by the criminal code, thereby strengthening its ability to enforce the law.

Because the debate over the FECA amendments of 1976 went on far longer than anticipated, the FEC went out of business for about two months. The Supreme Court had ordered the commission reconstituted in thirty days and then extended that deadline by twenty days. But, in the end, 111 days elapsed between the *Buckley* decision and Ford's signing of the 1976 law reconstituting the FEC.

The FEC's loss of authority between late March and late May was more than a bureaucratic nuisance. Its period of limbo fell in the midst of the 1976 presidential primary campaign, when public matching funds were being distributed by the FEC for the first time under the terms of the 1974 FECA amendments. The commission's temporary inability to provide these funds left a number of presidential hopefuls strapped for cash and wholly reliant on private donations.

Whether this hiatus had an impact on the 1976 presidential race remains unclear. Democrat Jimmy Carter, the party's front-running candidate when the FEC stopped giving out money, lost nine of the last fourteen primaries but still won the nomination. Meanwhile, Republican Ronald Reagan, who was challenging Ford for renomination, was forced to go into debt because of the dearth of public funds. Nonetheless, Reagan won primaries in Texas, Indiana, Georgia, and Alabama during this period in the face of the financial superiority of Ford's organization.

The Carter Years

The return of the White House to Democratic control in early 1977 buoyed the hopes of advocates of public financing for congressional elections. In addition, another long-time roadblock—Wayne Hays—had been forced from office by scandal the year before.

However, while President Jimmy Carter made public financing a major legislative priority, the proposal did no better than meet with committee approval during his four-year term.

In June 1977, the Senate Rules Committee reported a bill extending public financing to Senate general elections. It was abandoned on the Senate floor in the face of a filibuster by Republicans and Southern Democrats. Once again, the Southerners feared that extending public financing to congressional races would encourage Republican opposition in states long dominated by the Democrats. During the same year, a public financing measure was shelved in the House Administration Committee after Republicans and several Democrats succeeded in attaching a "killer amendment" to extend it to primaries—thereby raising the cost of the program to several hundred million dollars.

In 1978, House advocates were defeated twice in parliamentary maneuvers designed to bring a public financing measure to the House floor. Common Cause found itself in the unusual position of siding with House Republicans against the House Democratic leadership. The lobbying group charged the Democrats with harming the cause of public financing by promoting a bill to reduce contributions to candidates from political party committees. With Republican party committees then enjoying a 10-to-1 advantage in cash on hand over their Democratic counterparts, the bill was attacked by House Republicans as "piggy."

In 1979, a further attempt at public financing of congressional elections (assigned the bill number HR 1 to underscore its importance) failed to get out of committee. Several Democrats representing safe districts joined a unified Republican minority to kill the bill.

The House later that year voted a $70,000 aggregate limit on the amount a House candidate could accept from all PACs per election. The provision, sponsored by Reps. David Obey, D-Wis., and Tom Railsback, R-

Ill., had strong support from Common Cause and organized labor. But the Obey-Railsback bill died in the Senate under the threat of a filibuster.

Another Revision of FECA

Congress in 1979 did approve yet another significant overhaul of the Federal Election Campaign Act. The FECA amendments of 1979[19] was the fourth major campaign finance measure passed by Congress during the 1970s.

The amendments were intended to be noncontroversial to ensure passage. They were designed largely to reduce the paperwork burden on campaigns by easing the reporting requirements imposed on candidates and political committees. They thus represented a relaxation of some of the constraints that earlier reforms had placed on those in the political process.

However, several of the changes—particularly those expanding the role of state and local parties in federal elections—were to have far-reaching and often controversial effects during the 1980s.

The 1979 FECA amendments were in many respects a response to the observations and complaints of those regulated by federal campaign law. During the late 1970s, considerable discussion was held regarding the effects of FECA and the 1974 and 1976 amendments on the conduct of campaigns and the outcome of elections. In August 1978, the House Administration Committee commissioned Harvard University's Institute of Politics to study the impact of the original law and ensuing amendments.

The study, which took a year to complete, singled out three problems: The law set individual contribution limits too low, it imposed burdensome reporting requirements on campaigns, and the role of political parties was weakened.[20] The report recommended numerous legislative changes, several of which were influential when possible revisions to FECA were taken up by the Senate Rules Committee in mid-1979.

Perhaps the greatest controversy during the debate centered around the conversion of excess campaign funds to personal use. The Senate, whose internal rules prohibited personal use of campaign contributions by both sitting and retired members, inserted a statutory ban on such a practice in its version of the 1979 amendments. But the House, whose rules barred sitting members from converting campaign funds but allowed retired members to do so, did not include the ban in its version of the legislation. With the 1980 legislative reapportionment on the horizon, more House incumbents than usual would face the possibility of involuntary retirement, and several looked upon their campaign treasuries as a kind of consolation prize in the event of defeat.

In a compromise, the 1979 FECA amendments barred the conversion of campaign funds to personal use but exempted all House members in office at the time of the law's enactment: January 8, 1980. This provision became popularly known as the "grandfather clause." But the compromise did not end the controversy. Throughout the 1980s, calls were made for repeal of the grandfather clause, as numerous media stories reported on members who, in some cases, converted hundreds of thousands in campaign dollars to personal use.

Finally, in a November 1989 pay raise package, Congress did away with the grandfather clause—as of January 1993. This gave senior House members a few years to decide whether to retire and take advantage of campaign treasuries that, in several cases, exceeded half a million dollars.

Meanwhile, in response to complaints that public financing of presidential campaigns had eliminated the role of state and local parties in those contests, the FECA amendments of 1979 allowed state and local parties to underwrite voter registration and get-out-the-vote drives on behalf of presidential tickets without regard to federal financial limits. This provision, which came to be known as the "soft money" loophole, also applied to campaign material used in volunteer activities, such as buttons, bumper stickers, brochures, and yard signs. In addition, the law permitted this type of material to make passing reference to a presidential candidate without having it count against the spending limits.

The growth of volunteer activities fueled the soft money debate of the 1980s, as presidential campaigns took full advantage of the 1979 FECA amendments to far exceed the official spending ceiling imposed by law.

An Evolving FEC

Since beginning its operations in 1975, the FEC has been a focus of considerable controversy. Some criticism of the commission is inevitable, for inherent in the creation of an agency to regulate elections rests a philosophical dilemma: How closely can elections be regulated to preserve the integrity of the electoral process and still allow for free and untrammeled political exchange?

Commission Structure. In accord with the 1976 FECA amendments, the FEC is composed of eight members: the secretary of the Senate and the clerk of the House, or their designees, who serve ex officio and without the right to vote; and six voting members appointed by the president and confirmed by the Senate. The terms of the appointments are staggered and are for six years each. No more than three of the voting appointees may be affiliated with the same political party. The commission elects from its members a chair and a vice-chair—each of a different political party—and the chair serves a term of only one year to prevent a particular party or interest from dominating agency decisions and actions.

In 1979 the Campaign Finance Study Group of Harvard University's Institute of Politics recommended that the FEC chair be appointed to a four-year term and be made responsible for administering the agency. The chair's responsibilities also should include appointing the staff director and general counsel and preparing the agency's budget. Under existing law, the commission decides administrative and fiscal business by majority vote, which means four affirmative votes; the chair represents the agency and presides over the commission meetings, but has little authority. The Harvard Study stated:

> This intentionally "weak" commission structure creates . . . problems that need to be addressed: an absence of adequate accountability on the part of appointed officials, indirect delegation of responsibility to staff without adequate policy direction; and the likelihood that the staff, faced with such absence of direction, will either focus on non-controversial, minor paperwork matters, or, worse, assume policy-making functions properly reserved to publicly accountable officials.[21]

In 1981 Common Cause made similar recommendations in a study of its own. The organization agreed with the Campaign Finance Study Group that much of the blame for the agency's administrative inefficiency and lack of clear direction must be directed at Congress. "It is quite clear that the Congress was uncomfortable with the concept of a strong and independent commission established to protect the public's interest in clean and competitive elections," said the Common Cause study. "Instead, when forced to establish an election commission in the face of public outrage over Watergate, Congress deliberately weakened the commission with structural defects and a continuing congressional presence that undermines the very concept of independent enforcement."[22]

Appointments. The process of appointing members to the Federal Election Commission has been a continuing source of conflict. The opposing influences of labor and business frequently are brought to bear on appointments. The conservative and liberal wings of both parties screen each nominee, giving special attention to his or her views. Expertise and political cronyism often vie as criteria for appointments. As might be expected, appointments to the FEC have been strongly influenced by the appointees' political connections and leanings.

The commission is charged with administering the FECA, disbursing public funds to presidential candidates, enforcing the expenditure and contribution limits, and providing comprehensive disclosure of political receipts and expenditures. Observers believe the FEC is or should be at the center of campaign finance reform. But the FEC looks over its shoulder continually for fear Congress is watching—and would disapprove. Congress controls the annual budget of the FEC, and, as a result, the commission is less able to carry out its central responsibility to make the

Federal Election Campaign Act—with its wide scope and extreme complexities—work smoothly and fairly. The commission has not found a commanding vision that would give the FECA credibility and widespread acceptance.

The Federal Election Campaign Act vests the Federal Election Commission with its authority and designates its responsibilities regarding federal election practices. Although the FEC has jurisdiction over civil enforcement of federal political finance laws, it does not have formal authority to act as a court of law.

Voluntary Compliance. A major goal for the commission has been to induce voluntary compliance. After enactment of the FECA, expertise in fulfilling compliance requirements began to develop in the private sector, as candidates and political committees turned to lawyers, accountants, and computer specialists for advice on how to comply. Once it began functioning, the Federal Election Commission issued numerous booklets, manuals, and guides to ease the burden of compliance. It established a toll-free "hot-line" to answer questions, and it holds seminars throughout the country to educate candidates and committee staffs about their responsibilities under the law.

Prior to the establishment of the FEC, the Department of Justice had sole authority in cases of campaign finance law violation. From 1975 to 1979, the FEC and the Justice Department divided jurisdiction by mutual agreement. All "serious and substantial" violations of the act were the responsibility of the Justice Department, and the commission handled less serious violations. The 1979 amendments, however, gave the commission "exclusive jurisdiction" over all civil matters relating to the act. The Justice Department can pursue unilaterally criminal enforcement matters or follow through on referrals from the commission. Such referrals, which usually require the commission's determination of a "knowing and willful" violation that cannot be resolved through the agency's own resources, have not been common. Further, most provisions of the act do not easily lend themselves to criminal violation. Thus the Department of Justice regularly refers reporting and organizational offenses to the commission.

The act specifically mandates the commission to encourage voluntary compliance with the law, and the commission has committed itself to correct or prevent violations by seeking conciliation before resorting to civil enforcement actions. Candidates and committees, however, may agree to conciliation for a variety of reasons. The exceptional pressures of time and publicity may make a candidate under investigation by the FEC reluctant to choose any other course. Further, fines levied by the FEC regularly are less than the anticipated costs of litigation. Finally, although the FEC does not formally adjudicate, the commission does interpret matters of law, determine matters of fact, and publicly declare violations of law. These powers cannot be easily ignored.

Complaints regarding federal elections must be approved by a majority of the six-member FEC; only later can redress and nonvoluntary enforcement be sought through litigation or through referral to the attorney general. The fact that the FEC membership is divided equally between the two major parties sometimes has made a majority of four difficult to obtain because it requires some element of bipartisanship.

The agency has had to spend considerable time and resources defending itself, often at the expense of administration and enforcement of the law. Budgets are not keeping up with inflation. The constant drumfire of criticism has sapped much of the commission's vigor, strength—and support. A major criticism of the FEC is that it exercises its enforcement powers too selectively, resulting in unjustified costs and burdens on campaigns that must now employ lawyers and accountants to ensure compliance.

Defenders of the commission contend that many of the criticisms are unfair because the agency is required to follow the law enacted by Congress and is too often blamed for merely implementing the law. In this view, the fault may lie in the law, but the FEC gets the static. The continuing objections to most facets of the commission's work are bound to inhibit the healthy functioning of the agency—diminishing its moral authority in administering and enforcing the law.

The most approved and respected functions of the FEC are its disclosure activities—including the easy availability of information through its automated facilities in a ground floor office—and the compilations of political fund data through its computer services. The FEC can be faulted for not more clearly articulating its many accomplishments in this area, and sometimes for its slowness in compiling data in meaningful fashion. Budgetary considerations, however, do slow the compilation process.

In fairness, FEC problems spring less from the agency's shortcomings than from Congress's reluctance to create a truly independent commission. It is the kind of commission Congress wants, as is apparent in the congressional influence on appointments to the FEC. That, in turn, is reflected in the occasional failure to deal with major campaign finance issues, including a number of cases in which the commission acted only after being forced to do so by the federal courts.

Past and Prologue

By the beginning of the 1980s, the United States had in place a system of election regulation that had taken most of the previous decade to enact and "debug." Federal elections were subject to strict rules for disclosure of spending and contributions, with the role of the wealthy donor greatly diminished by the availability of public funding in presidential races and the presence of contribution limits in both presidential and congressional contests. PACs were legitimized. The Federal Election Commission was established to administer and enforce the laws. Unlike the negative reforms of prior decades, which attempted to prevent abuses by telling candidates and interests what they could not do, public financing in the presidential campaigns represented a step forward in that it provided a substitute for less desirable forms of political money. The new structure put in place at the federal level served as a model for many states and localities to reform their election laws, although those changes in many instances differed significantly from the statutes adopted by Congress.

In 1980, Ronald Reagan's landslide victory returned the Senate to Republican control for the first time in a quarter of a century. The House remained in Democratic hands, but reform elements there saw little opportunity for change during Reagan's first term, and campaign finance languished as an issue. It was not until 1986, when the Democrats recaptured control of the Senate, that election reform again was to move toward the top of the congressional agenda.

4 Sources of Funds

The 1976 Supreme Court ruling on campaign finance left areas where "big money" might still influence campaigns—notably the unlimited spending permitted certain candidates in their own campaigns and the unlimited expenditures permitted efforts independent of a candidate. However, the Court upheld the $1,000 individual contribution limit, which reduced the possibility of a candidate becoming beholden to a few large donors. Then, after 1979, "soft money" entered the picture, bringing a return to some very large contributors. The Court also upheld the $5,000 political action committee (PAC) contribution limit and the legitimization of PACs.

Why People Give

No single purpose or goal explains why people donate money to political campaigns. Most contributors have a mixture of reasons for making contributions, whether they are given to candidates, to PACs, or to political parties.[1]

Many people donate money to political campaigns simply because they are asked to make a contribution. For many reasons, a good number of contributors find it difficult to turn down a fund-raising solicitation—just as in any charitable drive. Other individuals contribute to campaigns out of a sense of civic duty or because they sympathize with a particular candidate or cause that is being advocated.[2]

Others may give to a PAC out of a sense of loyalty to their employer or a group with whom they identify, be it a corporation, labor union, or membership organization. Concern for government policy espoused by a candidate motivates some to make contributions, while personal identification with a candidate, party, or PAC may inspire others. And others want favorable treatment from—or at least access to—government officials or those who solicit them. Contributors seek the good will of elected officials and hope to have a basis for talking—even about the time of day. Indeed, some do want a quid pro quo—a job, a contract, or a policy.

However, some contribute for reasons of ego and self-esteem: to be invited to dine at the White House; to be on the dais during a speech or in a reception line; to be able to call the senator by his or her first name or, even better, to have the senator call the donor by his or her first name. For wealthy individuals seeking status, a few thousand dollars are hardly a sacrifice.

In short, motivations for giving money are similar to those for participating in politics generally: public policy reasons; social reasons that include friendship with a candidate or enjoyment of the social aspects of politics; and the furtherance of business or professional goals.[3]

Fund-Raising Strategies

Candidates receive the vast majority of their campaign dollars from individual contributions. In 1989-1990, 53 percent of gifts to congressional campaigns came from individuals, some raised by direct mail and others raised through solicitations made for events such as barbecues and cocktail parties held in the members' districts.[4] Even though personal solicitations may produce significant campaign income, many candidates understand that district-based appeals are important because everyone who attends an event is a potential voter.

Individuals who give larger contributions—for example, $500 or more—rarely do so as the result of a mail solicitation. Many contributions are to purchase tickets to dinners and other events, especially when the president or a national leader is speaking. Typically a candidate or a solicitor visits or telephones prospective donors as a follow-up to a mailed invitation.

When candidates are unable to adequately finance a campaign from constituents within a state or district, however, they seek funds from political action committees, political parties, lobbyists, and out-of-staters often in Washington, D.C. Or they spend personal funds. Another source is the personal PACs of presidential candidates or party leaders—sometimes called leadership PACs—which contribute to favored party candidates.

American politics has shifted from neighborhood precincts in which the political parties contested to socioeconomic bases representing a common occupation or ideology—often without party consideration. People give because they share ideas and concerns that PACs advance, and they seek to elect candidates with congenial views. Out-of-state funding helps to nationalize politics, directing candidates to national issues and away from the provincial interests of a state or district.

Given that more public policy is formulated in Washington than in state and local communities, the trend toward nationalization of campaign fund raising is inevitable. As government has expanded and increased its role in the economy and in social issues, affected interests have become more active in politics. In general, the greater the impact of federal government decisions, the more people are likely to be interested in politics and in organizing political action committees to raise funds for sympathetic candidates.

As the federal government divests itself of some of its programs and the states take on new or added policy responsibilities, state-level funding and giving by affected interests increase accordingly. Fund raising at the state level often occurs in the state capital, though considerably less out-of-state interest and fewer PACs may exist.

Candidates want to win. Campaign costs are high. Only a limited number of local people can or will give. So candidates start their fund raising early, based on where they think the money is. And incumbents spend more and more time raising money, taking time away from their duties as elected officials. Overall, the higher the political spending, the greater the need for money, and the more the concern about where to get campaign funds, the deeper the attention candidates will pay to the public policy interests of individuals or groups that have money and are willing to give it.

Direct Mail

To raise political contributions from a great number of individuals, some candidates solicit funds through broad-based direct mail campaigns. Direct mail is most successful for candidates who are to the left or right of the political spectrum or who identify themselves with a set of issues that arouse deep emotions.

In general, direct mail campaigns are most effective for presidential candidates and for those outside the political mainstream. The use of direct mail made a financial success of Sen. George McGovern's 1972 presidential campaign, even though he lost by a large margin to Richard Nixon in the general election. Like Barry Goldwater in 1964 and George Wallace in 1968, McGovern was considered a factional or fringe candidate. And like both Goldwater and Wallace, McGovern succeeded in getting financial support from large numbers of small contributors.

In the prenomination period, McGovern raised some $3 million dollars through direct mail at a cost of about $1 million. Most of the money was received in contributions of $100 or less. In the general election, his direct mail efforts gathered $12 million, costing the campaign $3.5 million.[5]

McGovern began using direct mail during the days when he criss-crossed his mostly Republican state of South Dakota, keeping lists of contacts and potential contributors. Once he won a U.S. Senate seat, he continued to add to the list and broadened it extensively when his anti-Vietnam War activities launched him into the national spotlight.

McGovern invariably appealed for funds at the conclusion of his television broadcasts, which were timed to coincide with direct mail appeals that already were in the mail. The strategy paid off: At the time it was the most successful direct mail campaign in American political history. It far exceeded Barry Goldwater's direct mail effort of 1964, which had raised some $5.8 million.

Ronald Reagan sent out mailings too late to reap many rewards for his 1976 presidential bid, but four years later, he was more successful than any other candidate in raising funds through direct mail. His campaign used a mailing list made available by Citizens for the Republic, a PAC that Reagan formed in 1977 to help keep his name prominent and to launch his 1980 presidential bid. Reagan's treasurer noted that, through late April 1980, almost 50 percent of Reagan's campaign funds came from direct mail appeals.[6]

Direct mail has been less of a factor in more recent presidential bids. In 1988, Republican Jack F. Kemp enjoyed the most successful direct mail effort. Of the $16 million dollars raised by the Kemp campaign, $5.6 million came from direct mail contributions.[7] But matching funds enhanced the success of the mail drive by doubling contributions up to $250.

Direct mail appeals generally are most effective for candidates running for national office. The technique is too costly for most Senate and House candidates and requires more lead time than House candidates have in a two-year cycle. In recent years, increasing competition for political donations has diluted the effectiveness of direct mail appeals. Nevertheless, most ideological or issue PACs and a few Senate and House candidates have come to rely heavily on direct mail to raise needed funds.

For example, in 1988 conservative Republican representative Robert K. Dornan raised more money for his Orange County, California, congressional seat than any other candidate running for the House. In total, he raised $1.7 million in contributions of about $25, two-thirds of which came from ideologically conservative contributors outside of California.[8]

Mostly through nationwide direct mail campaigns, conservative North Carolina Republican senator Jesse Helms has raised unprecedented amounts of money for each of his bids for office. In 1978, he received about $7.5 million. Six years later, in his highly competitive Senate race against former Democratic governor James B. Hunt, Jr., Helms's fund-raising success was greater: In that year, 1984, he raised what was at the time a record $16 million.

However, of the $16 million spent by Helms's campaign, approximately 40 percent or about $6.5 million was spent on fund raising (mainly direct mail), leaving only about $9.5 million to use against Hunt. Thus, because of his out-of-state direct fund raising, Helms's spending advantage in North Carolina was somewhat less than the total spending the press reported during the campaign.

Much of the Helms spending on fund raising was out of state. Helms spent a number of years prospecting mailing lists and had a hard core of supporters across the country built up through the National Congressional Club, a PAC he sponsors. In 1984, Helms had about 180,000 contributors and 700,000 contributions. The large numbers, resulting from Helms's style of seeking to broaden his financial bases, are unusual in Senate campaigns, but as in presidential campaigns will not work for most centrist candidates. His 1990 reelection campaign was based again on a successful direct mail drive for funds, with results similar to 1984.

Political Party Committees

Generally, Republican party committees have enjoyed much more fund-raising success than their Democratic counterparts. As the Democratic party increased its direct mail efforts, the gap narrowed. However, the GOP still raises much more than the Democrats.

The Republican fund-raising success is, in large part, the result of its effective direct mail. The Republican National Committee (RNC) has relied on mail appeals since 1962, when it launched its first national sustaining fund membership drive and collected $700,000. The effort gained each succeeding year, and in 1972, a presidential election year, the RNC raised $10.1 million, $4.1 million more than the year preceding. In the post-Watergate years, the Republican party vigorously began rebuilding itself by launching aggressive fund-raising campaigns.[9] A 1978 law allowing national party committees to mail at a nonprofit rate of 3.1 cents enabled the RNC to expand its direct mail efforts even further. In the following year, the RNC mailed 18 million fund-raising letters and netted $12 million from 550,000 contributors.

Throughout the 1980s, the GOP raised several times as much as the Democratic party did from individual contributions. In 1980, the RNC reportedly received almost $26.5 million from small donations—most of which came in the form of $25 contributions given in response to direct mail appeals. In that election cycle, the RNC, together with the two other Republican party committees—the National Republican Congressional Committee and the National Republican Senatorial Committee—raised $169.5 million. In that same election cycle, the Democratic party raised only $37.2 million. In 1982, the gap was even wider: The Republican party raised $215 million—fully five times more than the Democratic total of $39.3 million.

By the end of the 1980s the Republicans still held a significant advantage over the Democrats, but the Democrats were catching up. In the 1988 election, the Republican party raised $267.1 million, twice what the Democrats raised ($135.2 million). The Republicans also received a much higher percentage of donations from individual contributors than the Democrats—87 percent to 66 percent. That ratio stayed stable in the 1990 elections. In that year, 86 percent of the $207.2 million the

Republican party raised was from individual contributors; for Democrats, only 64 percent of $86.7 million. The average contribution to the Republicans also is consistently less than that to the Democrats.

The Republican direct mail drive crested in 1986, and receipts, while still high, have been declining since for both election and nonelection years. Similarly, the Democratic effort and those of numerous ideological PACs have experienced diminishing returns. Among the reasons are contributor-fatigue, a changing salience of issues, and, since 1991, a recession.

The national parties also seek funds in other ways—through annual and special dinners. Further, the Republicans have an Eagles program for $15,000 per year dues (the annual limit for an individual contribution to the national party is $20,000), which includes meetings in Washington, D.C., special visits to the White House, and seminars given by administration officials. The Democrats have a Democratic Business Council, also for $15,000 per year, which holds meetings in Washington or at various resorts where members can hear speeches, meet national leaders, and socialize. The senatorial and congressional committees of both parties also have fund-raising group activities. For example, the Democratic Senatorial Campaign Committee has a Leadership Circle, and the National Republican Congressional Committee has the President's Forum through which meetings are arranged with President Bush and also former presidents Ford, Nixon, and Reagan. The Republicans have a decided advantage in having popular former presidents.

Fund-Raising Events

Throughout the 1980s, as campaign costs escalated, candidates for federal office spent increasing amounts of time in activities related to fund raising. For House members, the pursuit of campaign donations is never-ending. While senators serve six-year terms, many of them are now starting to hold fund-raising events shortly after election and well in advance of reelection, so they can store up enough of a war chest to fend off any serious political opposition. Senators now must raise nearly $13,000 each week for their entire six-year terms to amass the average that a winning Senate race costs.[10] The strategy behind beginning fund-raising efforts early is to amass amounts of money large enough to deter the entry of serious challengers.

While a typical fund-raising event may still be the garden-variety campaign round-up at a local club, some hold glitzy fund raisers aimed at garnering large contributions from members of elite groups and industries. This is particularly true in presidential campaigns and in hotly contested races for the U.S. Senate. Often House members hold fund raisers in Washington, D.C., that seek contributions from lobbyists, PAC managers, and others who have never even been to their district. Such fund-raising events may be called "access opportunities"; in other words, a chance to mingle with an elected official and to at least be seen as supporting reelection. Incumbents often use their legislative committee assignments to enhance their fund raising. For example, congressional committees dealing with taxation—the Senate Finance and the House Ways and Means committees—are especially choice member assignments because they attract contributors interested in legislation being considered by them.

As candidates compete for scarce dollars, they have begun to lure more would-be contributors by staging increasingly fancy affairs. In 1990, Republican representative Al McCandless of California held a "Night of Stars" fund raiser that featured singer Sonny Bono, the mayor of Palm Springs.[11] In that same year, Democratic representative Don J. Pease of Ohio held a fund-raising event at the Arena Stage and New York Republican Bill Green held his at the Kennedy Center—both Washington, D.C.-area locations—and offered would-be contributors free tickets to the play *Shogun*.

During the few months preceding elections, fund-raising events are held so often and by so many candidates that many potential contributors receive invitations to far more events than they could possibly afford to—or want to—attend. On one morning in 1990, six fund-raising events were held simultaneously at one Washington, D.C., restaurant.[12]

Perhaps recognizing how tight their contributors' schedules had become, two Democratic representatives, Frank J. Guarini of New Jersey and William L. Clay of Missouri, used a gimmick—they hosted "no show" fund raisers that spared contributors from attending in exchange for mailing in their donations.[13]

Relatively unknown candidates often will invite popular celebrities to a fund raiser as a way to raise money quickly. One week before his June 1988 primary, California Republican Dana Rohrbacher had only 8 percent of the vote, according to a poll. Then Rohrbacher invited Lt. Col. Oliver L. North to his fund-raising party. At the time, North was experiencing a post-Iran-contra surge of popularity and was helping selected candidates to obtain free media exposure simply by attending their events. The strategy paid off: In that night Rohrbacher raised $80,000, helping him to win the primary, beating seven other candidates, with 35 percent of the vote.[14]

Star-studded fund-raising events that court contributions from movie moguls, actors, rock stars, and other wealthy Hollywood entertainment industry persons are most common in presidential campaigns. Increasingly, presidential hopefuls are finding it necessary to make pilgrimages to Hollywood to seek campaign dollars and, perhaps more importantly, to capture the vocal support of popular celebrities.

Given the wealth of the Hollywood community, candidates have an easy time gathering large amounts of donations from particular fund-raising events. During his bid for the 1988 Democratic presidential nomination, Delaware senator Joseph R. Biden, Jr., raised $435,000 from a single, Beverly Hills fund-raising event.[15] In 1984, Jesse Jackson did not spend much time courting the Hollywood elite, but he did for his 1988 presidential bid. In October of 1987, Jackson held a birthday party that drew an impressive array of Hollywood entertainers, who gave him even more support as his credibility rose.[16]

Producer Norman Lear asked each of the 1988 Democratic presidential hopefuls to come to his home to be interviewed by a gathering of top Hollywood personalities. All of the candidates accepted, with the expectation that they might be able to impress people who would then help them raise money.[17] Other Hollywood groups, such as the Hollywood Women's Political Committee, also held similar events. These grilling sessions were an inevitable part of the process of wooing Hollywood celebrities for the contributions and exposure they could provide.

Republican candidates in 1988, particularly front-runners George Bush and Robert Dole, managed to avoid spending much time at Hollywood fund raisers. Instead, both candidates collected a significant amount of money from Los Angeles corporate leaders and businesspersons. In one night, Bush raised $1.1 million for the RNC Presidential Trust.[18]

The biggest star in political fund raising normally is the president. President Bush was credited with having raised $90 million in a year and a half of speaking at 115 fund-raising events in thirty-five states, benefiting party committees and candidates.[19] Vice President Dan Quayle tallied some $17 million raised in the same time period.[20] The party not controlling the White House has a harder time raising money, in part because the American tradition does not specify a single and acknowledged leader of the party not in power. Even the Speaker of the House, the majority leader of the Senate, former presidents, or former presidential candidates simply do not have the same fund-raising appeal as a sitting president or vice president.

Bundling

In the 1980s, as criticism of PAC spending grew and limits on PAC and party gifts made campaign contributions lose value through inflation, certain PACs, political parties, and corporate executives turned to an alternative method of fund raising: "bundling" contributions. Bundling is a technique whereby contributions are collected from individuals who have made out their checks to a designated candidate. An intermediary or conduit is involved; it may be a PAC or a party committee that provides individuals with a list of suggested candidates for whom a contribution is encouraged. The committee will then send the collection of individual contributions to a candidate in a "bundle."

Although the bundled contributions technically are a collection of individual campaign gifts, candidates receiving them can identify the contributions as being from a particular PAC or industry.

Bundling is not new, but the extent to which it is now used is new to the election process. The technique was invented by the Council for a Livable World (CLW), an organization that raises funds for candidates opposed to nuclear proliferation. In 1962, CLW bundled contributions for George McGovern in his Senate race. The method was identical to those used today: CLW mailed campaign information to supporters and asked them to send the council checks payable to McGovern.[21] CLW is still actively bundling contributions and along with an adjunct, Peace PAC, funneled $1.4 million to Senate and House candidates for the 1990 campaigns.

PACs are not the only bundlers. Industry executives also raise considerable amounts of money for candidates. The technique carries less stigma than PAC gifts and, perhaps more significantly, if properly executed, can give higher amounts of money to political campaigns (no one individual can give more than $2,000 to a single candidate). A PAC is limited to giving any individual candidate $10,000, but, for example, thirty corporate executives can each give $2,000, for a total of $60,000.

In 1989, Disney chief executive officer Michael D. Eisner held a $250-a-head fund-raising event in his Beverly Hills home for Democratic New Jersey senator Bill Bradley. Shortly afterwards, Bradley's campaign received separate bundles of checks from executives of Warner, Paramount, MCA, and Disney.[22]

A newer-style version of the bundling technique is employed by a "political donor network" called EMILY's List (an acronym for Early Money Is Like Yeast).[23] Formed in 1985, EMILY's List was formed to raise early campaign money for Democratic women candidates who support the Equal Rights Amendment and abortion rights. Members of EMILY's List pay $100 in dues and pledge to donate at least $100 to two or more candidates on EMILY's List choice of candidates. The network has been very successful. In 1990 EMILY's List raised $1.5 million in bundled contributions for fourteen women candidates.

Groups from all sides of the political spectrum, not just liberals, have adopted the technique of bundling. In the 1980s, the Associated Life Insurance Group National Policyholder Advisory Committee (ALIGNPAC) channeled money to selected members of the Senate Finance and the House Ways and Means committees at a time when both panels were considering various tax proposals that would affect the life insurance industry. The bundled funds included $150,000 to Oregon Republican senator Bob Packwood, who was chairman of the Finance

Committee, and $50,000 to House Ways and Means Committee chairman Dan Rostenkowski, an Illinois Democrat.[24] ALIGNPAC's bundled contributions were controversial and were criticized by the press. "ALIGNPAC's money stands out because . . . it illustrates how easily special interest groups can get around election laws when they wish," wrote *Wall Street Journal* reporter Brooks Jackson.[25]

Lincoln Savings and Loan director Charles H. Keating, Jr., used the bundling technique when he funneled thousands of dollars in contributions to five senators who intervened on his behalf with federal regulators. And Wall Street firms use bundling to make contributions to elected officials at the state and local levels who may be helpful in floating government bond issues.

PACs and individuals are not the only bundlers. The National Republican Senatorial Committee funneled some $6.6 million to Senate candidates in 1986,[26] resulting in protracted complaints to the Federal Election Commission (FEC), litigation, and finally a substantial fine.

Some advocates of campaign finance reform argue that bundling is just as bad as PAC contributions. Fred Wertheimer, president of Common Cause, believes that bundling is a deliberate attempt to evade PAC contribution limits and should, therefore, be outlawed. "It's a direct threat to the integrity of the system," he said. "If the contribution limits are to have any impact, you have got to stop bundling."[27] Bundling is legal, but several campaign finance reform proposals have called for outlawing the practice or tightening the restrictions to its use.

Trends in Giving since the 1970s Reforms

Ironically, the laws of the 1970s led to an institutionalization of the special interests political reformers sought to eliminate. Following enactment of the 1974 amendments, which imposed limits on the amounts individuals may contribute to candidates, the once key role of the large donor was replaced by that of the elite fund raiser. No longer could a W. Clement Stone contribute millions of dollars or a Stewart R. Mott hundreds of thousands, so candidates were forced to broaden their financial bases. Persons with access to networks of proven contributors or with mailing lists to be prospected for potential donors became increasingly important because they could help to raise big money in smaller sums. Elite solicitors who can bring in large amounts of money are few, direct mail fund raising is expensive and not feasible for most candidates, and the number of fund-raising dinners and other events that donors will attend is not unlimited.

Political Action Committees. Political action committees helped fill the void created by loss of the "fat cat." Sponsored by corporations or labor unions or membership groups with political interests, PACs share two characteristics essential to fund raising: Access to large aggregates of like-minded persons and internal means of communication. PACs collect numerous small contributions that they combine into larger, more meaningful amounts that are then contributed to favored candidates—all at no cost to the candidates' campaigns. In this sense PACs can be considered solicitation systems, reaching out to thousands of corporate employees or union members whom candidates would find prohibitively expensive to ask for money from separately. PACs are willing to undertake the task because the money raised goes to candidates or party committees that support their causes.

The reforms of the 1970s sought, among other things, to tighten restrictions on the kinds of illegal contributions uncovered by Watergate-related investigations and to diminish the influence of special interest groups and wealthy contributors in the electoral process. While reducing the role of the large individual contributor, the changes, particularly the low contribution limits, served to increase—or at least to make more visible—the roles played by special interests. The establishment of political action committees was sanctioned by the 1971 and 1974 laws.

A PAC normally is organized by a business, labor, professional, agrarian, ideological, or issue group to raise political funds on a voluntary basis from members, stockholders, or employees for the purpose of combining numerous smaller contributions into larger, more meaningful amounts that then are contributed to favored candidates or political party committees. A PAC can contribute up to $5,000 per candidate per election (that is, $5,000 in a primary and another $5,000 in the general election) provided the committee has been registered with the Federal Election Commission for at least six months, has more than fifty contributors, and has supported five or more candidates for federal office.

The 1980s witnessed an explosive growth in registered political action committees. The number went from a total of 2,551 in 1980 to 4,172 in 1990—an increase of 64 percent. However, the number of PACs reached its peak in 1988, when the tally hit 4,268. The decline from 1988 to 1990 was largely a result of a reduction in the number of nonconnected or ideological committees, a category that had grown more rapidly in number than any other grouping of PACs in the early 1980s. In 1980, only 374 nonconnected PACs were registered; exactly ten years later their numbers had risen to 1,062. Currently corporate PACs still outnumber every other category, with a total number of 1,795 registered at the end of 1990—49 percent more than existed ten years before. In 1990, trade/membership and health PACs totaled 774 (198 percent more than in 1980); labor PACs, 346 (16 percent more than in 1980).[28]

A great surge in PAC spending also occurred in the 1980s. In the 1980 election cycle, PACs raised and spent more money and contributed more to federal candidates than in the two previous election cycles combined. PACs gave federal candidates a total of $60.2 million. Throughout the decade, PACs spent more in each succeeding federal election campaign, until leveling off in 1988 and 1990. PAC spending increased 28.9 percent between the 1981-1982 and 1983-1984 election cycles. Expenditures in 1985-1986 were 23 percent higher than the $113 million spent in 1983-1984. PAC gifts in 1987-1988 totaled 14 percent more than in 1985-1986. But in 1989-1990, PACs gave federal candidates $159.3 million, virtually the same amount they gave in 1987-1988—$159.2 million.[29]

No clear reasons exist for why PAC spending is slowing or why the number of PACs has diminished. Corporate mergers and buyouts have led to the combining of some PACs. Some suggest that PACs are victims of their own unreasonable expectations or that PACs already have fulfilled their potential and that the law of diminishing returns gives some PACs, particularly small ones, less incentive to stay involved in the political process. Others believe that media criticism, the so-called "PAC attack," has made sponsors and participants wary.

Correlating the number of PACs to productivity may be misleading. The top 100 PACs in the 1989-1990 cycle contributed $74.5 million to federal candidates, or 46.7 percent of the total given by all PACs.[30] Some 64 PACs reported at least $1 million in total receipts, while 669 raised $100,000 or more. However, 870 PACs had no dollar activity, and 1,054 spent $5,000 or less.[31] These figures indicate that large amounts of money are handled by relatively few PACs.

Because many PACs are tied to corporations, trade associations, and unions with legislative interests, critics charge that wholesale vote-buying is occurring. Studies of congressional behavior have indicated, however, that personal philosophy, party loyalty, and an aversion to offending voters are more influential factors than campaign contributions in determining positions taken by members of Congress.

PACs, however, have created public relations problems at a time when Congress already is held in low regard by the American public. If PACs have not spawned vote-buying, they have created a system in which money and access to legislators have become intertwined. Not only have reformers criticized PACs but also, in recent years, has the Republican congressional leadership. Furthermore, President Bush called for their elimination in his 1991 State of the Union address. The irony is that Republicans in the 1970s and early 1980s championed business PACs and encouraged their development. Not surprisingly, when business PACs started to give more to Democratic incumbents, Republicans reversed their position—at least in their rhetoric if not in practice.

PACs have their defenders, who maintain they merely represent competing interests inherent in the U.S. pluralistic system and are not nearly as monolithic as portrayed, and some cancel others out. Defenders note that at a time when many bemoan declining citizen involvement in the electoral process, PACs have increased participation by their rank-and-file. Finally, they contend that efforts to abolish PACs would be ineffective. PAC money would not disappear; instead it would be channeled into less visible, less traceable channels such as soft money and independent expenditures.

The Impact of Ideological PACs. The number of PACs not connected to a corporation, trade association, or labor union grew tremendously in the 1980s. Of these nonconnected PACs, ideological committees saw the greatest proliferation and had the greatest effect on the federal election process. However, ideological PACs hit their peak in the 1985-1986 election cycle. Since then, their number has diminished and the amounts they raised and spent on behalf of candidates decreased considerably.

Ideological committees are comprised of both liberal and conservative groups that have broad-based political agendas. But ideological PACs also include single-issue groups such as gun lobbies and abortion rights and anti-abortion committees. Also among the ideological PACs are women's PACs, environmental PACs, and civil rights PACs, which are interested in a range of issues and hence not identifiable as single-issue PACs.

Many ideological PACs, such as the National Committee for an Effective Congress and the American Conservative Union, have been longstanding players in the election process. But a large number of the most active conservative PACs first became heavily involved in the late 1970s and increasingly active in the 1980s—parallel to the popular conservative views of the Reagan era. Among these were the National Conservative Political Action Committee (NCPAC), the National Congressional Club, the Fund for a Conservative Majority (FCM), and the Committee for the Survival of a Free Congress—groups representing the New Right, a loosely knit coalition of politically conservative individuals, PACs, think tanks, and publications intent on gaining political influence to promote their conservative agenda and moral orthodoxy.

However, conservatives were not the only ideologues to form successful political action committees. Several liberal groups—Democrats for the 80s, the National Abortion Rights Action League, Fund for a Democratic Majority, and Independent Action—also have been active.

In the early 1980s, the financial role of PACs grew with their dramatically increasing numbers. In those years, ideological PACs dominated the scene and grew faster than corporate, labor, or trade association PACs. In the 1981-1982 election cycle, nonconnected PACs, many of which were ideological committees, reported spending almost $65 million, more than any other category of PACs and about $22 million more than corporate PACs.

In that same election cycle, six of the ten leading money raisers among PACs and five of the leading spenders were ideological groups. No ideological PACs, however, were included among the ten leading contributors to candidates. These PACs contribute only a small portion of their total receipts directly to candidates, as low as 2 percent in some cases, because, unlike corporate, union, and trade/membership/health PACs, they have no sponsors and thus must use treasury or dues money to pay for fund raising and operating costs.

But ideological PACs' tactics also explain why they have so little money left to give to candidates. Their leaders maintain that they prefer to spend large amounts of their money for candidate-training schools, polls, and consultants, all of which show up on disclosure reports as operating expenses, not contributions to candidates. A number of these committees also make substantial independent expenditures.

In the 1985-1986 election cycle, ideological PACs raised $118.4 million, $38 million more than corporate PACs and more than twice what labor union PACs raised. But by 1990, the fortunes of ideological PACs clearly began to wane. They raised $72.4 million, $32 million less than in 1988. Meanwhile, for the 1988 and 1990 elections, corporate and labor PACs began raising more than ideological committees. In 1990, for example, corporate PACs raised $106.3 million; labor PACs, $89.0 million.[32] Furthermore, only two ideological PACs were on the list of top ten PAC money raisers and none was on the list of top ten contributors to federal candidates for the 1990 elections.

A 1983 study of PACs characterized the fund raising and spending of nonconnected PACs as "entrepreneurial." Connected committees, the study said, with a more "participatory" style, tended more than nonconnected PACs to support incumbents and to spend in ways that suggest their donors have some influence on spending decisions. "The decision-makers for non-connected PACs," the study concluded, "have no responsibility—not even nominal responsibility—to any cohesive group of donors who share a profession or workplace. Thus the leaders are free to pursue ideological, challenger-oriented strategies or to spend independently of any candidate organization."[33] Not so for corporate and labor PACs, which have definite constituencies to please.

Leadership PACs. Another category of PACs is the thirty-two or so operated by members of Congress. Variously called leadership PACs or member-affiliated PACs, they represent an effort by members to raise funds above and beyond their principal campaign committees. They use their leadership positions within the Senate and House, and their committee and subcommittee chairmanships and memberships, to raise money that they mainly contribute to other candidates to enhance their present leadership positions, achieve new leadership positions, seek presidential nominations, rally support for legislative bills or public policy issues they care about, or simply help out friends or party members being challenged. Some use the money to travel for speech making at party or candidate fund-raising events. Presidential candidates have used their PACs to undertake travel and other activities in advance of establishing personal campaign committees. In 1990-1991, some gave to party redistricting committees and operations within their states.

Leadership PACs are controversial. Some say they are simply additional ways for special interests to generate multiple PAC contributions and thus greater influence. Some object on grounds they develop "personality cults" around members who established them. Others defend leadership PACs as improving the political process by providing party solidarity, helping to protect vulnerable incumbents, enhancing leadership and issue potential, and imposing chances for mobilizing support for or against legislation. While the so-called personality cult leads to raising money in the name of the leader instead of the party, for example, many leaders help party senatorial and congressional campaign committees to raise money as well.[34]

The Decreasing Role of the Individual Contributor. In recent years, as candidates have been spending more and more time seeking funds from PACs, parties, and out-of-state lobbyists, many people have begun to lament that individuals play a lesser role in the federal election process. However, even as PACs have gained influence, the ultimate source of all political contributions is the individual. That is true whether contributions are given to a PAC, a political party, or an individual candidate. The PACs or party committees are merely channels through which individuals give.

Clearly, individuals still play a substantial role in the federal election process and contribute far more dollars to federal candidates than political action committees do. In the 1987-1988 and the 1989-1990 federal election cycles, contributions from individuals accounted for more than half the contributions to congressional candidates. By contrast, contributions from political action committees were about 30 percent in those years. Altogether, individual contributions accounted for $249.5 million of the $471.2 million raised in the 1990 election cycle.

A study conducted by Citizen Action concluded that two-thirds of the $516 million that House and Senate candidates raised in the 1987-1988 election cycle came in the form of large individual contributions—defined as gifts of $200 or more. Twenty-seven percent came in the form of gifts that were at least $500.[35] Only five states—California, Florida, New Jersey, New York, and Texas—accounted for 45 percent of the large contributions given.

The Citizen Action report also found that a great number of large individual donors gave gifts to candidates running outside of their states.

Donations were tracked by zip code, and ten—which included the wealthiest addresses in the country—accounted for 12 percent of all large individual contributions. The top one-hundred zip codes accounted for 25 percent of all large individual gifts. A subsequent Citizen Action study confirmed the trend by showing that, in the 1990 federal election cycle, a single Manhattan zip code (10021) contributed $3.5 million more than all the large donors in twenty-eight states.[36]

Independent Expenditures

In the early 1980s, independent expenditures—those made by individuals or groups without consultation or cooperation with a candidate's campaign organization—became an important form of spending in federal elections. Starting in 1980, as individuals and groups became more familiar with the law, the importance of independent expenditures increased significantly as a means of circumventing the contribution limits and supplementing candidate spending in early primary states with low spending ceilings and in later primary states when presidential candidates might be approaching the national spending limit.

Independent spending survived two major court challenges and has been sanctioned by the U.S. Supreme Court. In 1980, the FEC and Common Cause challenged the practice of independent spending and filed suit against a number of groups that had announced plans to spend money on behalf of Ronald Reagan's candidacy. The FEC and Common Cause charged that such spending violated a provision of federal election law that prohibited organized political committees from spending more than $1,000 on behalf of a candidate eligible to receive funds. A federal district court threw out the suit and also struck down the provision of law in question, calling it an unconstitutional restriction of the First Amendment rights of individuals and groups. Common Cause and the FEC appealed the decision to the Supreme Court, which in the fall of 1980 reached a 4-4 deadlock on the case, thereby leaving independent spending unaffected in 1980.[37]

To prevent a large amount of independent spending in the 1984 election, the FEC and the Democratic National Committee in 1983 brought suit against two groups—NCPAC and FCM—that announced plans to conduct massive pro-Reagan independent expenditure campaigns. The case did not make its way to the Supreme Court until late November 1984, after the general election, in which groups and individuals spent nearly $20 million on behalf of federal candidates. Most of that money—$15.8 million—was spent on behalf of Reagan.

In March 1985, the Court, in a 7-2 decision, struck down the provision of the act that limited PACs' ability to spend money on behalf of candidates.

Writing for the majority, Justice William H. Rehnquist declared that the provision failed to serve a compelling government interest, such as avoiding corruption or the appearance of it, and that, accordingly, the provision's restrictions of First Amendment rights would be upheld. In dissent, Justice Byron R. White took issue with the Court's identification of money and speech, arguing, as he had in the *Buckley* decision, that the First Amendment protects the right to speak, not the right to spend.[38]

Following the Court's decision, groups and individuals spent $8.8 million on behalf of and $1.4 million against federal candidates in the 1986 federal elections. The marked dip from the 1984 figures reflects the difference in spending between presidential and nonpresidential election years.

By 1987-1988, total independent expenditures decreased for the first time since spending began. At $21.4 million, spending was down from the $23.4 million of the comparable presidential election four years earlier.

Through the 1980s, far more independent money went in favor of Republican candidates than Democratic candidates. For example, in 1988 presidential campaigns, $13.7 million was spent for Republicans as compared with only $2.8 million for all Democrats. At the same time, $4.2 million in negative spending targeted Democrats, while $409,000 was spent against Republicans. In the 1988 election, independent spending amounts were down a bit, but negative independent spending was the highest it had been since 1982.[39]

In congressional elections, independent spending tends to mirror patterns in direct PAC gifts: a heavy emphasis is placed on supporting incumbents. One reason that a PAC may lean toward independent expenditures is to get the attention and appreciation of an incumbent.

While independent spending is an important factor in political finance, its relevance should not be overrated because only a small number of PACs engage in independent expenditures. Independent expenditures, however, could become much greater and much more of a factor, if reform legislation outlawed PAC giving in its present form.

Perhaps the most well known independent expenditure in 1988 was made by a group of Californians called the Committee for the Presidency, which advocated George Bush's election. The group spent $92,000 to produce a television spot that featured the story of a Massachusetts felon named Willie Horton, who raped a woman after he was released from prison on a furlough program. The flurry of press attention surrounding the ad made Willie Horton a major issue of the campaign against Michael Dukakis, who granted the furlough.

Individuals also may engage in independent spending. Los Angeles businessman and pro-Israel advocate Michael R. Goland made extremely large independent expenditures in 1984, spending more than $1 million of his own money to finance an independent effort to defeat then Illinois Republican senator Charles Percy, first in the primary, then in the general election. Percy lost to Democrat Paul Simon. Goland used his money to pay for ads that criticized Senator Percy's voting record on American policy toward Israel, the handicapped, school nutrition, and draft registration.[40] Goland also spent money on behalf of other candidates he believed were pro-Israel.[41]

Goland's independent expenditures were legal despite complaints made to the FEC. However, in 1986, Goland violated federal election laws by arranging a series of illegal contributions to a third party candidate as part of an effort to help California Democratic senator Alan Cranston get reelected. Goland was later convicted and sentenced to three months in a "jail-like facility." His conviction marked the first time a political donor was sent to jail for evading campaign limits in a Senate race.[42]

Goland's crime was that he repaid fifty-six individuals—employees and associates—who agreed to give a total of $120,000 to American Independent candidate Edward B. Vallen. It is illegal to be reimbursed for political contributions, or, in other words, to give in the name of another. The money financed television advertisements that described Vallen as a far better candidate than Cranston's chief opponent, Rep. Ed Zschau. The effort was meant to deflect votes away from Zschau, whom Goland suspected was anti-Israel.[43] No evidence surfaced indicating that either Cranston or Vallen knew about Goland's illegal contributions.

Soft Money

Soft money has become a major issue in debates about campaign finance reform. The term "soft money" refers to funds that are raised from sources outside the restraints of federal law but are spent on activities intended to affect federal elections. By contrast, "hard money" is raised, spent, and publicly disclosed under federal supervision. Some have called the use of soft money a healthy development, claiming that it encourages citizen participation and helps to revitalize state and local party committees. However, since large sums of soft money have been used in recent presidential campaigns—some as large as $100,000 from a single source—some have called for federal regulation or even the complete prohibition of such donations.

Federal law exempts several types of state and local activity from the federal contribution and expenditure limits. State and local party committees can spend money for voter registration and get-out-the-vote drives and for grass-roots campaign materials, such as yard signs, campaign buttons, bumper stickers, and party tabloids. Federal law also allows these committees to spend unlimited amounts of money to distribute slate cards, sample ballots, palm cards, or any other printed listings of names of three or more candidates for public office.

In these types of exempted activity, only the portion of the costs that benefits federal candidates has to be paid with hard money, and thus is subject to federal limits. The remainder may be paid from funds raised under applicable state laws, which often permit corporate and labor union political contributions and give much freer rein to individual and PAC contributions.

Some suggest that soft money is a loophole of the Federal Election Campaign Act that encourages just the kind of large individual contributions that the law was designed to eliminate. But soft money was sanctioned by the 1979 FECA amendments, which were, in part, a conscious effort by Congress to empower state and local party committees in federal campaigns.

In the three presidential election cycles in the 1980s, soft money became an ever more integral part of federal campaign finance. For 1980, $19 million in soft money was spent in federal elections; for 1984 the number grew to $19.6 million; by 1988, $45 million.

Robert A. Farmer, the chief fund raiser of the Dukakis-Bentsen campaign, started the 1988 drive for soft money by announcing an effort to raise $50 million in such private donations. "I refuse to apologize," said Farmer. "For the past three elections, the Republicans have hit a Mack truck through campaign loopholes. Our objective has been to create a level playing field."[44] Farmer later admitted that the plan was a strategic error because it triggered a Republican response in the form of Team 100, which raised soft money funds. That effort was orchestrated by Farmer's Republican counterpart, Robert A. Mosbacher.

Both Farmer and Mosbacher raised $22 23 million in soft money. Among their sources were corporations and labor unions, which are not allowed to contribute to federal candidates but may give at the state level in many cases. Many donors gave well beyond federal limits, which seems to have violated the spirit of the campaign finance limitations of 1974.

The Keating Affair

Developments in the savings and loan debacle of the late 1980s brought to public attention the role that soft money can play in congressional elections. One institution, Lincoln Savings and Loan, was accused of receiving special attention as a result of the $1.3 million in political contributions made by its president—Charles Keating—his family, and associates.

In 1988, federal regulators were closely scrutinizing Lincoln Savings. Facing pressure, Keating made or arranged direct contributions to five senators: John Glenn, D-Ohio, $34,000; Alan Cranston, D-Calif., $47,000;

John McCain, R-Ariz., $112,000; Dennis DeConcini, D-Ariz., $55,000; and Donald W. Riegle, Jr., D-Mich., $76,000. In addition, Keating gave substantial soft money to several other senators. He arranged for $200,000 in soft money to go to the National Council on Public Policy, a committee operated by Glenn. He also arranged $850,000 in soft money contributions to go to committees working on voter registration and get-out-the-vote drives in California. One of these committees was operated by Cranston's son. Keating also gave $85,000 to the California Democratic State Central Committee for voter activities and $95,000 to the California Republican State Central Committee.[45]

The five senators were dubbed the "Keating Five" and were accused of having engaged in an extraordinary effort to help Lincoln Savings. Initially, four of them, and then in a second meeting, five, summoned the chairman of the Federal Home Loan Bank Board and key officials to discuss proposed actions against Lincoln Savings, including the possibility of delaying action against the institution. When the relationship of Keating to the five senators became public, all the senators denied doing favors for him because of his political donations. Senators DeConcini, McCain, and Cranston claimed they were simply doing constituency service because Keating's holdings were mostly in Arizona and California. In a news conference, Keating said: "One question, among many, has had to do with whether my financial support in any way influenced several political figures to take up my cause. I want to say in the most forceful way I can: I certainly hope so."[46]

A number of members of Congress, not only some among the Keating Five, returned to Keating and his associates their contributions, and some went further to refund all contributions from savings and loan PACs or individual officers. Several contributed the amounts to the U.S. Treasury.

The Senate Ethics Committee appointed a special counsel and held extensive hearings. After reformulating the recommendations of the special counsel, the committee found that the conduct of Senators Riegle and DeConcini "gave the appearance of being improper and was certainly attended with insensitivity and poor judgment," that Senators Glenn and McCain "exercised poor judgment" in selected circumstances, and that Senator Cranston was considered most culpable. The committee extended its investigation to receive Cranston's rebuttal. The case was delayed because of Cranston's extensive preparation of his defense. In a plea bargain with the Ethics Committee, seeking to avoid a censure vote, and based in part on consideration of his personal illness, Cranston received a reprimand derived from "substantial credible evidence [that he] engaged in an impermissible pattern of conduct in which fundraising and official activities were substantially linked." Cranston accepted the reprimand "with remorse" but declared that his intentions were proper, that he had violated no Senate rule, and that others have behaved similarly. Some senators sought to vote censure but in the end refrained from pursing the action.[47]

The Lincoln Savings scandal, among other matters, raises questions of the proper and ethical definition of "constituency service." Can a member of Congress provide assistance to a contributor on the same basis, or must it be on a different basis, as a noncontributor constituent? Is it possible to distinguish the number of jobs that may be lost if a company does not get a contract, from the influence of the company's owner or its PAC? While a member of Congress has limited hours and cannot meet with everyone who wants an appointment, in recent years, meeting with a contributor triggers reform-minded groups and investigative journalists to raise doubts, whatever the merits of the case.

Ambassadorships for Large Donors

A number of the Team 100 donors were nominated by the Bush administration to become ambassadors to foreign countries. The practice of rewarding large donors with high-placed federal jobs has been a time-honored practice, but nevertheless, the Bush administration encountered great criticism at confirmation hearings for several of these nominations. Senators, political analysts, and foreign service officers charged that Bush's appointments were simply rewards for large financial contributions to his presidential campaign. In particular, they disapproved of the appointment of Joy A. Silverman to become the ambassador to Barbados. Silverman, whose nomination was blocked by the Senate, had no college degree and no foreign policy experience.[48] "Such appointees may well possess qualifications beyond personal wealth or fund-raising prowess," said Democratic senator Paul Sarbanes of Maryland. "But even when that is true, the appearances are that they bought their jobs."[49]

Although controversy persists about the practice of rewarding large contributors with high government posts, the 1980s witnessed a decline in the number of ambassadorships being rewarded to large contributors, until the Bush administration reversed the trend.

The practice had been put into sharp focus when one Watergate investigation revealed that following the 1972 election President Nixon appointed 319 persons to high-level positions (including ambassadorships) and that all had won confirmation. Fifty-two of these appointees, or 17 percent, were recorded as having contributed $100 or more to the Republicans. Their gifts totaled $772,224, with $703,654 of that going to the Nixon campaign.

The appointment of Ruth Farkas, a sociologist and a director of Alexanders, a New York department store, generated the most controversy of any of Nixon's appointments. According to testimony during the

Watergate hearings, Farkas reportedly had balked at an offer of an ambassadorship to Costa Rica, saying, "Isn't $250,000 an awful amount of money for Costa Rica?"[50] Farkas, who actually gave a total of $300,000, was the single largest donor of the group being investigated.

Several individuals felt the repercussions of the Farkas affair. Herbert E. Kalmbach, President Nixon's personal lawyer, was imprisoned for fund-raising activities relating in part to his participation in creating "ambassadorial auctions," which were illegal because federal law prohibits the promising of federal jobs in return for financial support.

Since Watergate, the practice of appointing large donors to high government posts has generally diminished, although all presidents who have been elected have encountered criticism for rewarding fat cats with jobs.

Although Jimmy Carter pledged that he would take the selection of envoys out of the realm of politics, his appointment of Ohio real estate developer Marvin L. Warner as ambassador to Switzerland was controversial because Warner had arranged a fund-raising breakfast that netted $20,000. Carter also was criticized for his appointment of Cleveland businessman Milton Wolfe to become ambassador to Austria because Wolfe arranged a fund-raising event that collected $80,000 for Carter in one evening.

Questions also arose about Reagan's appointments of large donors to ambassadorships. The American Foreign Service Association claimed that the "vast majority" of Reagan's appointees to foreign posts were "relatively undistinguished as public figures."[51] Former U.S. ambassador to the Soviet Union Robert Toon accused the Reagan administration of using diplomatic posts as "a dumping ground for defeated politicians and Republican financial backers."[52] Toon was particularly critical of four of Reagan's appointees.

Of eighty-seven ambassadors appointed by President Bush in the first nine months of his administration, forty-eight were friends and supporters—a higher rate than those made by Presidents Carter and Reagan at a similar time in their terms.[53]

The Wealth of Candidates

Since 1932, a number of presidents were considered wealthy when they took office. The list includes Franklin D. Roosevelt, Dwight D. Eisenhower, John F. Kennedy, and Lyndon B. Johnson. However, personal wealth was a significant factor only in Kennedy's nomination. For the rest, their personal assets had little if any effect on their nomination and subsequent election. The same is true for other candidates who ran for the presidency. Though both Adlai E. Stevenson and Barry Goldwater had personal fortunes, their wealth did not seem to enhance nor hinder their campaigns.

Although Jimmy Carter, Ronald Reagan, and George Bush were considered wealthy when they ran for the presidency, their money was not considered a major factor in their successful quests for nominations, either. However, wealth benefits a candidate indirectly. For example, because of his family's successful peanut warehouse business, Carter was able to guarantee personal loans to his campaign during a difficult time in 1976 when matching government funds were not available because of legal challenges to the then-new public financing system for presidential campaigns. And Reagan's wealth enabled him to devote full attention to his presidential campaign. Other potential candidates, from the presidential to the local level, may have difficulty going without salary or income while campaigning for office.

While wealth may not have made a difference in recent presidential campaigns, it has been a source of controversy. The case of the Rockefeller family is the most conspicuous example. When he appeared before the House Judiciary Committee in 1974 as the vice president designate, Nelson Rockefeller testified that he and members of his family had spent more than $17 million on the various political campaigns he had run in eighteen years of public service. He said that family spending is necessary because "it's very difficult for a Rockefeller to raise money for campaigns. The reaction is, 'Why should we give money to a Rockefeller?' "[54]

Passage of the Federal Election Campaign Act of 1971 diminished the role that personal wealth could play in federal campaigns. In the 1976 *Buckley v. Valeo* decision, the Supreme Court declared the FECA's limitations on a candidate's contributions to his or her own campaign unconstitutional unless public funding is provided and accepted. This ruled out such limits in congressional campaigns, but restrictions remained in force for presidential campaigns if the candidate accepted public funding.

Because federal funds are not provided for congressional elections, there is no limit on the amounts these candidates may contribute to their own political campaigns. Sen. John Heinz of Pennsylvania spent several million dollars from his fortune to finance his successful Senate bid in 1976. In the primary, Heinz, who was then a member of the House of Representatives, ran against former Philadelphia district attorney Arlen Specter. Ninety percent of the funds Heinz used in that race—$585,765 out of a total of $673,869—came in the form of personal loans. Specter spent only $224,105—a third of what Heinz did—in the primary; Specter was able to lend his campaign $38,744. Counting the general election contest, which he also won, Heinz made loans to his campaign amounting to $2,465,500.

In 1982, several candidates contributed extremely large amounts to their own campaigns, including Democrat Mark Dayton of Minnesota, who spent $6.9 million personally in a bid to defeat Republican senator David Durenberger; and New Jersey Democrat Frank Lautenberg, who gave or lent $5.1 million to his Senate campaign against Rep. Millicent Fenwick, who gave or lent $877,000 to her own cause. Dayton lost, but Lautenberg won.

For his 1984 Senate campaign, Sen. John D. Rockefeller IV of West Virginia used more than $11 million of his own money to help defeat his opponent, Republican John R. Raese. The strategy was not a new one for Rockefeller, who served two terms as governor of West Virginia from 1977 to 1985. In his 1980 gubernatorial campaign, Rockefeller spent more than $12 million of his own money to finance his competitive race against former governor Arch A. Moore, Jr., who was trying to stage a comeback. Rockefeller's use of his own money engendered some resentment among voters and even inspired a bumper sticker that read, "Make Him Spend It All, Arch."[55] Perhaps because of public pressure, Rockefeller, after winning his U.S. Senate race in 1984 , decided not to dip into his pockets to finance his 1990 reelection. But then he encountered criticism for accepting PAC contributions. He remarked, "You can spend your own money or you can go out and raise it. We've been roundly criticized for doing both."[56]

The most notable case of self-financing in 1988 took place in Wisconsin, where Democrat Herbert H. Kohl, a multimillionaire, spent more than $7 million of his own money to win a Senate seat. Kohl also had the distinction of being the only 1988 Senate winner to refuse PAC money. He made a public virtue of his ability to finance his campaign almost entirely out of his own fortune. His campaign slogan was "Nobody's Senator But Yours,"[57] meaning he would not be beholden to any contributors. In the general election, Kohl spent $500,000 more than his challenger, state senator Susan Engeleiter, and won 52 percent of the vote.

Even with the limitations on personal spending by candidates who accept public funds, wealth still brings candidates incalculable advantages. Wealthy candidates make news, and publicity about their families draws attention—all part of the process of building valuable name recognition. A budding politician from a wealthy family frequently is able to run for high office at the outset of his or her political career, whereas men and women of less wealth—with the possible exception of actors, athletes, and astronauts—usually begin at lower elective levels and earn their way up the political ladder from office to higher office.

Other advantages for wealthy candidates derive from their access to wealthy friends. Well-connected persons obtain credit with ease and can guarantee that loans or bills will be paid. Their ability to pick up the tab at lunches and dinners, to phone long distance without worrying about the cost, is helpful, too.

Superficially at least, wealthy candidates seem less likely to seek personal gain from public office. They may incur fewer obligations and thereby preserve more freedom of action—and wealthy candidates such as Kohl have at times used just such an argument in their campaigns.

Wealthy candidates can lose, however. But political realities continue to favor them. Wealth propels, quickens, and catalyzes. And it is only folklore that the average American admires the impecunious candidate who wins elections on a shoestring. Voters often cast their ballots for the well-to-do individuals with expensive organizations and substantial war chests. American voters have been strongly drawn to the Roosevelts, Tafts, Kennedys, and Rockefellers.

A common concern exists that the wealthy are over-represented in politics. However, wealthy officeholders often represent those who might not otherwise have a strong voice in government. This tradition goes back to the Virginia squire who was the first president of the United States and carries up to Massachusetts senator Edward M. Kennedy, who regularly voices the interests of minorities and the poor.

The main problem of wealth in elections may not be so much in the outcome of financially imbalanced contests but in depriving the voters of potential leaders who do not have the money to even consider running for office.

Patterns in Political Giving

In the years between 1972 and 1986, the tax credit individuals could claim on their federal income tax returns was considered an important incentive for making contributions. Until the Tax Reform Act of 1986 repealed the provision, individuals could subtract from their tax liabilities one-half the amount of contributions they made to candidates, PACs, and political party committees, up to a limit, after 1978, of $50 for individuals and $100 for married couples. To date, the repeal of the political tax credit has not had a measurable effect on political contributing, since political income has continued to rise.

Just as myriad reasons exist for people to donate to campaigns, a variety of types of persons make contributions. While there is no such thing as a "typical contributor," analysis shows some prevailing characteristics of people who make political donations. One study of the role of individual contributors concluded that they are more active in other aspects of the political process than noncontributors.[58] Their additional participation often includes not only voting but also trying to persuade others to support a particular candidate or party, publicizing a candidate or campaign,

Table 4-1 Percentage of National Adult Population Making Political Contributions, 1952-1988

Year	Polling organization	Contributions		
		To Republican	To Democrat	Total[a]
1952	SRC	3	1	4
1956	Gallup	3	6	9
	SRC	5	5	10
1960	Gallup	4	4	9
	Gallup			12
	SRC	7	4	11
1964	Gallup	6	4	12
	SRC	6	4	11
1968	SRC	4	4	9[b]
1972	SRC	4	5	10[c]
1974	SRC	3	3	8[d]
1976	Gallup	3	3	8[e]
	SRC	4	4	9[f]
1980	CPS	7	3	13.4[g]
1984	CPS	5	4	12.5[h]
1988	CPS	4	3	7.2[i]

Sources: Survey Research Center (SRC), succeeded by the Center for Political Studies (CPS), University of Michigan; Angus Campbell, Philip E. Converse, and Donald E. Stokes, *The American Voter* (New York: John Wiley and Sons, 1960), 91; 1980 data from Ruth S. Jones and Warren E. Miller, "Financing Campaigns: Macro Level Innovation and Micro Level Response," *Western Political Quarterly* 38:2 (June 1985); 1984 data from Ruth S. Jones, "Campaign Contributions and Campaign Solicitations: 1984" (Paper presented at the annual meeting of the Southern Political Science Association, Nashville, Tennessee, November 6-9, 1985); Gallup data from Roper Opinion Research Center, Williams College, and American Institute of Political Opinion (Gallup Poll). Reprinted from: *Financing the 1988 Election*, Herbert E. Alexander and Monica Bauer, 1991, by permission of Westview Press, Boulder, Colorado.

[a] The total percentage may not add up to the total of Democrat and Republican contributions because of individuals contributing to both major parties, to nonparty groups, or to combinations of these.

[b] Includes 0.7 percent who contributed to George C. Wallace's American Independent party.

[c] Includes contributors to the American Independent party.

[d] Includes 0.7 percent who contributed to both parties and 0.8 percent who contributed to minor parties.

[e] Includes 1 percent to another party and 1 percent to Do Not Know or No Answer.

[f] Republican and Democratic figures are rounded. The total includes 0.6 percent who gave to Both Parties, 0.4 percent to Other, and 0.3 percent Do Not Know.

[g] Includes persons who gave to special interest groups. As some 6.8 percent of those surveyed fell into this category, it appears that many contributed in two or all three categories.

[h] Includes persons giving to groups supporting and opposing ballot propositions and candidates.

[i] Includes 0.5 percent who gave to both parties or to candidates from both parties.

volunteering, and attending rallies and fund-raising events.

Although the costs of running a campaign have risen dramatically over recent decades, the percentage of Americans donating to candidates and parties has not changed much since 1956 (see Table 4-1). Although the figures in Table 4-1 are subject to a polling error of up to four percent, their replication over the years gives confidence that the upper and lower parameters of giving are accurate. The variation from year to year shows no recent trend line.

A steady increase in the number of contributors took place in the 1950s through 1968, when it dropped. The number rose again in 1972, only to drop once more in the post-Watergate period. From 1952 to 1988, between 4 and 13 percent of the total adult population said they contributed to politics at some level in presidential election years. Clearly, some persons contribute in more than one category.

One recent study of patterns of giving concluded that

> While it is true that more and more people are now asked, by phone and mail, to make political contributions, the response rate is generally very low. Modern technology notwithstanding, face-to-face appeals continue to be the most effective way of soliciting political contributions. There does not seem to be a large, undifferentiated electorate just waiting for an invitation to contribute to campaigns.[59]

The data in Table 4-1 seem to bear out this conclusion.

5 The Costs of Elections

John Quincy Adams, the sixth U.S. president, argued that the presidency should be neither sought nor declined. "To pay money for securing it directly or indirectly," he asserted, was "incorrect in principle."[1] However noble these sentiments, all presidential candidates since George Washington have had to worry about campaign costs. From torchlight parade to "telethon," someone has had to pay expenses.

Before 1972, measuring all the costs of presidential campaigns was difficult because money traditionally was spent at the national, state, and local levels, with no central accounting system. However, more historical information is available about presidential elections, because of their prominence, than for most other categories of election campaigns.

Early Campaigns

Since the Republic's founding, printing has been the most basic campaign expense. In 1791, Thomas Jefferson asked Philip Freneau to come to Philadelphia; gave him a part-time clerkship for foreign languages in the State Department; and made him editor of the *National Gazette*, the subsidized organ of the Anti-Federalists. The Federalists had been financing their own paper, the *Gazette of the United States*, with money from Alexander Hamilton, Rufus King, and printing subsidies.[2]

The system of newspapers supporting, and being supported by, one political faction or another quickly developed. Editors' fortunes rose and fell with the political success of their patrons. Newspapers vilified candidates mercilessly, and various factions spun off their own papers.

Much early campaigning for the presidency took place in newspaper columns. As late as 1850, when a wealthy backer wanted to further the political ambitions of James Buchanan, he contributed $10,000 to help start a newspaper for Buchanan's support.[3] In 1860, Abraham Lincoln secretly bought a small German weekly in Illinois for $400 and turned it over to an editor who agreed to report on the Republican party and to publish in both English and German.[4]

During the early 1800s, books, pamphlets, and newspapers were handed from person to person until they no longer were readable. All the campaign publicity caused a reaction that seems modern by today's standards. A letter written to the *Charlestown Gazette* complained, "We are so beset and run down by federal republicans and their pamphlets that I begin to think for the first time that there is rottenness in the system they attempt to support, or why all this violent electioneering?"[5]

By 1840, more than just the printed word was used to spread the story. Pictures, buttons, banners, and novelty items appeared. According to one observer, William Henry Harrison's campaign had "conventions and mass meetings, parades and processions with banners and floats, long speeches on the log-cabin theme, log-cabin song books and log-cabin newspapers, Harrison pictures, and Tippecanoe handkerchiefs and badges."[6]

Active campaigning by presidential candidates is a recent phenomenon. Andrew Jackson retired to his plantation, the Hermitage, after he was nominated, although his supporters did hold torchlight parades and hickory pole raisings. Political rallies came into their own in the mid-1800s. Campaigns provided an opportunity for a widely scattered population to meet and socialize. In those days, audiences judged orators by the length—not the content—of their speeches. Therefore, two or three hour orations were not uncommon.

Stephen A. Douglas barnstormed the country in his 1860 campaign against Lincoln, a practice not tried again until 1896, when William Jennings Bryan, the "Boy Orator," traveled eighteen thousand miles giving some six hundred speeches to at least five million people.[7] By contrast, his opponent, William McKinley, sat on his front porch and let the people come to him. Special trains were run to his hometown of Canton, Ohio, with the railroads cooperating by cutting fares. McKinley did not have to travel because wealthy industrialist and Republican National Committee chairman Mark Hanna organized fourteen hundred people to go around the country to speak on McKinley's behalf. Hanna also spent a great deal of money to publish and distribute more than 120 million pieces of McKinley campaign literature. The volume of campaign mail is even more remarkable considering that U.S. citizens in 1896 numbered only 71 million.[8] The exact costs of these early forays into personal campaigning by Douglas and Bryan are not known, but because both candidates lost, they probably were not considered worthwhile expenses.

Modern Campaigns

Politics is big business and has become a major industry. In 1952, the first year in which total political costs were calculated, the bill for electing people to local, state, and federal office was $140 million. By 1988, another presidential election year, the cost of American elections at all levels of government skyrocketed to $2.7 billion.[9] The costs of electing candidates to higher office were nineteen times higher in 1988 than in 1952.

The data in Table 5-1 show the amounts spent by national party and candidate committees on major party presidential candidates in general elections since 1860, though the figures before 1912 are less reliable. A general upward movement in spending has taken place, with some startling differences in particularly intense contests. Much of the increase is related to the growth in size of the electorate and to general inflation. If expenditures are calculated on a per-vote basis, the sharp rise in costs began with the 1952 elections, the year, significantly, when the freeze on licensing of new television stations ended. In the next four years, the number of commercial stations quadrupled.[10]

In addition to paying for radio and television advertising, candidates have become more dependent upon the use of direct mail appeals and of high technology and the political consultants needed to apply it to campaigns: pollsters, media specialists, fund raisers, and computer experts. Higher levels of competition also are a factor in the escalating spending. And greater availability of data because of reforms in the law provided more disclosure of candidates' finances. Therefore, although by comparison costs have risen dramatically in recent years, much candidate spending went unrecorded prior to the adoption of comprehensive financial disclosure laws. The steady progression in spending in presidential election years from 1952 to 1988, at all levels—federal, state, and local—is shown in Table 5-2, with percentage increases.

The rate of spending has, however, begun to slow. For example, in 1990, candidates for Congress spent $445 million, the lowest amount that had been spent in six years and $14 million less than spent in 1988. However, incumbents' spending is still increasing, while challengers are spending less money in their campaigns. For example, in 1990, all Senate candidates spent $180 million, a 10 percent decline from 1988. Incumbent senators, however, spent 12 percent more than they did in 1988 and outspent their challengers by a ratio of more than 2-to-1.[11] Spending by House candidates in 1990 shows a similar trend. While overall spending increased by 3 percent to $265 million, incumbents' spending increased by 21 percent. More significantly, these incumbents outspent their challengers by a ratio of more than 3.5-to-1.[12]

No single factor accounts for campaign finance inflation. And certain categories of campaign spending are more pronounced in some campaign years than in others. The best way to understand why costs have risen is to look at different categories of spending over the course of several years.

During the 1987-1988 election cycle a total of $2.7 billion was spent on political campaigns for local, state, and federal offices (see Figure 5-1). The people who spent the money included candidates, committees, and organizations, and individuals trying to influence the election process. The

Table 5-1 Costs of Presidential General Elections, 1860-1988

Year	Republican Spending	Republican Candidate	Democratic Spending	Democratic Candidate
1860	$ 100,000	Lincoln°	$ 50,000	Douglas
1864	125,000	Lincoln°	50,000	McClennan
1868	150,000	Grant°	75,000	Seymour
1872	250,000	Grant°	50,000	Greeley
1876	950,000	Hayes°	900,000	Tilden
1880	1,100,000	Garfield°	335,000	Hancock
1884	1,300,000	Blaine	1,400,000	Cleveland°
1888	1,350,000	Harrison°	855,000	Cleveland
1892	1,700,000	Harrison	2,350,000	Cleveland°
1896	3,350,000	McKinley°	675,000	Bryan
1900	3,000,000	McKinley°	425,000	Bryan
1904	2,096,000	T. Roosevelt°	700,000	Parker
1908	1,655,518	Taft°	629,341	Bryan
1912	1,071,549	Taft	1,134,848	Wilson°
1916	2,441,565	Hughes	2,284,590	Wilson°
1920	5,417,501	Harding°	1,470,371	Cox
1924	4,020,478	Coolidge°	1,108,836	Davis
1928	6,256,111	Hoover°	5,342,350	Smith
1932	2,900,052	Hoover	2,245,975	F. Roosevelt°
1936	8,892,972	Landon	5,194,741	F. Roosevelt°
1940	3,451,310	Willkie	2,783,654	F. Roosevelt°
1944	2,828,652	Dewey	2,169,077	F. Roosevelt°
1948	2,127,296	Dewey	2,736,334	Truman°
1952	6,608,623	Eisenhower°	5,032,926	Stevenson
1956	7,778,702	Eisenhower°	5,106,651	Stevenson
1960	10,128,000	Nixon	9,797,000	Kennedy°
1964	16,026,000	Goldwater	8,757,000	Johnson°
1968	25,402,000	Nixon°	11,594,000	Humphrey
1972	61,400,000	Nixon°	30,000,000	McGovern
1976[a]	21,786,641	Ford	21,800,000	Carter°
1980[b]	29,188,188	Reagan°	29,352,767	Carter
1984[c]	40,400,000	Reagan°	40,400,000	Mondale
1988[d]	46,100,000	Bush°	46,100,000	Dukakis

Sources: 1860-1888 Republican and 1860-1900 Democratic: The best available figures, although disputed, are from U.S. Congress, *Congressional Record,* 61st Cong., 2d sess., April 18, 1910, 4931, as cited in Louise Overacker, *Money in Elections* (New York: Macmillan, 1932), 71n. 1892-1924 Republican and 1904-1924 Democratic: Overacker, *Money in Elections,* 73. 1928-1944: Louise Overacker, *Presidential Campaign Funds* (Boston: Boston University Press, 1946), 32. 1948: Alexander Heard, *The Costs of Democracy* (Chapel Hill: University of North Carolina Press, 1960), 18, 20. 1952-1960: *Financing Presidential Campaigns: Report of the President's Commission on Campaign Costs* (Washington, D.C.: Government Printing Office, April 1962), 10. 1964-1988: Compiled by the Citizens' Research Foundation and reported in Herbert E. Alexander, *Financing the 1960 Election* (Princeton, N.J.: Citizens' Research Foundation, 1962); Alexander, *Financing the 1964 Election* (Princeton, N.J.: Citizens' Research Foundation, 1966); Alexander, *Financing the 1968 Election* (Lexington, Mass.: Heath Lexington Books, 1971); Alexander, *Financing the 1972*

Table 5-1 (continued)

Election (Lexington, Mass.: Lexington Books, 1976); Alexander, *Financing the 1976 Election* (Washington, D.C.: CQ Press, 1979); Alexander, *Financing the 1980 Election* (Lexington, Mass.: Lexington Books, 1983); Herbert E. Alexander and Brian A. Haggerty, *Financing the 1984 Election* (Lexington, Mass.: Lexington Books, 1987); and Herbert E. Alexander and Monica Bauer, *Financing the 1988 Election* (Boulder, Colo.: Westview Press, 1991).

* Indicates winner.

[a] Public funding was first used for presidential elections in 1976. The Republican National Committee spent an additional $1.4 million on Ford's campaign. The Democratic National Committee spent an additional $2.8 million on Carter's campaign.

[b] In 1980, the Republican National Committee spent an additional $4.5 million on Reagan's campaign. The Democratic National Committee spent an additional $4 million on Carter's campaign.

[c] In 1984, the Republican National Committee spent an additional $6.9 million on Reagan's campaign. The Democratic National Committee spent an additional $2.7 million on Mondale's campaign.

[d] In 1988, the Republican National Committee and Democratic National Committee each spent an additional $8.3 million on their presidential candidates' campaigns.

spending covered efforts by numerous independent organizations to register and turn out voters, as well as the cost of administering ideological group committees and maintaining national, state, and local political party organizations.

The $2.7 billion represents a 50 percent increase in estimated actual costs of the 1984 election, which were $1.8 billion. This increase was far greater than the 13.5 percent increase in the consumer price index for the period between January 1, 1984, and January 1, 1988. A storm of criticism concerning rising campaign costs has developed, with critics arguing that candidates now are forced to spent too much time raising money. These critics also maintain that special interest groups, which satisfy candidates' needs for campaign dollars, are an ever-growing threat to the integrity of the election and governmental processes.

Compared with other categories of spending, however, the amount spent on political campaigns is low. The $2.7 billion spent on the 1987-1988 elections is about the same as the nation's two leading commercial advertisers—Procter and Gamble and Philip Morris—spent in 1987 to proclaim the quality of their products.[13] And what was spent on campaigns in 1988 is just a small fraction of what is spent on cosmetics or gambling and represents just 1 percent of the $1.9 trillion spent by federal, state, and local governments in the same year.

As with other kinds of expenditures, no universally accepted criterion exists to determine when political spending becomes excessive. Reformers perpetually push for limits on spending but constitutionally that cannot

Table 5-2 Total Political Spending at Federal, State, and Local Levels, 1952-1988

Year	Spending	Percentage increase
1952	$ 140,000,000	NA
1956	155,000,000	10.7
1960	175,000,000	12.9
1964	200,000,000	14.2
1968	300,000,000	50.0
1972	425,000,000	41.6
1976	540,000,000	36.4
1980	1,200,000,000	122.0
1984	1,800,000,000	50.0
1988	2,700,000,000	50.0

Sources: 1952-1956: Alexander Heard, *The Costs of Democracy* (Chapel Hill: University of North Carolina Press, 1960). 1960-1968: Compiled by the Citizens' Research Foundation and reported in Herbert E. Alexander, *Financing the 1960 Election* (Princeton, N.J.: Citizens' Research Foundation, 1962); Alexander, *Financing the 1964 Election* (Princeton, N.J.: Citizens' Research Foundation, 1966); Alexander, *Financing the 1968 Election* (Lexington, Mass.: Heath Lexington Books, 1971); Alexander, *Financing the 1972 Election* (Lexington, Mass.: Lexington Books, 1976); Alexander, *Financing the 1976 Election* (Washington, D.C.: CQ Press, 1979); Alexander, *Financing the 1980 Election* (Lexington, Mass.: Lexington Books, 1983); Herbert E. Alexander and Brian A. Haggerty, *Financing the 1984 Election* (Lexington, Mass.: Lexington Books, 1987); and Herbert E. Alexander and Monica Bauer, *Financing the 1988 Election* (Boulder, Colo.: Westview Press, 1991).

Note: NA = Not Applicable. Figures rounded. Percentage increases each four-year period.

happen unless legislation is enacted to provide public financing for congressional candidates who agree to limit their spending.

The Impact of Radio and Television

Television first became a prominent political tool in the 1952 presidential election. Since then, television advertising costs have commanded a growing share of campaign costs. Some have charged that the money is being used to promote less appealing candidates—wealthy ones, perhaps, or those who can entice voters into buying an agency-designed image without revealing much about their true political selves.[14]

Critics also warn of the power of political broadcasting. Political scientist Louise Overacker noted that as far back as 1928 spending on radio spots "dwarfed" all other campaign expenditures. In that year, according to Overacker, $550,000, or 18 percent, of the Democratic National Committee's funds went to bring "Al Smith's voice into every home in the United States." Writing in 1932, Overacker predicted that "future campaigns are likely to be fought largely through the microphone."[15]

Clearly, recent election campaigns have demonstrated that the micro-

Figure 5-1 The Campaign Spending Dollar in 1988

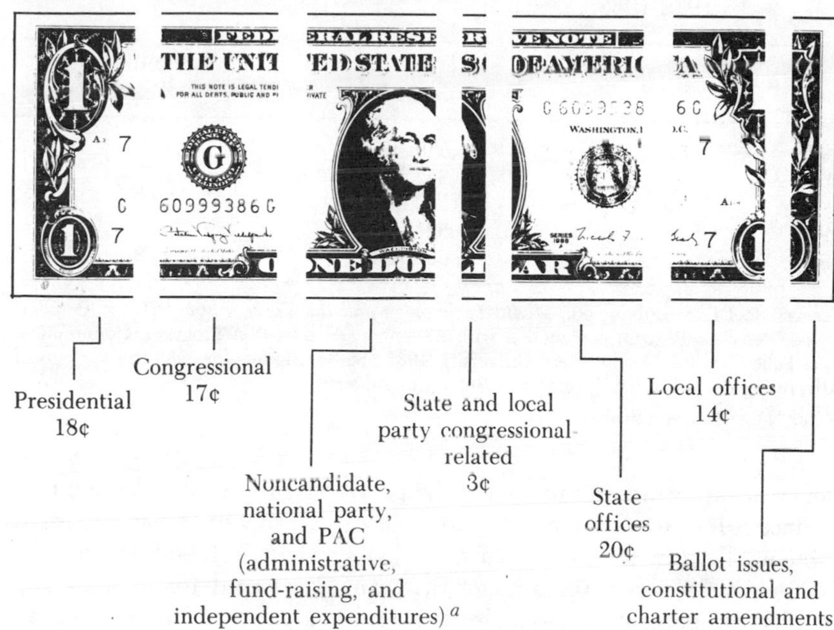

Note: PAC = political action committee.

[a] Not including party and PAC contributions to presidential and congressional candidates; party and PAC contributions to these candidates are included in the presidential and congressional categories.

phone and the airwaves are the venues through which many politicians voice their messages and fight their political battles. And the quantum jump in campaign spending that began in the 1950s clearly can be attributed in some measure to the use of television and radio advertising.

Candidates spent what then was considered a tremendous amount of money on broadcasting in the 1968 elections. That year, Richard Nixon had a carefully programmed campaign calling for noncontroversial television spots and live regional broadcasts that featured the candidate answering prescribed questions from a panel of well-rehearsed supporters. The total of $58.9 million that the Federal Communications Commission (FCC) reported spent in 1968 by candidates at all levels was 70 percent above the $34.6 million expended on political broadcasting just four years earlier. The 1972 broadcast spending totals were only slightly higher than the 1968 totals, but broadcast expenditures declined as a proportion of total political spending from about 20 percent in 1968 to 14 percent in 1972. Among the reasons for this decline were the emergence in importance of

Table 5-3 Costs of Political Advertising in Presidential Election Years, 1972-1988

Year	Total cost	Percentage increase
1972	$ 24,580,100	NA
1976	50,842,200	10.7
1980	90,570,000	78.7
1984	153,824,000	69.6
1988	227,900,200	48.3

Sources: Joel L. Swerdlow, ed., *Media Technology and the Vote: A Source Book* (Boulder, Colo.: Westview Press in conjunction with Annenberg Washington Program, Communications Policy Studies, Northwestern University, 1988), 83-84. Figures for 1988 from "Political Advertising on Television," Television Bureau of Advertising, n.d.

Note: NA = Not Applicable.

nonbroadcast communications and the provisions of the 1971 election law.

Since 1972, the amount of paid political broadcasting has increased substantially, but the rate of increase has slowed considerably since the 1976 elections, when the amount that candidates paid for broadcasting rose by 107 percent over the elections four years earlier (see Table 5-3).

The surge in spending for broadcast advertising has spawned public concern about television's influence on politicians and the electoral process. But the degree to which television has taken over the political process is a matter of perspective.

Television's critics maintain that many, if not most, political candidates now rely almost solely on expensive television commercials to promote their campaigns and that those ads manipulate the unsuspecting voting public. Some argue that the amount of paid advertising should be restricted. Others go further and argue that television ads should be banned altogether and that broadcast stations should provide free air time to candidates as a condition of their broadcast licenses.[16]

Others want to regulate the content of political ads. One proposal would require campaign commercials to be at least one minute long to force candidates to reveal more of their political thinking. Another would require candidates, party chairpersons, or interest group leaders to appear on camera for the entire duration of the commercial, without use of graphics or simulations.

Given the Supreme Court's interpretation of the First Amendment as applied to speech in political campaigns, it is doubtful that some of the proposals would pass constitutional muster. Furthermore, whether these proposals would necessarily reduce campaign costs or enhance political communication is uncertain.

In fact, television accounts for a far smaller proportion of campaign budgets than most people believe. Over every four-year period, elections are held for more than 500,000 state, local, and federal public offices in the United States. Most candidates for these positions never buy advertising or even get close to a television camera. Usually only serious candidates for major offices—presidential, senatorial, gubernatorial, and mayoral in big cities—make substantial use of television advertisements. Only about half of the House candidates purchase television time, and its cost often represents just a small portion of their campaign spending. Even in races where television advertising is essential, such as in presidential contests, the extent of its use varies according to campaign strategy and circumstances.

A Television Bureau of Advertising study estimated that $228 million was spent on political broadcasting in 1988. That figure represents only 8.4 percent of total political spending, which was $2.7 billion for the 1988 elections. This small percentage tends to dispel the commonly accepted notion that television is a large political expense, that television ads are pervasive in U.S. campaigns, and that they have changed the American political landscape.

The extent of television's use is widely dependent on a particular candidate's strategy and ability to pay for broadcast time. For example, in the 1988 presidential primary contests, five major presidential candidates spent $12.7 million on television air time (excluding production costs). That means that only six percent of the $199.6 million of the candidates' campaign expenditures went toward television.

In contrast, the amount that both George Bush and Michael S. Dukakis spent on television advertising in the 1988 general election campaign was substantially higher. In that contest, television expenditures were $52.5 million (57 percent) of the $92.2 million total, or 48 percent of the combined candidate and party coordinated expenditures within the candidates' control, which amounted to $108.8 million.[17]

Presidential candidates find paid political advertising to be an essential tool for their general election races. Faced with the daunting prospect of trying to communicate effectively with more than 170 million potential voters in a two-and-a-half-month period, candidates have little choice but to turn to television. In the political primary season, candidates find television to be a less useful tool, even though they may begin campaigning a year or more before the nominating conventions. In the preelection year, television is considered ineffective. Once the election year begins, the low expenditure limits imposed by law on publicly funded candidates in Iowa and New Hampshire restrain spending for broadcast advertising in those two key states. After voters in those states make their choices, the field of candidates narrows, leaving fewer candidates to purchase advertising time.

Candidates in seriously contested U.S. Senate or gubernatorial campaigns also spend an enormous percentage of their campaign budgets on paid political advertising. Robert Squire, a prominent political consultant who generally works for candidates who are facing stiff competition, said this about broadcast costs: "One rule of thumb is that half the campaign money goes to paid media, and with our fee, it goes up to about 60 percent." Campaign finance analysis of recent hotly contested U.S. Senate and gubernatorial campaigns confirms Squire's observation. In the 1986 California race for the U.S. Senate, Democratic senator Alan Cranston spent $6.2 million on television time and $800,000 on commercial production costs, which amounted to 57 percent of the $12.3 million he spent. His Republican opponent, Rep. Ed Zschau, spent $6.5 million on broadcast time alone, more than half his total of campaign expenditures.

The Congressional Research Service studied how much a select number of Senate and House candidates spent on broadcasting costs in 1988. The study, which looked at the campaign finances of eighteen Senate candidates and sixty-three House candidates (all of whom ran in competitive races), found that House candidates spent less than their Senate counterparts on broadcast time. On average, Senate candidates spent 43 percent of their budget on air time, while House candidates spent only 25.1 percent.[18]

In general, television is simply not cost-efficient for most House, state legislature, county, and municipal campaigns. House candidates whose districts are covered by the costliest media markets—such as New York City, covering forty congressional districts in a tri-state area—are more likely to spend their money on direct mail rather than on television time that blankets not only their district but sections of huge metropolitan areas most of whose residents are unable to vote for the candidate.

Candidates who use television advertising do so primarily for two reasons: They find it cost-effective and they believe that it works. This is so for heated campaigns for major office, mainly general election contests. Even in those categories, some want to use television but cannot afford it because their fund raising has not kept pace with their perceived spending needs.

It is misleading to think that television advertising has taken over the election process. Clearly, candidates in tough races have to focus more of their energy and spend more of their funds on political ads. But for most political campaigning, which is local, television has hardly changed the face of American politics.

FCC Audit. Preliminary findings of a Federal Communications Commission audit of thirty television and radio stations in five selected cities during part of the 1990 election year indicated that political candidates were charged more than other customers to broadcast advertisements. In one city during one week, all candidates paid in excess of the highest rate paid by any commercial advertiser. In another case, candidates paid an average of $6,000 for a thirty-second spot announcement, although the average cost for commercial advertisers was $2,713. The FCC also found that some stations created new classes of time for candidates, called "news adjacencies," for which no comparable commercial rates existed; hence, higher charges were made.[19]

One reason for these excessive charges is that most candidates seek to buy fixed air time, specifically aiming their message to reach certain audiences. Such time traditionally has drawn higher rates than preemptible air time, wherein no guarantee can be made that a spot will be broadcast if other advertisers are willing to pay higher rates for the time. But if an election is imminent, candidates often are willing to pay higher rates for the time periods the consultants and media buyers tell them they need. Ultimately, the results of the audit moved the FCC to rule that broadcasters must stop charging premium rates for political advertising on television and radio.

Since 1972, federal law has required broadcasters to sell political time at the lowest unit charge, giving candidates a price comparable to the lowest rate sold to a most favored advertiser for a spot in a comparable time period. Some broadcasters auction off certain time periods to the highest bidder, political or commercial. Some stations have not been fair to political candidates, and some political consultants and time buyers have not bargained for the lowest unit rates required by law. Moreover, some observers maintain that high television costs are a cause of negative advertising because candidates cannot afford softer positive spots but instead must resort to hard-hitting negative spots to get their messages across.[20]

Production Costs. Buying air time represents only part of the broadcast advertising costs. Commercials to fill the time must be made and distributed. Production costs are difficult to pinpoint because of the design of the FEC disclosure forms. For example, the costs of writing, producing, and running the spot may be hidden in other categories of the disclosure form, such as the unspecified "consultant" category.

A rule of thumb regarding television and radio advertising is that the production costs range between 10 percent and 33 percent of the air-time charges. These include costs of consultants' fees, preparing the commercials, editing and duplicating them, and sending them to stations for broadcast.

The Professionalization of Politics

As campaign technology has become increasingly sophisticated and as candidates need to spend more time packaging an image for their broadcast ads, the amount that candidates have spent to hire political consultants has risen substantially.

An unpublished study conducted on the 1988 Senate race of one

California Democrat showed that consultants are becoming so expensive that candidates are having trouble paying for other key campaign costs, such as broadcast advertising. The study criticized Democratic lieutenant governor Leo T. McCarthy for not spending enough on television advertising when he unsuccessfully ran against Republican senator Pete Wilson. McCarthy raised $8.7 million but spent less than half on broadcast commercials. The McCarthy campaign, the study said, spent too much of its limited funds on consultants: $500,000 for advertising and strategy consultants; $116,000 for a management consultant; $232,000 for pollsters; and $1 million for press, research, and other consulting costs.

However, a *Los Angeles Times* study of 1990 congressional candidates showed that, on average, candidates for the U.S. House of Representatives spent only 8 percent of their funds for consulting fees—far less than the 25 percent they spent on ads. The study showed a similar trend in the Senate races, where candidates spent only 5 percent of their costs on consultants and 35 percent on advertising.[21] Clearly consulting costs may be higher in individual campaigns. In most major campaigns, candidates consider the services consultants offer to be an essential component of modern-day campaigning.

Candidates feel they must retain political specialists, whatever their costs. Some consultants run the candidate's entire campaign, advising on basic strategy, such as what issues the candidate should stress or how best to utilize limited time and funds. Others specialize in polling, fund raising, organizing volunteers, or media advertising. Some consultants deal with only particular aspects of a campaign; for example, putting voters' names on computer tapes for direct mail appeals, fund raising, or election day get-out-the-vote reminders. And the complexities of election laws have led candidates to hire election lawyers and political accountants to ensure that they comply with the laws.

The proliferation of consulting firms points to the increasing professionalization of electoral politics. This trend may be irreversible but has been criticized on the ground that many profit-making companies, perhaps located in Washington, D.C., or New York City, have no base or interest in the candidate's constituency and often supplant established party organizations and traditional volunteer campaign staffs. Few party organizations, however, are geared to provide services with the competence and reliability that some professional consultants demonstrate. Moreover, campaign managers often have looked upon volunteers as of marginal help, seeing amateur efforts as more of a burden than a boon.

In presidential campaigns, the increase in the number of primary election contests and the growing length of the prenomination campaign period also have contributed to increasing professionalization and rising costs. In 1968, only fifteen primaries were held during which about 40 percent of the party convention delegates were chosen. In large part because of the movement toward greater mass participation in the Democratic party's selection of delegates to its presidential nominating convention, the number of primaries gradually was increased to diminish the influence of the party hierarchy and to make the choice of the party responsive to the electorate. In 1988, thirty-six states, Puerto Rico, and the District of Columbia held presidential primaries. Devising strategy and getting competent help to implement it requires professional assistance.

In prenomination contests candidates are required to reach mass audiences. Newspaper and broadcast advertising and other means of communicating with large numbers of people are far more expensive than the means formerly employed to influence state and interest group leaders who used to control the delegate selection process.

The campaign finance reforms enacted in 1974 helped lengthen the prenomination campaign period, thus increasing the candidates' costs. Because candidates no longer may rely on large contributors to cover campaign start-up costs, they generally begin their fund raising early to gather from many small contributors the needed seed money. The costs of such fund-raising drives are significant. So are the costs of the campaign publicity required to generate the name recognition candidates hope will inspire potential contributors to donate to their campaigns.

Fund-Raising Costs. For many candidates, spending on direct mail can be almost as substantial as expenditures on television advertising. In many House campaigns, particularly those covered by the most expensive electronic media districts, spending on direct mail is essential to reach specific audiences. According to a Congressional Research Service study, selected candidates spend almost as much on mailing costs as on broadcast advertising.

The study focused on the campaign finances of sixty-three House candidates and eighteen candidates for the Senate in competitive campaigns. The median amount spent on mailing costs for House candidates was 15 percent, half what they spent for television ads, but twice what they spent for radio, seven times what they spent for print advertising, and three times what they spent for polling services. For the eighteen Senate candidates, the median amount spent on mailing was 10 percent, less than one-fourth of what they spent for television advertising. Nevertheless, what they spent on mailing was twice what they spent for radio, five times what they spent for print advertising, and more than double what they spent for polling services.[22]

It is impossible to determine, however, to what extent mailings were sent to communicate with voters, as opposed to fund-raising appeals, as the study did not ask candidates to make that distinction. But the results of a 1990 *Los Angeles Times* study show that House and Senate candidates spent, on average, 16 percent and 24 percent, respectively, of their funds on fund raising and direct mail.[23]

Contributions do not magically appear; potential donors must be asked to give. Just as direct mail is costly, so are dinners and other events for which tickets are sold. When a fund-raising event is said to have been a million-dollar dinner, that figure invariably represents gross receipts. Costs for food, drinks, flowers, band, and other amenities may cut deeply into the net profit.

Compliance and Legal Expenses. Among the political experts increasingly employed are election lawyers and political accountants. Elections laws are complex and candidates need to be in compliance with them. Often a screening committee is formed to ensure that contributions are legal or an election agency is called upon to issue an advisory opinion about a fund-raising event or a political accountant is hired to keep the books and make the required disclosure of campaign receipts and disbursements on time. Five to 10 percent of campaign budgets now may be allocated to meet bookkeeping and legal expenses.

In addition, some incumbents are spending increased amounts of their campaign funds to combat ethics charges that threaten their political careers. The Federal Election Commission has issued several rulings stating that spending campaign funds for such expenditures is legal. And the House Standards of Official Conduct Committee has generally sanctioned the practice.

Even when ethics charges do not end up in court, politicians can spend considerable money in their own defense. For example, no charges were filed in the probe of House Speaker Jim Wright, D-Texas. However, the Speaker spent $282,000 on legal advice, a cost so high that he held fund raisers to help pay for them.[24]

But Wright was not alone. Many members of Congress have been dipping into their campaign coffers to fend off encroaching legal battles. In 1989, New York representative Robert Garcia spent $130,000 to combat criminal charges. Nevertheless, he was convicted on charges of conspiracy and extortion.[25] Massachusetts Democratic representative Barney Frank set up a special legal defense fund to pay for legal charges incurred from an ethics inquiry that resulted from his association with a male prostitute. Although the fund is separate from Frank's campaign committee, it is subject to the same federal election law requirements as his principle campaign committee.[26] The defense costs of the Keating Five were immense, as were the costs to the Senate for a special prosecutor and enhanced staff for the Senate Ethics Committee.

Why Spend So Much?

One reason candidates seem to spend so lavishly is that little scientific evidence is available about the incremental value in additional votes resulting from various levels of campaign spending and about the effectiveness of different campaign techniques. Traditionally, candidates spend as their supporters expect them to or as their opponents spend—and then some. New techniques win acceptance and to some extent displace older ones, but few candidates are willing to pioneer with unconventional methods alone. For example, although the electronic media are now widely used, the print media still comprise major expenditures in most campaigns. Campaign posters, bumper stickers, and buttons abound although their effectiveness has not been measured scientifically. Common sense persists that these kinds of expenditures promote candidates' name recognition while doing the conventional things people expect serious candidates to be able to afford.

New uses of old techniques also develop. For example, computer technology has made generating printed matter easier, bringing increased use of direct mail that can be specially targeted to groups of potential voters or contributors. Campaign strategies, and thus spending, are further altered by changes in the law. Contribution limits have required candidates to reach a broader base of financial support by soliciting more small contributions. And according to a provision in the 1974 amendments to the Federal Election Campaign Act (FECA), a candidate for the presidential nomination must receive a minimum number of contributions in twenty states to qualify for public funds. This requires organization, networking, and fund-raising acumen.

Perhaps half of all campaign spending is wasted—but no one knows which half. In any case, political campaigns are not comparable to advertising campaigns selling products such as soap because the candidate's personality and unanticipated events both impinge on campaigns in ways that cannot be controlled as easily as the environment for selling commercial products.

Relatively speaking, the dollar price of U.S. elections is not high. The $2.7 billion spent for campaigns in 1988 was a fraction of 1 percent of the amounts spent by federal, state, county, and municipal governments—and that is what politics is all about, gaining control of governments to decide policies on, among other things, how tax money will be spent. The $500 million spent to elect a president in 1988, including prenomination campaigns and minor party candidates, was only a little more than what Americans spend in one year on cosmetic surgery. And compared with what is spent in other nations on elections, the U.S. total is not excessive—the average costs fall somewhere near the middle, clustered with costs in India and Japan. The cost per voter in Israel is far higher than in the United States.

Still, a high price is paid because of the irrational, irresponsible ways in which some money is raised and spent. Less concern should be focused on the actual costs of campaigning than on the need to raise and expend money in ways conforming to democratic ideals.

Political scientist Stanley Kelley, Jr., has described four subcampaigns in the election process: to raise money, to seek the support of party leaders, to seek the support of interest group leaders and memberships, and to hold a public campaign directed to the electorate.[27] The subcampaign directed at the party activists—the people who volunteer to work and who thereby relieve some financial pressures on the campaign—could be added to the list. Undoubtedly, more expenditures are aimed at reinforcing potential workers and voters inclined to support the candidate than at converting voters not so inclined.

Political costs tend to be high because the political season is relatively short and the intensity is greatest just before an election. The American system of elections creates a fiercely competitive political arena within a universe full of nonpolitical sights and sounds that are vying for attention, too. Candidates and parties must compete not only with each other but also with big businesses with large budgets, advertising on a regular basis, often through popular entertainment programs on television and radio.

American politics is candidate-oriented. Unlike most other democracies, where political parties choose the candidates, the United States has costly campaigns for nomination. Federal, state, and local elections are held simultaneously in many jurisdictions, resulting in long ballots, which means competition for exposure in the media is increased among the numerous candidates. In addition, ballot measures, bond issues, state constitutional amendments, and other issues attract money and spending to the political arena. And, the political party system needs to be supported year in and year out, whether an election is due to take place or not. Considering all these opportunities for political spending, it is not surprising how much is spent on American politics.

Classifying Expenditures

The perceived needs of political campaigns are reflected in the amounts allocated to various categories of expenditures. How money is spent reveals strategies for winning elections, informs the controversy about high campaign costs, and tells much about challenger problems. Data on where the money goes are relatively less studied than where the money comes from because, despite full disclosure of campaign funds, disbursements are difficult to classify. For example, should consultants' fees be classified separately or with media?

Spending in selected 1988 House races is presented in Table 5-4. In each case, the winners were incumbents who spent more. The challengers raised more than many do, and the incumbents raised less than some with or without serious competition.

Table 5-4 Categories of Spending in Selected 1988 House Campaigns

Congressional district and candidate	Category of spending					
	Organization	Fund raising	Travel	Advertising	Consulting	Total
Florida Ninth District						
Michael Bilirakis (R)[a]	$115,102 (61%)	$26,515 (14%)	$18,032 (9%)	$ 14,812 (8%)	$15,091 (8%)	$189,554
Oregon Fifth District						
Denny Smith (R) °	170,437 (31%)	17,013 (3%)	9,442 (2%)	292,718 (53%)	58,612 (11%)	548,225
Michael Kopetski (D)	270,305 (80%)	442 (<1%)	6,119 (2%)	15,388 (4%)	46,107 (14%)	338,107
New Jersey Ninth District						
Robert G. Torricelli (D) °	242,728 (62%)	27,853 (7%)	29,742 (8%)	37,711 (9%)	55,648 (14%)	393,684
Roger J. Lane (R)	18,556 (32%)	1,850 (3%)	628 (1%)	35,531 (60%)	2,000 (3%)	58,566

Source: "'Always Running Scared,'" *National Journal*, June 16, 1990, 1456.

Note: R = Republican; D = Democrat. These figures do not include unitemized disbursements, campaign contribution returns, or loan and debt repayments.

° Indicates winner.

[a] Ran unopposed.

Table 5-5 Distribution of Campaign Expenditures Reported by Thirty Highest-Spending Candidates in Seattle-King County, Washington, 1989

Purpose	Amount	Percentage
Media advertising	$997,714	30.6
Mailings	600,117	18.4
Personnel (including consultants)	571,702	17.6
Printed material	511,401	15.7
Name display	219,933	6.8
Voter data	134,489	4.1
Fund raising	88,727	2.7
Telephone	68,913	2.1
Office	60,211	1.8
Miscellaneous	4,318	0.1

Source: Adapted from Public Disclosure Commission, *Where the Money Goes: A Review of Campaign Vendors* (Olympia, Wash.: Public Disclosure Commission, June 1990), 19-20.

Note: Percentages do not add to 100 because of rounding.

The variation in spending on advertising reflects the contours of the districts, whether television advertising is financially feasible, and whether the candidate is an incumbent or challenger. For example, challengers needing name recognition tend to spend as much as possible on media. The relatively high percentages spent on organization are little acknowledged because the conventional view is that so much is spent on television. In Senate races that may be true, but not in many House contests. Organizational costs include rent, salaries, office supplies, printing, telephones, and maintaining lists for fund raising and voter contact. They also may include registration and get-out-the-vote activities. Organizational activity brings the candidate exposure and visibility and enhances networking with constituents and potential voters.

One study of spending in California county and city campaigns found only 38 percent directed to voter contacts, mainly by means of campaign literature, while 62 percent could be counted generally as overhead, fund raising, and the maintenance of campaign organizations. In nonelection years, even less—only 13 percent—was devoted to voter contact.[28]

The Public Disclosure Commission of the state of Washington categorized the expenditures of the thirty highest-spending candidates on the ballot in 1989 (see Table 5-5). All were local candidates in the Seattle-King County area.[29] The various expenditures help to explain why, even in local campaigns, so many activities costing so much money are considered necessary to be reelected or, for a challenger, to win.

Personal Uses of Campaign Funds

While the high costs of politics usually are explained as the need to communicate with voters, not all money is spent on such purposes. A newspaper reported that one House incumbent from Florida used campaign money to buy a $30,000 auto; a Pennsylvania representative spent $6,600 on professional baseball and football tickets; and another spent $3,000 to commission a portrait of his father, a former member of Congress.[30] Another newspaper account revealed that a New York City councilman used campaign funds to buy and insure a car, to contribute to his favorite charities, to take trips to Israel and the Soviet Union, and to eat at expensive restaurants.[31]

Another spending issue relates to the use of campaign funds to pay personal living expenses, such as a mortgage on a house or health insurance. On the one hand, a challenger may have given up a job to campaign while the incumbent is drawing a public salary. Under the law, candidates have discretion over the deployment of campaign funds.[32] On the other hand, under House rules, most incumbents cannot convert campaign funds to personal use.

Consideration must be given to a number of questions: Is donor intent relevant? Are such payments legitimate so long as they further the goal of the campaign—that is, to win? Would donors agree? And if nonwealthy individuals are able to run for office by taking living expenses, should this use of campaign funds be allowed? Otherwise, is public office narrowed to those who can afford to run, say, for a year, without salary? Also, should campaign funds be used to pay the travel expenses of a candidate's spouse? Should he or she not be encouraged to attend political events?

The ultimate in personal use of campaign funds was achieved through the 1979 FECA amendments. In what was called a "grandfather clause," House members of the Ninty-sixth Congress exempted themselves from a provision prohibiting conversion of leftover federal campaign funds to personal use after leaving office. From 1979 to 1991, some seventy-three members disposed of almost $6.4 million for nonelection-related expenditures. Some retirees established PACs with the funds, some gave the money to charitable causes or established scholarships at colleges, but some used the money for legal fees and others for personal uses. Since the money is treated as income, taxes must be paid on it.[33] A gradual phase-out was enacted with the 1989 pay raise and will be completed in January 1993. The Senate had phased out the diversion of campaign funds in 1980.

The Price of Incumbency

Reelection rates are high and thus lead to concerns about incumbency advantage, which entails use of government resources for personal political gain by those in power. Determining the line between legitimate representational functions and partisan political activities can be difficult. Controversial, for example, is the federal government's franking privilege, which allows members of Congress, under certain circumstances and at certain times, to send mailings to constituents—free of charge. Through these mailings, legislators inform their constituents of pending legislation and other matters. An additional benefit is the achievement of widespread name recognition, which may be translated into votes at the next election.

Incumbents have been charged with using their status as officeholders to run a "permanent campaign." A network of supporters is nurtured year in and year out, consultants are retained on an ongoing basis, legislative expertise is touted to appeal to political action committees, events are sought in which the incumbent can be seen and heard. Increasing amounts of government time are spent on raising funds, not on government business. Furthermore, many incumbents now are professional politicians who have not made a living any other way and thus are primarily interested in protecting their job security. They are left, as a result, more vulnerable to ethical lapses, particularly because they spend considerable time officially and unofficially mingling with the wealthy and the powerful, who can help them win reelection.

Power of Money

Among the conclusions that can be drawn about political spending are several that cast doubt about some of the conventional wisdom regarding the financing of election campaigns—particularly questions about the relationships of spending to winning and about incumbency advantage.

The complaint most frequently voiced is that the cost of campaigning has skyrocketed to heights beyond reason. A related charge is that election outcomes are determined by amounts spent. Actually, in a number of contests, candidates who spent less were victorious over those who were better funded. Perhaps the best example occurred in 1986, when the Democrats regained control of the Senate. Five Democratic challengers beat Republican incumbents who outspent them by ratios of at least 2-to-1. In the 1990 Senate race in Minnesota, Democratic challenger Paul Wellstone won, despite being outspent 8-to-1. Wellstone's victory derived partly from his tagging Rudy Boschwitz, the incumbent, as a captive of special interests and partly from some innovative spot television announcements—spots that critics generally decry as unedifying. Wellstone's victory demonstrated an important principle, which can be termed "the doctrine of sufficiency." Enough money must be spent to get a message across to compete effectively but outspending one's opponent is not always necessary—even an incumbent with a massive ratio of higher spending.

Other examples at other levels exist as well. In the Texas race for governor in 1990, Ann Richards spent $11 million to Clayton Williams's $20 million, yet Richards won. Williams spent some $9 million of his personal fortune in the losing campaign. In Florida in 1990, Lawton Chiles not only was outspent 2-to-1 and won in his campaign for governor, but also ran a truly reform campaign of "people versus money." He refused to accept contributions in excess of $100 and group or political action committee gifts, but he managed to raise more than $5 million from seventy-five thousand individual contributors.

In 1990, Sen. Bill Bradley of New Jersey outspent his challenger by a ratio of 10-to-1 but received only 51 percent of the vote. Instead of demonstrating the waste of excessive spending by incumbents, the Bradley case showed the value—to him—of high incumbent spending. The huge amounts Bradley spent proved essential, for he might have lost had he spent less.

The safest strategy for incumbents who may be in highly competitive districts or states is to raise sufficient money to scare off potentially viable opponents as well as to guard against eleventh hour surprises such as Bradley encountered. Having cash available to pour into television when polls indicate trouble is comforting. This explains in part the hoarding of money by incumbents, for fear they will not have enough time to raise needed funds just before an election.

Initiatives and Referenda

The 1980s witnessed a great surge in the use of initiatives, the process by which citizens petition to place public policy measures on the ballot. In fact, initiatives are a major growth industry in American politics. As of 1991, twenty-five states and the District of Columbia allowed citizens to pass legislation through the use of initiatives and referenda, while these and additional states required constitutional amendments and bond issues to be on the ballot.

Some political analysts claim that citizens are turning toward direct democracy because they are frustrated when contentious issues become gridlocked in their state legislatures. In many states, legislators are more than willing to let the issues be decided through initiatives because a public voting record could offend potential voters or monied contributors.[34]

The growth of single-issue constituencies also accounts for the increase in number of initiative campaigns. Environmental activists, insurance reformers, and other such groups are becoming more sophisticated and have found the direct democracy route to be an effective tool.

The high point in initiatives and referenda spending occurred in 1988, when $225 million were spent, pro and con. This included the cost of signature gathering to place initiatives on the ballot. In California alone, some $139.8 million were spent in the 1988 primary and general elections. Although prohibited from contributing to candidates in some states, corporations, labor unions, and trade associations are free to contribute or spend unlimited amounts favoring or opposing ballot issues, according to *First National Bank of Boston v. Bellotti.* The courts have held that while candidates may be corrupted by contributions, issues cannot be, even if one side spends more than the other.

Despite the widely held notion that corporations or unions opposed to reform initiatives can squelch an impecunious citizens' group, results from the 1988 election are evidence that those who spend the most money sometimes lose. For example, the Ralph Nader-backed insurance reform initiative, California's Proposition 103, won with 51 percent of the vote, even though the insurance industry spent almost $30 million on direct mail and advertising to defeat it. Nader's forces expended little more than $2 million, with virtually no money spent on advertising. Five initiatives relating to insurance rates were on the ballot in California, and some $84 million, including the $32 million for Proposition 103, were spent pro and con.[35] For a Los Angeles municipal initiative, the Occidental Petroleum Corporation spent $8 million in an attempt to preserve its oil drilling rights near a public beach. However, environmental groups defeated the company's efforts, spending only $3 million. And in Maryland, the National Rifle Association (NRA) was soundly defeated when it tried to repeal a state ban on the sale and manufacture of cheap "Saturday Night Special" handguns. The NRA's defeat came after the group spent $6 million.[36]

Those with the most money do not always lose, however. In Massachusetts, utility interests successfully managed to defeat an effort that would have shut down two of the state's nuclear power plants. The utility interests spent $8 million while backers of the proposal spent only $1 million.[37]

Predictions have been made that spending for initiatives and referenda will continue to grow, especially in states where the legislature and the governor are split between the two political parties. Political stalemates and legislative gridlocks encourage special interest groups to resort to direct democracy to launch their political agendas. Even in defeat, the process of collecting signatures for the ballot may provide the groundwork for future fund raising by identifying a large base of political donors; then, the mailing lists may be sold.

6 Skirting the Limits in 1988

An examination of the 1988 presidential election provides a vivid illustration of how modern campaign finance laws operate and how drastically different campaigns now are from the privately funded campaigns held prior to 1976.

The Structure of Campaign Financing

Derived mainly from the Federal Election Campaign Act (FECA) of 1971, the Revenue Act of 1971, and the 1974 FECA amendments, the laws that applied to the 1988 presidential campaigns limited the amounts of money that could be contributed and spent. As a result, the importance of the individual wealthy donor was diminished. The Federal Election Commission (FEC) administered the law and certified the disbursement of public funds. The funds are government subsidies and are derived from the federal income tax checkoff.

Three kinds of public funding were available for different phases of the campaigns. During the prenomination period, matching funds of up to about $11.6 million (adjusted for inflation) were provided for qualifying candidates seeking the nomination for president; accompanying expenditure limits were $23.1 million, plus exceptions. Grants of $9.2 million (adjusted for inflation) were made to each of the major parties to arrange for and run the national nominating conventions. Lesser amounts would have been provided for qualifying minor party conventions, but none was eligible in 1988. For the general election period, a flat grant of $46.1 million (adjusted for inflation) was given to each major party candidate; this amount also served as the candidates' expenditure limit. Smaller amounts were available for minor party candidates, although none qualified.

The Prenomination Period

In the prenomination period, a candidate faced a $1,000 limit on individual contributions and a $5,000 cap on political action committee (PAC) donations. To receive public funds, a candidate had to qualify for eligibility by collecting $5,000 through individual contributions of $250 or less in each of twenty states. The federal government matched one public dollar for each privately raised dollar from an individual contributor up to $250. Regardless of the ultimate amount collected, the federal government capped its contribution at $11.6 million—half the limit for prenomination spending. PAC donations were not eligible for matching grants.

Every four years changes are made to the expenditure limits to keep pace with inflation, based on increases in the consumer price index. However, the upward adjustments were not enough to account for the escalation of campaign costs. For example, from 1984 to 1988, the cost of a thirty-second commercial shown in Des Moines during a top-rated television show rose 80 percent from $1,000 to $1,800 while the inflation rate was 13.5 percent.[1]

The $1,000 contribution limit helped shape prenomination campaign strategies. Although the limit achieved its intended effect of eliminating large gifts from "fat cat" contributors, it also provided an edge to well-known politicians and forced lesser-known candidates to gear up their fund-raising campaigns much earlier.

The limit altered fund-raising patterns in unforeseen ways. The role once filled by large contributors was taken by well-connected individuals, called "elite fund raisers," who could persuade a large number of people to contribute the $1,000 maximum. Candidates also were forced to rely more on direct mail solicitations—in many instances the most effective way of reaching small contributors—and on the specialists who orchestrated them. Entertainers, whose services were volunteered and therefore not subject to the $1,000 limitation, were enlisted to hold benefit concerts for candidates.

Under the 1988 financing limits, each candidate was allowed to spend $27.7 million during the run for the nomination: $23.1 million for campaign activities and $4.6 million, or an additional 20 percent above and beyond spending for the campaign itself, to defray fund-raising costs.

The Tax Checkoff. The Presidential Election Campaign Fund is funded by tax dollars voluntarily earmarked on individual federal income tax returns—$1 on a single return, $2 on a joint return (see Figure 6-1). The checkoff neither increases the amount of taxes owed nor decreases any refund due. Once a presidential candidate meets the qualification requirements, the FEC determines eligibility and certifies amounts of funds to which the candidate is entitled. The certification is submitted by the FEC to the U.S. Treasury, which makes the payments from the Presidential Election Campaign Fund.

The feasibility of public financing has depended on the taxpayers' willingness to participate in the tax checkoff. Until now, the system has provided more than enough money to cover the public funds certified to presidential prenomination and general election candidates and to the major parties for their national nominating conventions. Certifications by

Figure 6-1 Federal Income Tax Checkoff for Presidential Election Campaign Fund

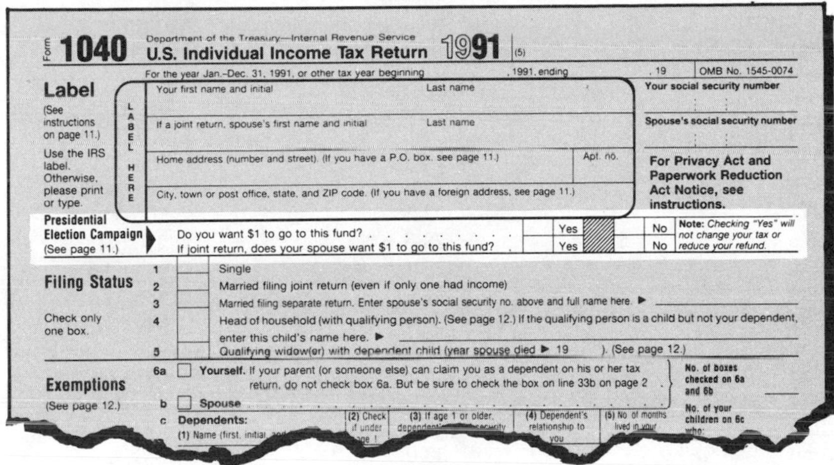

Form **1040** Department of the Treasury—Internal Revenue Service
U.S. Individual Income Tax Return **1991** (5)

For the year Jan.–Dec. 31, 1991, or other tax year beginning , 1991, ending , 19 OMB No. 1545-0074

Label (See instructions on page 11.) Use the IRS label. Otherwise, please print or type. LABEL HERE

Your first name and initial | Last name | **Your social security number**

If a joint return, spouse's first name and initial | Last name | **Spouse's social security number**

Home address (number and street). (If you have a P.O. box, see page 11.) | Apt. no.

City, town or post office, state, and ZIP code. (If you have a foreign address, see page 11.)

For Privacy Act and Paperwork Reduction Act Notice, see instructions.

Presidential Election Campaign (See page 11.)
Do you want $1 to go to this fund? . . . . Yes | No
If joint return, does your spouse want $1 to go to this fund? . Yes | No
Note: *Checking "Yes" will not change your tax or reduce your refund.*

Filing Status
Check only one box.
1 Single
2 Married filing joint return (even if only one had income)
3 Married filing separate return. Enter spouse's social security no. above and full name here. ▶
4 Head of household (with qualifying person). (See page 12.) If the qualifying person is a child but not your dependent, enter this child's name here. ▶
5 Qualifying widow(er) with dependent child (year spouse died ▶ 19). (See page 12.)

Exemptions (See page 12.)
6a ☐ **Yourself.** If your parent (or someone else) can claim you as a dependent on his or her tax return, do not check box 6a. But be sure to check the box on line 33b on page 2 . . | **No. of boxes checked on 6a and 6b**
b ☐ **Spouse** . . . . | **No. of your children on 6c who:**
c **Dependents:** (1) Name (first, initial, and ... | (2) Check if under age 1 | (3) If age 1 or older, dependent's social security ... | (4) Dependent's relationship to you | (5) No. of months lived in your ...

the FEC totaled $70.9 million in 1976, $100.6 million in 1980, $133.1 million in 1984, and $177.8 million in 1988.

Inflation and eligibility of candidates in the prenomination and general elections and of major parties for their conventions have begun to erode the balance of the Presidential Election Campaign Fund. While private money has found several channels into presidential campaigns, the flow of public funding has slowed considerably. The Presidential Election Campaign Fund will face some cash flow problems in the 1992 campaign but will be running at a substantial deficit by the 1996 race unless action is taken.[2]

Taxpayer support for the checkoff declined by more than 30 percent since 1981 when participation was at an all-time high of 28.7 percent (see Table 6-1). The 1990 returns revealed 19.9 percent participation generating revenues of $32.4 million.[3]

While the FEC is stepping up efforts to educate taxpayers about the checkoff, several commission members contended that Congress will have to decide to raise the checkoff amount, make a one-time grant to keep the fund out of debt, or scrap the checkoff in favor of public funding through continuing legislative appropriations—a perilous possibility given U.S. budget deficits.[4]

State Limits. Candidates were subjected to additional limits on expending their allotted $27.7 million. Spending in a primary or caucus was restricted to an amount based on the state's voting-age population times 16 cents plus a cost-of-living adjustment.[5] However, these limitations became

Table 6-1 Federal Income Tax Checkoff, 1973-1990

Calendar year	Percentage of returns with checkoff [a]	Total amounts checked off
1973	7.0	$ 2,427,000
1974	[b]	27,591,546
1975	24.2	31,656,525
1976	25.5	33,731,945
1977	27.5	36,606,008
1978	28.6	39,246,689
1979	25.4	35,941,347
1980	27.4	38,838,417
1981	28.7	41,049,052
1982	27.0	39,023,882
1983	24.2	35,631,068
1984	23.7	35,036,761
1985	23.0	34,712,761
1986	23.0	35,753,837
1987	21.7	33,651,947
1988	21.0	33,013,987
1989	20.1	32,285,646
1990	19.9	32,462,979

Sources: Federal Election Commission. Reprinted from: *Financing the 1988 Election*, Herbert E. Alexander and Monica Bauer, 1991, by permission of Westview Press, Boulder, Colorado. Data for 1990 from Federal Election Commission, "Presidential Fund-Income Tax Checkoff Status," press release, September 1991.

[a] The percentages refer to returns of the previous year, for example, the 27 percent of 1981 tax returns that indicated a one- or two-dollar checkoff directed $39,023,882 into the Presidential Election Campaign Fund in calendar year 1982.

[b] The 1973 returns were the first to have the campaign fund checkoff on the first page. To compensate for the presumed difficulty of locating the separate form in the previous year, taxpayers were permitted to check off $1 for 1972 as well as 1973. Since this option did not exist in any other year, percentage figures for those returns would be misleading.

unrealistic in a time of media-dominated, regional campaigning. They forced candidates to engage in subterfuges that made a mockery of the law and further confused the issue of spending limits.

The primary campaigns in New Hampshire, for example, had a spending limit of $461,000—a small sum given the perceived political importance of winning or placing well in the contest that traditionally has launched or destroyed presidential hopefuls. However, candidates found ways to assign spending to their national headquarters, to surrounding states, or to fund-raising costs, which are subject to separate accounting procedures. For example, autos were rented in Massachusetts for use in New Hampshire and credited against the higher Massachusetts limit. The FEC allowed 80 percent of the television time purchased on

Boston stations—reaching 80 percent of the New Hampshire population—to be included in the Massachusetts limit, where the primary was not held until later. Candidate Richard A. Gephardt made requests for contributions in his television ads, then allocated half the costs of the ads to fund raising, and, by doing so, avoided consuming his New Hampshire allocation.

By sanctioning such maneuvers, the FEC allowed candidates to avoid exceeding the state limits in ways that cast doubt on the entire process.[6] Worse, documented overspending resulting in FEC fines, imposed long after the event, merely equal to the amount of the limit's excess. The penalties were viewed as a cost of doing business because pragmatic politicians considered the spending essential. As Professor L. Sandy Maisel wrote, "Certainly the intent of the law was not to create incentives for candidates to cheat on the state-by-state limits, because the consequences of being caught cheating were less serious for a campaign than the consequence of losing a caucus or primary."[7]

The absurdity of the state limits became obvious when the aggregate spending was totaled. For all fifty states, it was $70 million, almost three times the $27.7 million candidates could legally spend nationwide. Thus, to stay within the limits, candidates needed to allocate funds carefully in early primary and caucus states, micromanage limited monies in key states, and not campaign in some states at all.

Presidential PACs. Another circumvention or activity not counted against the expenditure limits was the use of presidential PACs. Presidential PAC spending for 1988 was more than twice the combined amounts spent in advance of the 1980 and 1984 elections. Once a person declared his or her intention to run for the presidency and registered a principal campaign committee with the FEC, the meter began to run on expenditure limitations. Candidates avoided these limits by remaining undeclared for as long as possible, creating PACs to support precandidacy political activity such as travel, development of fund-raising lists, and issues development. According to political scientist Anthony Corrado, precandidacy PACs since 1980 had become "one of the biggest loopholes in the federal campaign-finance system."[8]

More than $25 million was spent by PACs for undeclared presidential candidates. The PACs of George Bush, Robert Dole, and Jack Kemp accounted for 85 percent of it. Democratic candidates spent less than $2 million, and Michael S. Dukakis did not have a presidential PAC.[9]

Although the FECA required full disclosure of funds, limited individual contributions to $1,000 for presidential candidates, and mandated a limit on expenditures for both the nomination and the general election, the precandidacy PACs allowed undeclared candidates to accept contributions of up to $5,000 for each year the PAC was functioning.

General Election Campaigns

For the 1988 general election, the presidential nominee of each major political party—Republican Bush and Democrat Dukakis—received full public financing. Each candidate was given a flat grant of $46.1 million from the federal government, which could have been supplemented by a limited amount of funds—$8.3 million—by the candidate's party. With that exception, the two presidential nominees were theoretically barred from raising private funds. But those restrictions bore little resemblance to the realities of the campaigns.

Independent Expenditures. Independent expenditures are a means of getting around both the contribution and expenditure limits. By rulings of the U.S. Supreme Court, independent expenditures cannot be limited if they are made by an individual or PAC on behalf of a candidate but undertaken without the collaboration or cooperation of the candidate or the candidate's campaign. Independent expenditures also may be negative—against a candidate instead of for one.

Independent expenditures declined between 1984 and 1988; nevertheless, in the presidential campaigns, some $14.3 million was spent in this category. Independent expenditures played a crucial role in the general election. Dukakis's campaign was hurt by explosive ads featuring a felon named Willie Horton, who, while on a prison furlough program in Massachusetts, had escaped and brutally raped a Maryland woman. These commercials, designed to question Dukakis's record on crime, were produced and aired not by the Bush campaign but by two independent spending groups and were further widely disseminated by being shown on television news programs.

Soft Money. The most troubling element of the 1988 general election campaigns was the extensive use of "soft money." In contrast to "hard money" regulated by the FECA, soft money was subject to neither the limits nor the disclosure requirements of federal law. Soft money refers to funds channeled to state and local party organizations for voter registration, get-out-the-vote efforts, and similar volunteer activities. These state and local party affiliates, outside the jurisdiction of federal law in these activities, then spent the money on behalf of the party ticket, but having an impact on the election of federal candidates.

Because soft money was raised primarily by officials of the presidential campaigns, critics charged that it was benefiting candidates while undermining the contribution and spending limits. Because presidential candidates helped to raise the money, questions surfaced about whether they were violating the legal provisions by which they agreed to restrictions on private fund raising during the general election in return for public subsidies. Because soft money permitted the collection of unlimited donations from individuals, critics said it was a throwback to the days of the very large contributor.

Soft money was sanctioned by the 1979 amendments to the FECA and was present in presidential campaigns throughout the 1980s. What distinguished 1988 from past elections was its quantity. More than twice as much—$45 million—was spent than during the 1980 and 1984 general elections combined.

In 1980 and 1984, the Republicans had far outstripped the Democrats in raising soft money. That changed dramatically in 1988 when the Democrats raised $23 million for the Dukakis campaign while the Republicans raised $22 million for the Bush effort. The Republicans claimed 267 contributors of $100,000 or more; the Democrats, 130.[10]

Although the FEC and others viewed soft money as a way to empower state and local political party committees to participate in federal elections, the return of the very large contributor eroded the concept behind the funding structure embodied in the FECA. Public funds were intended to provide most of the money serious candidates needed to present themselves to the electorate. In addition to large individual contributions, soft money offered a pathway into presidential politics for direct corporate and labor donations. The former was barred at the federal level in 1907 and the latter in 1943.

But thirty states permitted direct corporate contributions, and forty-one allowed direct labor contributions. Consequently, a donation could be channeled by a party's national operatives from organizations, such as corporations, in a state that barred corporate contributions to a committee in a state that allowed them.

Other sources of funds in the presidential general election campaigns were labor unions, which in the 1988 cycle spent $30 million for activities such as voter registration drives and partisan communications to their memberships; corporate spending; and candidate compliance costs.

The 1988 Presidential Election

In the 1987-1988 election cycle, political candidates and committees at all levels—federal, state and, local—spent $2.7 billion on political campaigns. Electing a president cost approximately 18.5 percent of that or $500 million, which represented a 54 percent increase from the $325 million spent in 1984.[11] The costs of running for president rose seventeenfold from 1960 through 1988.

Despite the bleak appearances, the long-term trends were not as alarming. When adjusted for inflation, presidential campaign costs increased only fourfold since 1960. The steep rise in spending in the 1988 cycle can be attributed in part to the intense competition for the parties' nominations, which was not present in 1984 when President Reagan faced little opposition (although the Democrats had a spirited contest).

Spending by or on behalf of presidential hopefuls amounted to $233.5 million for nomination campaigns. The two major parties spent a total of $40.4 million on their conventions. More than $208.3 million was spent on the general election campaigns.

The intense competition for the nominations in both parties cost candidates $212 million, double the amount in 1984.[12] Public funds accounted for 31.7 percent or $67.2 million, thus making the U.S. government the largest single contributor.[13] Independent expenditures totaled $4.2 million for all prenomination candidates, $3 million of that on behalf of Bush and $656,000 in negative campaigning. Independent expenditures on behalf of Democratic candidates were only $81,600, but negative spending in opposition to Democratic candidates was $658,600, including $396,000 against front-runner Dukakis and $163,800 against Jesse Jackson.

The costs of the nominating conventions for the Democrats and Republicans ran to approximately $22.4 million and $18.0 million, respectively. The federal government provided each party $9.2 million.

While the spending limit was $54.4 million for the general election, the amounts actually spent by or on behalf of the Republican and Democratic candidates totaled $93.7 million for Bush and $106.5 million for Dukakis—figures accounted for by inflation and the widespread use of soft money and independent campaigning.

The Prenomination Campaigns

With President Reagan leaving office at the end of his second term, the Republican field was wide open in 1988, and numerous Democrats opted to vie for their party's mantle. For the first time in twenty years an incumbent president was not running for reelection. But the roads to the nominations had changed since the reforms of the 1970s, and the federal campaign financing structure proved unable to respond to the highly competitive campaigns in both parties and to innovations such as "Super Tuesday."

In the Democratic contest, all seven candidates needed exposure. As political scientist Clyde Wilcox suggested, "Campaign spending matters most when little-known candidates contest the nominations, and matters considerably less when the candidates are well known and when free media provide voters with sufficient information to make up their minds."[14]

Michael Dukakis had the most money, allowing him to win by spending the most and surviving the entire campaign season. Jesse Jackson had much more money than in 1984, but he received notable media attention throughout the campaign season with the result that his spending was less important than for the others. He won or came in second in several primaries and caucuses where he was outspent.

On Tuesday, March 8, 1988, the nation experienced the closest thing it had seen to a national primary in recent history—it was called "Super Tuesday." The Democrats held twenty state primary or caucus elections; the Republicans, seventeen. The result was a change in the way candidates raised money and scheduled the use of their resources.

Although "Super Tuesday" was important, the candidates did not put their entire campaign budgets on the line for it. Difficult choices had to be made to ensure that funding was available for the duration of the long presidential season. Candidates could not spend the $5 million most experts said was necessary to campaign effectively by buying such things as spot announcements in approximately fifty media markets. Candidates used political broadcasting judiciously, focusing on a state or an area, because the cost would have been prohibitive to cover the many media markets in all the states participating in "Super Tuesday."

Spending on television accounted for only 6 percent of prenomination expenditures. Relatively low television spending in the primary and caucus period was explained by a number of factors. Retail politics in Iowa and New Hampshire, for example, stressed personal, event-to-event campaigning and did not demand much electronic advertising. Also, less spending occurred in Iowa, for example, because TV costs were low. In New Hampshire, meanwhile, spending was limited to avoid exceeding expenditure ceilings; television broadcasts in the state came out of Boston stations, which had an expensive market.

George Bush's successes were related more to his status as vice president, to his impressive résumé, and to the political debts people owed to him than to his spending. He won decisively on "Super Tuesday" despite being outspent in twelve states.[15] However, if leading spenders such as Robert Dole or Marion G. "Pat" Robertson had remained competitive with Bush through the California primary and the Republican convention, they would have been unable to spend much money in the primaries and caucuses after "Super Tuesday" without violating the overall $27.7 million spending cap. Even without such competition, Bush was forced to curtail his schedule a month before the convention to ensure his spending levels did not violate legal limits.[16]

In contrast, Dukakis's main opponent was Jackson, whose spending did not approach the upper limits of the Bush, Dole, and Robertson campaigns. Nevertheless, Dukakis had a decided advantage in early fund raising. For example, by the end of 1987 he had raised more than twice as much as his closest competitor, Richard Gephardt. Dukakis's funding advantage enabled him to sustain his campaign through some rocky outcomes in Iowa and elsewhere.

Table 6-2 Adjusted Disbursements of Presidential Prenomination Candidates, 1988

Candidate	Amount
Democratic	
Bruce Babbitt	$ 3,349,508
Joseph R. Biden, Jr.	3,735,650
Michael S. Dukakis	28,157,137
Richard A. Gephardt	10,297,103
Al Gore	12,328,351
Gary Hart	3,276,852
Jesse Jackson	19,391,092
Lyndon LaRouche	3,843,590
Paul Simon	9,593,686
Democratic subtotal	$ 93,972,969
Republican	
George Bush	$ 30,643,977
Robert Dole	26,458,398
Pierre S. "Pete" du Pont IV	8,031,549
Alexander Haig	2,029,205
Jack F. Kemp	16,512,967
Marion G. "Pat" Robertson	30,887,865
Republican subtotal	$114,563,961
Minor Party	
Lenora Fulani	$ 2,127,347
Minor party subtotal	$ 2,127,347
Total	$210,664,277

Source: Federal Election Commission, *FEC Reports on Financial Activity, 1987-1988: Final Report, Presidential Prenomination Campaigns* (Washington, D.C.: Federal Election Commission, August 1989), Table A6, 10.

Note: Amounts not all subject to expenditure limits. Amounts as of December 31, 1988.

For a range of spending in 1988 by candidates seeking the presidential nominations, see Table 6-2.

Bush had a similar early advantage in fund raising, made apparent by the ease with which a sitting vice president was able to raise large numbers of the maximum $1,000 contributions. Bush overspent in 1987 on a large and expensive organization, requiring him to conserve carefully during 1988.

Individual contributions that were made after January 1, 1987, were eligible for matching funds for candidates who qualified. However,

Table 6-3 Dukakis Campaign Receipts for 1988 Presidential Election

Source	Amount (in millions)
Fund raising	
Direct mail	$ 2.4
Other sources	17.0
Legal and accounting funds	2.5
Matching funds	9.0
Transfer from Massachusetts gubernatorial campaign surplus	.4
Total	$ 31.3

Source: Dukakis campaign staff.

Note: The $27.7 million limit applied to expenditures, not receipts. Furthermore, some spending, such as from the legal and accounting funds, are not charged to the limit.

payouts to candidates cannot be made until the election year, and so candidates anticipating public funds may take out loans based on the expected funds. A number of candidates borrowed money in late 1987.

Additionally, by the end of 1987, Joseph R. Biden, Jr., Gary Hart, Paul Laxalt, and Patricia Schroeder had withdrawn from the contests. Hart reentered and exited a second time in March 1988. Not counting Hart, these candidates raised more than $5 million.

The Dukakis Campaign. In broad outline, the Dukakis campaign receipts are revealing (see Table 6-3). Direct mail raised $2.4 million, with a 3.5 percent response rate from past contributors and a 1.5 percent response rate from new contributors. The net mail receipts, after costs, were $1.6 million, but with matching funds amounted to $3.4 million. As a result, matching funds provided an incentive for direct mail campaigns.

Dukakis took the high road by deciding not to accept PAC contributions. However, his campaign made maximum use of top business managers who raised money from among their colleagues, particularly those in high-tech companies in Massachusetts and on Wall Street where he had close ties.[17] Thus his campaign was able to get ten or twenty contributions in amounts of $1,000 each from corporate executives. PAC contributions would have been limited to $5,000 for each corporation.

The regional receipts showed a strong eastern bias, with the exception of California. The three states providing the most contributions were Massachusetts ($7,044,251), New York ($3,012,645), and California ($2,282,128).

Table 6-4 Dukakis Prenomination Campaign Expenditures for the 1988 Presidential Election

Category of expenditure	Amount
Headquarters	$ 12,344,807
Media Placement	3,796,914
Media Production	1,463,085
Polling	428,620
Scheduling/travel	4,347,183
States	5,689,298
Total	$ 28,069,907

Source: Dukakis campaign staff.

In all, 114,000 contributions were counted, and the average donation was $171. Dukakis almost matched Dole by collecting 7,184 individual contributions of $1,000 each. Kitty Dukakis, the candidate's wife, was credited with raising $500,000 at events where she spoke. Dukakis also had 1,046 members of his finance committee who raised at least $10,000 each, and 203 members of the campaign's board of directors were credited with fulfilling commitments to raise at least $25,000 each.

Dukakis's prenomination campaign expenditures are listed in Table 6-4. For a campaign that participated in almost every primary and caucus, the figures revealed relatively high national headquarters expenditures in relation to state campaigns and very high media production costs in relation to airtime costs.

The Bush Campaign. The Bush campaign spent the legal limit for the Republican nomination. Its receipts included three notable sources: $2,000 from the candidate and his wife, $670,567 from political action committees, and $16,500,000 in $1,000 amounts from 16,500 contributors. Fund raising cost 21 cents per dollar raised. An additional $3.7 million was raised to cover compliance costs.

Media spending was $3,197,696 for television time and $239,620 for radio time. Production costs were not available. Of these amounts, combined television and radio spending in Iowa totaled $142,443 and in New Hampshire $213,070.

Self Contributions and Loans. Under federal law, a presidential candidate who accepted public financing was limited to $50,000 in personal or family member contributions. According to the FEC, Bruce Babbitt contributed $41,000 to his own campaign; Richard Gephardt, $50,000; George Bush, $2,000; and Pierre S. "Pete" du Pont IV, $50,000.

Table 6-5 Political Action Committee Receipts: Presidential Prenomination Campaigns, 1988

Candidate	Receipts
Democratic	
Bruce Babbitt	$ 1,000
Joseph R. Biden, Jr.	150
Michael S. Dukakis	0
Richard A. Gephardt	661,320
Al Gore	506,870
Gary Hart	0
Jesse Jackson	46,400
Lyndon LaRouche	5,000
Paul Simon	288,812
Republican	
George Bush	670,567
Robert Dole	848,931
Pierre S. "Pete" du Pont IV	0
Alexander Haig	19,820
Jack F. Kemp	64,998
Marion G. "Pat" Robertson	8
Total	$3,113,876

Source: Federal Election Commission. Reprinted from: *Financing the 1988 Election*, Herbert E. Alexander and Monica Bauer, 1991, by permission of Westview Press, Boulder, Colorado.

FEC records show that Al Gore loaned $40,000 (repaid) to his own campaign; Paul Simon, $45,000; Alexander Haig, $50,000; and Pat Robertson, $25,000 (repaid).

PAC Contributions. The FEC also tabulated data on PAC contributions (see Table 6-5). Notably, Robert Dole, who retained his position as Senate minority leader during his presidential bid, received the highest amount of PAC contributions, even more than Bush, a sitting vice president and the winner of the nomination. PAC contributions accounted for 1.4 percent of total candidate funding. Republican candidates raised only marginally more from PACs than Democrats, $1.6 million versus $1.5 million. Babbitt, Dukakis, Hart, and du Pont refused to accept PAC contributions.

The Hart Campaign. In early 1987, former senator Gary Hart was a front-runner for the 1988 Democratic nomination, following his near-win in 1984. Yet Hart entered and withdrew twice from the Democratic contest. His first withdrawal was in May 1987 after the *Miami Herald* broke the story of his reported relationship with a young model, Donna Rice. He reentered the race but withdrew again after garnering just 1 percent of the Iowa caucus vote, 4 percent in the New Hampshire primary, and 3 percent of the "Super Tuesday" vote. By delaying the announcement of his second withdrawal until after February 24, he was able to collect more than $1 million from the presidential checkoff account.[18]

Before his first exit, from January to May 1987, Hart raised nearly $2.2 million. His second departure occurred under a cloud seeded by financial problems. The *New York Times* reported "Mr. Hart's re-entry into the race was at times overshadowed by his continuing inability to pay off more than $1 million in debts from his 1984 bid. In addition, he had to respond to new allegations raised in newspaper accounts in January about irregularities in his 1984 campaign finances." [19] These irregularities centered on a Los Angeles videotape entrepreneur, Stuart Karl, Jr.

According to one of Karl's employees, "Mr. Karl had been advised by Douglas Rosen, the [1984 Hart] campaign's finance director, to collect money from employees and reimburse them." [20] Karl allegedly funneled about $100,000 to Hart's campaign, as well as wrote personal checks for thousands of dollars for routine campaign expenses. A media consultant to the 1984 campaign, Raymond D. Strother, also raised funds: "It was like he didn't want to know about the money. The truth is, Gary Hart had absolutely no idea about the money being raised in his campaign." [21]

After the Federal Bureau of Investigation looked into the matter, the Hart campaign admitted receiving illegal contributions in 1984 and pledged to attempt to refund the money to Karl's employees. However, Hart's 1988 campaign manager, Susan Casey, said that "since the 1984 campaign is $1.1 million in debt, all that could be done was to add the questionable contributors to the list of debtors to be repaid." [22]

On March 25, 1988, the FEC ruled that Hart could not use leftover 1988 campaign funds to retire 1984 debts until the 1988 books had been audited and all questions about their propriety resolved, a process that took months.[23] Hart's 1984 creditors proved a continual embarrassment during the 1988 contest. The saga included stories about the use of federal marshals by one creditor to seize money at a fund-raising event in California and the unsuccessful attempt by two creditors to seize a $100,000 certificate of deposit.[24]

Money management problems pushed Hart out of the 1988 race for the last time. The main lesson one can draw from the Hart campaigns is that complex laws require careful management. Otherwise, cash flow problems abound, unpaid debts may become serious detriments to future campaigns, and lack of personal attention by the candidate can lead to financial disarray.

Financing the National Conventions

Candidates receive public financing in the pre- and post-convention periods. But in the second phase of the presidential selection process, it is the political parties that receive public funding to arrange and stage their national nominating conventions. At times in U.S. history, conventions have chosen candidates for president and vice president. But in recent years, conventions are events that ratify decisions made during the course of the primaries and caucuses and the wooing of delegates, well in advance of the conventions themselves.

The FECA ensured that conventions would be financially viable—without traditional reliance on special interests—by providing the public funds essential to the major parties that hold them. Like candidates' campaigns, convention costs have soared, driven up in part by the parties' wanting to produce good shows for the television viewing audience and by cities' desire to attract the millions of dollars of business the conventions bring with them. The public funds were thought to be adequate when first provided in 1976 but since have been increased by law at rates greater than for the candidates' campaigns. Furthermore, other sources have emerged to at least equal the amounts government provides. The parties used creative means to raise money beyond the federal limits for their 1988 national conventions.

U.S. taxpayers put up $9.2 million for each of the two major nominating conventions. But the Democratic convention in Atlanta cost more than double that—$22.4 million—with the remainder financed by the host city and host committees. Atlanta assembled a financial package that included a special tax on hotel guests to raise money to attract the convention to the city. This enabled the host committee, the Atlanta '88 Committee, to borrow $5 million from two Atlanta banks, which were the largest creditors.[25]

The Republican convention in New Orleans cost more than $18 million, with revenues drawn from the city and host committee, which relied mainly on corporate donations and the $9.2 million federal payment. Host committee funds for both Atlanta and New Orleans were raised privately, in amounts as large as $100,000, mainly from corporate or union contributions.

Ironically, public funding was designed to provide an alternative to private funds, but the latter still could be raised under increasingly easy guidelines. Every four years since public funding went into effect in 1976, the FEC has interpreted the law to permit more and more private money for operating the conventions and has exempted more and more expenditures from the spending limits. States and local governments hosting conventions are permitted to provide certain services and facilities, such as convention halls, transportation, and security services, and the costs are not counted against the parties' expenditure limits. Parties may accept such items as free hotel rooms and conference facilities if other groups holding conventions of similar size receive similar benefits. However, no other conventions approximate the size of the political conventions.

Local businesses and national corporations with local outlets were permitted to contribute funds to host committees or civic associations seeking to attract or assist the political conventions if they could reasonably expect a commensurate commercial return during the life of the convention. Both parties were able to arrange reduced-cost services by agreeing to designate airlines and others as "official suppliers" for the conventions. Costly lounges to which delegates were invited to relax with their corporate, labor, and trade association sponsors were in ample evidence at both conventions as well.

To date, the mix of public and private financing of the conventions satisfies the parties because it provides sufficient money and involves local participation. But the development every four years of new ways of introducing private money undermines the premise of the 1974 law that public funding would replace private funding. Besides questioning the rationale for the use of public funds at all, the infusion of large quantities of private money makes the accompanying expenditure limits meaningless.

The General Election

The third phase of the presidential selection process is the post-nomination or general election campaigns. The law considers the presidential and vice-presidential campaigns as one when applying public financing and expenditure limits.

The Democrats nominated Michael Dukakis in mid-July—a month before the Republicans had their own extravaganza to select George Bush—bolstering the Massachusetts governor's exposure and his ratings in the polls. Dukakis had to spread out his spending over a longer period until the November election, and Bush was able to recoup some standing in the polls after the Republican national convention and as the general election campaign began in earnest.

With the major parties' winnowing of candidates down to two, the campaign became more focused with media spending significantly increasing. While media spending accounted for about $40 million of the $212 million spent in the nominating campaigns by all candidates, the Bush and Dukakis camps each spent approximately $30 million on the media during the general election campaign. This $30 million represented almost two-thirds of the $46.1 million of the public funding they each received.

Consequently, general election public funding, in a sense, amounted to a major transfer of funds from the taxpayers to the broadcasters. The broadcasters, however, also provided significant free air time in the form of the presidential debates, daily news coverage, and other special programs, such as those on election day.

The Bush-Quayle campaign spent $31.5 million on media, not including production costs. Even so, that amount represented a large increase over the $22.9 million spent by Reagan-Bush in 1984. The Dukakis-Bentsen campaign spent $23.5 million on media, not counting production costs.

Soft Money. The most notable financial phenomenon during the general election was the search for soft money. Campaign efforts to raise soft money became as competitive and as high profile as the search for votes.

Both parties at the national level used the candidates' prenomination campaign operatives to solicit soft money. And it was raised in large individual contributions—much in excess of the federal contribution limitations—some as much as $100,000.

Robert A. Farmer, treasurer of the Dukakis-Bentsen campaign, started the drive for soft money by announcing an effort to raise $50 million. He wanted to achieve a level playing field with the Republicans. Farmer later admitted the plan was a strategic error because it triggered a Republican response in the form of Team 100, which raised $22 million in soft money;[26] the Democrats raised $23 million, less than half of Farmer's goal.

Dukakis capped these contributions at $100,000 and refused to accept any from corporations, labor unions, or PACs. However, before Dukakis was nominated, the Democrats had accepted soft money from corporate and labor sources for help in funding the Democratic national convention.

Republican soft money was raised in amounts as low as $1,000, for example, for tickets to the Gala Luncheon at the Republican national convention. The costs of the gala were part of the Republican soft money expenditures. So both conventions spent some soft money, and not all was spent in the general election campaigns. Additional hard money—tens of millions of dollars—was raised and spent by both Republicans and Democrats on combined hard money-soft money activities related to the campaigns. And additional soft money was raised and spent locally by state and local party committees in amounts not included in the national soft money totals.

Even with the misgivings surrounding soft money, it did play an important role in both voter outreach and party renewal.[27] Its use was originally tolerated under the FECA for funding voluntary activities and to allow state and local party committees to undertake registration and get-out-the-vote drives and phone banks. These are widely accepted functions that attract citizen participation—a highly valued role in a democracy.

Table 6-6 Sources of Funds, Major Party Presidential Candidates, 1988 General Election

	Candidate		
Source of funds	George Bush	Michael S. Dukakis	Type of campaign
Federal grant	$46.1	$ 46.1	Limited
National party	8.3	8.3	Limited/candidate controlled
State and local party	22.0 [a]	23.0	Unlimited
Labor [b]	5.0	25.0	Unlimited
Corporate/association [b]	1.5	1.0	Unlimited/candidate may coordinate
Compliance	4.0	2.5	Unlimited/candidate may coordinate
Independent expenditures [c]	6.8	.6	Independent of candidate
Total	$93.7	$106.5	

Source: Citizens' Research Foundation. Reprinted from: *Financing the 1988 Election,* Herbert E. Alexander and Monica Bauer, 1991, by permission of Westview Press, Boulder, Colorado.

Note: Figures are in millions.

[a] Includes money raised by the national party committee and channeled to state and local party committees.

[b] Includes internal communication costs (both those in excess of $2,000, which are reported as required by law, and those of $2,000 or less, which are not required to be reported; registration and voter turnout expenditures; overhead; and other related costs).

[c] Does not include amounts spent to oppose the candidates: $2.7 million against Dukakis, $77,325 against Bush, and $63,103 against Dan Quayle.

Soft money also freed up more public money for advertising, travel, and other expenditures directly associated with the presidential election campaigns.

Three Parallel Campaigns. Both parties expressed a need for a level playing field during the 1988 general election campaigns. And to accomplish that, soft money was solicited. But soft money was only one component of spending outside the candidates' expenditure limits. Analysis of the general election period revealed that at least three distinct but parallel campaigns were conducted either by each candidate or on his behalf (see Table 6-6).

The first campaign involved spending the $46.1 million flat grants from the U.S. Treasury. The money was supplemented by national party coordinated expenditures of $8.3 million, spending also controlled by the candidates' campaigns.

In the second campaign, spending was provided for but not limited under the law. It was financed in part by funds raised under FECA limits from private sources to pay the legal, accounting, and related costs the organization incurred in complying with the law. It also was financed in part by soft money spent by state and local party committees—in almost identical amounts by each major party. Additionally, funds were spent on the nominee's behalf in parallel campaigning by labor unions, trade associations, and membership groups on partisan communications with their own constituencies and on nominally nonpartisan activities directed to the general public. For example, Democratic senator Alan Cranston of California reportedly raised $12 million for tax-exempt groups carrying out voter registration and turnout drives among Democratic-leaning groups.[28] This type of parallel spending could be coordinated with spending by the presidential campaigns.

The third campaign also involved spending not limited under the law. Under *Buckley v. Valeo* and subsequent cases, individuals and groups were permitted to spend unlimited amounts to advocate the election or defeat of presidential candidates if these independent expenditures were made without consultation with the candidates or their campaign organizations.

The three parallel campaigns illustrate why expenditure limits seem illusory in a pluralistic system with numerous openings for disbursements sanctioned by law or court decisions. When freedom of speech and association are guaranteed, restricting money at any given point in the campaign process results only in new channels being carved through which monied individuals and groups can seek to influence officeholders and the outcome of elections.

The total amounts spent in the major party election campaigns were remarkable, not only for the totals raised and spent, but also because the Democratic candidate was the beneficiary of more spending than the Republican. This stark reversal from presidential elections in the twentieth century occurred for several reasons. First, unlike 1980 and 1984, the Democrats spent the full amount of party coordinated expenditures, $8.3 million. Second, unlike the previous two elections, the Democrats spent slightly more than the Republicans in soft money. Finally, the Democrats continued to take advantage of strong labor spending. But the best-financed Democratic campaign in history availed little as George Bush won the election.

Congressional Campaigns

The laws governing the financing of congressional elections constitute a hybrid system fashioned by legislation, judicial decision, Senate and House

Table 6-7 Congressional Campaign Expenditures, 1972-1988

Election cycle	Total	Senate	House
1971-1972	$ 77.3	$ 30.7	$ 46.5
1973-1974	88.2	34.7	53.5
1975-1976	115.5	44.0	71.5
1977-1978	194.8	85.2	109.7
1979-1980	239.0	102.9	136.0
1981-1982	342.4	138.4	204.0
1983-1984	374.1	170.5	203.6
1985-1986	450.9	211.6	239.3
1987-1988	457.0	201.2	256.5
1989-1990	445.2	180.1	265.1

Source: Citizens' Research Foundation compilation based on Federal Election Commission and other data.

Note: Figures are in millions.

rules, and FEC rules and opinions. The absence of public funding for candidates for the Congress means that no incentive exists for them to accept spending limits voluntarily. More than fifteen years after the Supreme Court ruled on campaign finance law, Congress had not enacted legislation to provide public funding and the accompanying expenditure limits for House and Senate races. Congressional campaigns thus are different from presidential campaigns. Congressional candidates can spend unlimited amounts of their own money as well as of other people's money.

The costs of congressional campaigns have increased sharply. Campaign expenditures totaled $445.2 million for House and Senate races in the 1990 cycle compared with $77.3 million during the 1972 election cycle (see Table 6-7). As in the presidential campaigns, however, the picture is not quite so dark when inflation is taken into account. Total spending decreased in the 1990 cycle to the lowest level in six years, representing the first drop since 1977, when the FEC began keeping computerized records. Another indicator exists in the average cost of a race: For the U.S. Senate, the average cost declined from $3 million in 1988 to $2.8 million in 1990, and for the House, from $269,000 in 1988 to $262,000 in 1990. However, no Senate elections were held in the two largest states—California and New York—and four incumbent senators faced no opposition from major party challengers, thus accounting for the decrease.[29] Also, these amounts are only averages of winners and losers, consisting of a great range of costs. Many winning campaigns cost far above the average.

All 435 House seats are up for election every two years, and in the aggregate they are costlier than the thirty-three or thirty-four Senate races decided at the same time. The costs of Senate seats vary according to the number of especially expensive elections that are held in super states such as California, New York, Texas, or Florida, or in some combination.

The erosion of the dollar has meant that the $1,000 maximum individual contribution lost more than 60 percent of its value between 1975 and 1990, and to make up for it, candidates increasingly have pursued PACs, which can contribute up to $5,000 per candidate per election.

The combination of escalating costs and increasing dependencies on certain sources, such as PACs, has given rise to complaints that political challengers are being priced out of the market while incumbents are remaining in office by relying excessively on special interest donations. PACs have focused more and more on campaigns for the Senate and House and have become the most controversial aspect of congressional financing. To put PAC funding in perspective, in 1990, PAC contributions represented 22 percent of total receipts for Senate candidates and 38 percent for House candidates. The differential, showing greater PAC dependency in House campaigns, is explained partly by the greater diversity of sources of funds available to Senate candidates, who represent statewide interests and are more in the news. However, in totals, in 1990, eighteen Senate candidates were PAC millionaires (candidates receiving $1 million or more)—only two challengers and one open seat candidate grouped with fifteen incumbents. Nine House candidates received $500,000 or more from PACs. The top PAC receipts among senators were Tom Harkin, D-Iowa, and Phil Gramm, R-Texas, with $1.8 million each, and among representatives the highest was Richard A. Gephardt, the majority leader, with $761,537.[30]

Although reformers believe PACs are inherently corrupting, leading congressional Republicans have targeted them for different reasons. They complain that PAC contributions have shown a distinct bias toward incumbent legislators, a significant majority of whom are Democrats controlling both the Senate and the House.

PACs have become a lightning rod in the debate over whether the advantages of incumbency have become excessive. In recent years, most House turnover has come through retirement or death, members seeking higher office, or the redistricting following the decennial census rather than through electoral defeat.

While Ronald Reagan won reelection in 1984 in an electoral vote landslide over Walter F. Mondale, the reelection rate of incumbents in the overwhelming Democratic House was 96 percent. Even in 1990 when many predicted public disenchantment with incumbents, the reelection rate was again 96 percent. In some years it has exceeded 98 percent. While some political scientists have concluded from these statistics that a "permanent Congress" exists, in fact, two-thirds of the members of the House have served fewer than twelve years,[31] and the Senate has witnessed a 44 percent turnover rate over a nine-year period.[32]

In 1988, while the average winning Senate campaign cost more than $4 million, many challengers failed to raise even a third of that.[33] In 1990, of the thirty-one Senate incumbents seeking reelection, four had no opposition, and another eleven faced challengers who never presented a credible financial or political threat. Again, in a year in which incumbents were thought to be in disfavor, only one sitting senator was defeated by a challenger who was outspent by a ratio of 8-to-1. The average cost of a winning Senate campaign declined from more than $4 million in 1988 to $3.9 million in 1990. Again, the lack of expensive campaigning in California and New York is part of the reason.[34]

While challengers frequently fail to attain financial competitiveness, money, according to political scientist Gary Jacobson, is a more important campaign resource for them than for incumbents.[35] At the same time, PACs are playing an increasingly important role in funding incumbents' campaigns. According to the FEC, 57 percent of PAC donations went to incumbents during the 1978 cycle; a decade later that figure had jumped to 74 percent.

Labor PAC support for Democrats, however, has been consistently strong. Substantial financial assistance has gone to many Democratic challengers. What has angered Republicans is that business and trade association PACs have shifted their loyalties toward Democrats. In 1988, 55 percent of business PAC money was given to Democrats, mostly to incumbents. Just six year earlier, Republican candidates had received 60 percent of business PAC dollars.[36]

A minority in both houses, Republicans contend that their inability to field competitive challenges to Democratic incumbents in many instances is because of a lack of financial support from, among others, business PACs. The PACs respond that the Republicans have failed to recruit credible challengers in the first place.

Two indices of spending bring findings worth consideration. Of the ten Senate candidates spending the most in 1990, only two lost—one an incumbent and one a challenger. The other eight, all incumbents, won.[37] Of the top eleven House spenders in 1990, only two lost and both were challengers.[38] Thus the results among highest spenders are mixed. However, most high spenders are incumbents, who generally have an easier time raising money, while challengers find it difficult to spend great amounts unless able to do so from personal funds. For example, in 1990, nine Senate candidates spent $100,000 or more of their own money—one, James W. Rappaport, spent personal funds totaling $4.2 million—but all lost.[39] In contrast, in 1988, of the nine Senate candidates who spent $100,000 or more of their own money, three won.[40] Thus both high overall spending and high personal spending may help candidates—more likely incumbents and open seat candidates than challengers—to win, but with no certainty.

Criticism of congressional candidates because of their continuous search for money is a byproduct of the escalating costs of campaigns. However, at the congressional level, the role of television has been overstated. In many House contests, particularly in densely populated urban and suburban areas, the boundaries of a House district are rarely contiguous with the viewership of a broadcast station. Consequently, it makes little sense to buy expensive television time to reach many people unable to vote in that district. In these instances, carefully targeted direct mail has been the medium of choice in communicating with voters. The statewide Senate races, however, do make extensive use of television, sometimes to the tune of 50 percent of general election campaign spending.

The Role of the Parties. The role of the political parties is one that transcends strictly financial issues. The reforms of the early 1970s sharply curtailed the financial involvement of the parties in both the national and congressional campaigns. However, the weakening of the political parties predates the appearance of campaign finance reform on the congressional agenda. The parties, in part, have fallen victim to a more educated, more transient, more independent-thinking electorate—a trend helped along by television.

Congress has been populated increasingly by nontraditional politicians who may ignore party structures in getting nominated and elected, then use some form of media to get their messages directly to the voters instead of relying on party promotions or declining party loyalties among voters.

Because the reforms of the 1970s placed strict limits on the amounts of money that national, state, and local party committees can give to candidates, the parties have lost some of their effectiveness. And the advantage has gone to institutions, such as PACs, that also can provide candidate support and contact with portions of the community. These changes are so basic that no legislation probably could succeed in reversing them. Added to these problems, the major parties at the national level are in debt. According to the FEC, at the end of 1990, the Republicans finished the year owing $8.3 million, while the Democrats owed $5.6 million.[41]

The parties are not without some clout, however. They benefit from soft money at the state and local levels. Moreover, the framework of the law permits coordinated expenditures under which national and state party committees can pay for certain candidate expenditures. The cap on coordinated expenditures is based on a formula of 2 cents per individual of voting age plus cost-of-living adjustments. In 1990, these expenditures in some cases amounted to large sums—as much as $2 million in a California Senate race. The House limit was $50,280.

Combining 1990 Senate and House races, the Republicans directly contributed $2.9 million to its candidates and spent an additional $10.7 million in coordinated expenditures. The Democrats gave $1.5 million to their candidates and spent another $8.6 million on their behalf. However, the level of coordinated spending by both parties declined along with their diminishing income. For example, the Republican party spent $14.3 million in the 1986 congressional campaign, while the Democratic party spent $9 million.[42]

The debate over the role of the parties is steeped in partisan motives. The Republicans, whose national party committees have outraised their Democratic counterparts in recent years, would like to substantially loosen—if not entirely remove—the current contribution limits and coordinated limits on party spending in congressional races. Predictably, because of the Republican party advantage in fund raising, the Democrats are leery of such proposals.

7 State and Local Experience

The drive for political finance reform since the early 1970s has not been limited to federal elections. Almost every state has changed its election laws in significant ways. Some states have imposed restrictions similar to those placed on presidential and congressional aspirants, while others have selected approaches markedly different from federal statutes. Some states have been innovative in their searches for satisfactory regulatory systems.

Many states that adopted campaign laws in the early 1970s had to alter them following the 1976 U.S. Supreme Court ruling in *Buckley v. Valeo*,[1] which found campaign spending limits to be unconstitutional unless they were tied to candidate acceptance of public financing. Although the *Buckley* decision brought about certain similarities between federal and state laws, no two states today are alike in their election statutes—any more than they are alike in their political cultures and traditions.

The period immediately following the *Buckley* case was not favorable to political finance reform either at the federal or state level. The initiative passed from reformers and their allies in the media to those most directly affected by the reform laws: officeholders and candidates, political parties, and interest groups.

But while the reform movement in Congress tries to recover the impetus it enjoyed in the years prior to the *Buckley* decision, reform at the state level has undergone a resurgence in recent years. Twenty-two states now have operative public funding or tax-assisted programs, a 16 percent increase since 1982. In addition, the legislatures of two of the nation's largest states, California and Illinois, approved public funding programs in 1984 and 1985—only to see them vetoed, however, when they reached the governor's desk. In response, California in 1988 adopted a ballot initiative providing public financing of campaigns for the state legislature. It was negated, however, by another issue on the same ballot prohibiting public funding.

Furthermore, three major American cities—New York, Seattle, and Tucson—instituted public financing campaigns during the latter part of the 1980s.[2] Two counties—Sacramento County, California, and King County, Washington—similarly enacted public funding programs, both by popular vote. And in June 1990, Los Angeles became the fourth city to undertake public financing, although its status remains clouded by litigation.

State Capitals and Financial Capital

The revival of interest in political finance reform at the state level stems in large part from the high cost of running for office, which, at the very least, is limiting the pool of people who can afford an election campaign. Increasing concern also exists that the abundance of money in state and municipal races is contributing to the appearance of impropriety, if not to the actual commission of illegal acts.

Just as congressional candidates are obtaining an ever-growing percentage of funds from political action committees (PACs), those seeking state office are relying increasingly on contributions from PACs, corporations, unions, and trade associations with interests before the legislative branch. According to the private California Commission on Campaign Financing, donations from these groups accounted for more than half of the money contributed to California legislative candidates during the 1986 election cycle.[3] In Maryland, Common Cause found that PAC contributions to state candidates during the 1986-1990 cycle almost doubled over the 1982-1986 period.[4] Other studies indicate a similar trend across the country, regardless of a state's geography, demography, or political leanings.

At the congressional level, more than three-quarters of PAC money goes to incumbents. Available evidence indicates that the percentage may be even higher in many states. The result is fewer competitive elections and heightened electoral advantage for those already holding office. In 1976, incumbents in the California Assembly were outspending challengers by a ratio of 3-to-1 in general elections. By 1984, this ratio had increased to 14-to-1. In 1986, it doubled to 30-to-1.[5]

The Mushrooming Cost of State Office

In 1976, spending in races for statewide office and state legislative seats stood at about $120 million. By 1984, it had risen to $325 million, and by 1988 to $540 million, a jump of 450 percent in twelve years.[6]

The escalating costs of running for state office coincide with the era of "New Federalism" initiated by the Reagan administration during the 1980s. This policy placed increased responsibility and power in the hands of the states, thereby enhancing the desirability of state executive and legislative office. While a governorship was once seen as a steppingstone to a U.S. Senate seat, it is significant that two U.S. senators—Republicans Paul S. Trible, Jr., of Virginia and Pete Wilson of California—opted recently to travel in the other direction; both decided to run for governor instead of remaining in "the world's most exclusive club." Trible lost; Wilson won.

The amounts being spent by gubernatorial candidates have risen proportionately with the desirability of these offices. In 1986, the average gubernatorial campaign—primary and general election for all candidates combined—exceeded $7 million.[7] In Florida, the combined primary and general election figure was just below $24 million; in California, $22.5 million. Just three years later, the 1989 race for governor in Virginia—a state a fraction of the size of Florida and California—saw candidates spend a total of $25.7 million.[8] In 1990, to fill the open seat in the California governorship race, expenditures rose to $43 million, almost double the amount spent four years earlier.

Even the states with the smallest populations are being affected in much the same manner. In 1988, candidates for governor of Montana spent a total of $2.7 million. The amount seems insignificant compared with sums spent in California and Florida, but it was more than was spent by all statewide and state legislative candidates in Montana just four years earlier.[9]

The upward spending spiral in statewide races can be explained in part by the increasing reliance on television advertising. In the 1990 Texas gubernatorial race, Republican candidate Clayton Williams by mid-October had spent $12 million on television advertising, and by some estimates had been seen eighty times by the average Texan.[10] By comparison, state legislative districts generally do not fall neatly within media markets, and expensive television advertising would be wasted on voters in surrounding districts.

Nevertheless, the cost of running for state legislative office is rising even faster than that of seeking statewide office. While television may be an inefficient promotional tool at that level, more and more sophisticated methods of targeting voters—through such means as direct mail and telephone calling—are being developed.

The increased responsibility placed upon state legislatures has been termed a "congressionalization" of some legislatures. Just as members of Congress consider their jobs to be full time—indeed, current ethics laws force them to consider their positions in that manner—many state senators and assemblymen are coming to regard themselves as professional politicians, not Jeffersonian "citizen-legislators." Consequently, candidates are willing to spend large sums of money to obtain or retain their posts.

Again, the situation in California is illustrative, but hardly unique. In 1978, total spending on state legislative races exceeded $20 million. In 1982, that figure more than doubled to $43 million. By 1986, it had reached $57.1 million.[11] In 1988, in just one California state senate district, $2.4 million was spent by all candidates during the primary campaign alone.

A survey by the National Conference of State Legislatures underscores the coast-to-coast nature of this trend. In the case of the Alaska senate, primary and general election costs rose 219 percent and 140 percent, respectively, between 1982 and 1988. For the Florida senate, combined primary and general election costs jumped 123 percent between 1982 and 1986. General election costs for the Connecticut senate were up 80 percent during that period.[12]

A 1990 study by Gary Moncrief of Boise State University offers further evidence. With inflation taken into account, Moncrief found that the average expenditure per candidate still increased almost 300 percent in races for the Oregon senate, 150 percent in contests for the Oregon house, and more than 90 percent in Washington senate races between 1980 and 1988. Even in states such as Idaho and Montana, where the concept of the "citizen-legislature" persists, Moncrief found inflation-adjusted increases of 11 to 30 percent during the early to mid-1980s.[13]

The Recent Push for Reform

Concerns about the costs of running for state office and the sources of much of the money received by the candidates have prompted both large and small states to act in recent years to impose limits on campaign contributions and expenditures (see Table 7-1) and to provide public financing of campaigns (see Table 7-2).

- 1986: An Arizona ballot initiative resulted in imposition of contribution limits on individuals and political committees and an aggregate limit on the amount candidates may accept from all political action committees. Passage of a Rhode Island campaign reform initiative forced the state legislature to develop a gubernatorial public funding program, which took effect with the 1990 election. Oregon enacted a law permitting taxpayers to "add on" a small sum to their tax bills to provide funding to the state's political parties. Florida adopted a law providing partial public funding for gubernatorial and state cabinet candidates in the 1990 elections, but the legislature's failure to provide adequate appropriations meant the law could not be implemented. The law was upgraded in 1991 with results yet to be seen.
- 1987: The Ohio legislature passed a law creating a checkoff by which taxpayers could direct that a small portion of their tax payments be given to the political parties.
- 1988: North Carolina adopted a tax add-on to help fund campaigns for governor and state cabinet officers; it already had a tax checkoff to support political parties. The Arizona legislature adopted a tax add-on to provide funding for political parties. Three states—Kentucky, Louisiana, and Massachusetts—adopted limits on contributions from political action committees.
- 1989: New Hampshire established a system of voluntary expenditure limits without public financing. Candidates who agreed to abide by the

Table 7-1 State Political Finance Regulation

State	Disclosure requirements	Contribution limits (individuals)	Contribution limits (organizations)	Tax credits/ deductions	Independent election agency
Alabama	Yes	No	Yes	No	No
Alaska	Yes	Yes	Yes	No	Yes
Arizona	Yes	Yes	Yes	Yes [a]	No
Arkansas	Yes	Yes	Yes	No	Yes [b]
California	Yes	Yes [c]	Yes [c]	Yes [d]	Yes
Colorado	Yes	No	No	No	No
Connecticut	Yes	Yes	Yes	No	Yes
Delaware	Yes	Yes	Yes	No	Yes
Florida	Yes	Yes	Yes	No	Yes
Georgia	Yes	Yes	Yes	No	Yes
Hawaii	Yes	Yes	Yes	Yes [a]	Yes
Idaho	Yes	No	No	No	No
Illinois	Yes	No [e]	No	No	Yes
Indiana	Yes	No	Yes	No	Yes
Iowa	Yes	No	Yes	No	Yes
Kansas	Yes	Yes	Yes	No	Yes
Kentucky	Yes	Yes	Yes	No	Yes
Louisiana	Yes	Yes	Yes	No	Yes
Maine	Yes	Yes	Yes	No	Yes
Maryland	Yes	Yes	Yes	No	Yes

continued

Table 7-1 (continued)

State	Disclosure requirements	Contribution limits (individuals)	Contribution limits (organizations)	Tax credits/ deductions	Independent election agency
Massachusetts	Yes	Yes	Yes	No	Yes
Michigan	Yes	Yes	Yes	No	No
Minnesota	Yes	Yes	Yes	Yes [d]	Yes
Mississippi	Yes	No	Yes	No	No
Missouri	Yes	No	No	No	No
Montana	Yes	Yes	Yes	Yes [a]	Yes
Nebraska	Yes	No	No	No	Yes
Nevada	Yes	No	No	No	No
New Hampshire	Yes	Yes	Yes	No	No
New Jersey	Yes	Yes [f]	Yes [f]	No	Yes
New Mexico	Yes	No	No	No	No
New York	Yes	Yes	Yes	No	Yes
North Carolina	Yes	Yes	Yes	Yes [a]	Yes
North Dakota	Yes	No	Yes	No	No
Ohio	Yes	No	Yes	No	Yes
Oklahoma	Yes	Yes	Yes	No	Yes
Oregon	Yes	No	No	Yes [d]	No
Pennsylvania	Yes	No	Yes	No	No
Rhode Island	Yes	Yes	Yes	No	Yes
South Carolina	Yes [g]	No	No	No	Yes

South Dakota	Yes	Yes	Yes	No	No
Tennessee	Yes	No	Yes	No	Yes
Texas	Yes	No	Yes	No	No
Utah	Yes	No	No	No	No
Vermont	Yes	Yes	Yes	No	No
Virginia	Yes	No	No	No	Yes
Washington	Yes	Yes	Yes	No	Yes
West Virginia	Yes	Yes	Yes	No	No
Wisconsin	Yes	Yes	Yes	No	Yes
Wyoming	Yes[g]	Yes	Yes	No	No

Sources: National Clearinghouse on Election Administration, Federal Election Commission, *Campaign Finance Law 90* (Washington, D.C.: Federal Election Commission, 1990); "State Campaign Finance Laws: The 1990 Legislative Session," *Campaign Practices Reports*, July 23, 1990; Federick M. Herrmann, *1990 Campaign Finance Update: Legislation and Litigation* (Los Angeles, Calif.: Citizens' Research Foundation, 1990); Ronald D. Michaelson, *1989 Campaign Finance Update: Legislation and Litigation* (Los Angeles, Calif.: Citizens' Research Foundation, 1990); Ronald D. Michaelson, *1988 Campaign Finance Update: Legislation and Litigation* (Lexington, Ky.: Council on Governmental Ethics Laws (COGEL), 1988).

[a] Tax deduction.

[b] A campaign finance initiative passed by Arkansas voters in November 1990 created a five-member Arkansas Ethics Commission effective as of January 1, 1991, to administer both the new campaign finance statute and a public ethics law passed by voters in 1988.

[c] For legislative campaigns only, but under litigation.

[d] Tax credit.

[e] The one restriction on Illinois involves a prohibition from making political donations by any individual who owns 5 percent or more of the stock in a horse racing organization.

[f] New Jersey's individual and organizational contribution limits apply only to the state's publicly funded gubernatorial election. No contribution limits currently exist in state legislative races.

[g] Unlike the other forty-eight states, which require both pre- and post-election reporting, South Carolina and Wyoming mandate only post-election filing. South Carolina does require that, two weeks prior to the election, candidates make a list of those contributing $100 or more available upon request. However, one must request such a list of the candidate's headquarters; it is not filed with the state.

Table 7-2 Public Financing and Tax-Assisted Funding in State Elections

State	System		Benefits			Elections			
	Checkoff	Add-on	Governor	Other offices	Parties	General	Primary	Expenditure limits	Year enacted
Alabama		X			X				1983
Arizona		X			X				1988
California		X			X				1982
Florida	[a]		X	X		X	X	X	1991
Hawaii	X		X	X		X	X	X	1978-1979
Idaho	X				X				1975
Indiana	[b]				X				1977
Iowa	X				X				1973
Kentucky	X				X				1976
Maine		X			X				1973
Maryland		X [c]	X			X	X	X	1974
Massachusetts		X	X	X		X	X		1975
Michigan	X		X			X	X	X	1976
Minnesota	X		X	X		X		X	1974
Montana		X	X	X		X			1975
New Hampshire	[d]		X	X		X		X	1987
New Jersey	X		X			X	X	X	1974
North Carolina	X	X [e]	X	X	X	X		X	1975-1988

Ohio	X				X				1987
Oregon		X[f]			X				1987
Rhode Island	[g]		X		X	X			1973-1988
Utah	X				X				1973
Virginia		X			X				1982
Wisconsin	X		X	X		X		X	1977

Sources: Citizens' Research Foundation.

Notes: Oklahoma enacted legislation, but its program has been discontinued. Some party funding may go to candidates in specific election campaigns, but in most states, parties are prohibited from engaging in primary election activity.

[a] In 1991, Florida passed a law creating a public financing program funded through a tax on filing fees and on contributions from political action committees.

[b] Indiana uses fees for customized license plates for funding subsidies to the major political parties.

[c] In 1982, Maryland suspended its add-on but will disburse previously collected funds in the 1994 gubernatorial election.

[d] In 1989, New Hampshire enacted a filing fee waiver for state and federal candidates.

[e] In 1988, North Carolina enacted a "candidates financing fund" with an add-on system that operates separately from the "political parties fund" checkoff established in 1975.

[f] In 1987, the Oregon legislature enacted an income-tax-based political party add-on long after a tax checkoff ended in 1981 because of a "sunset" provision; this program was automatically terminated effective tax year 1989 when minimum levels of participation set forth by statute were not met.

[g] In 1988, Rhode Island enacted a gubernatorial election fund to be financed by general appropriations in lieu of sufficient checkoff participation.

limits were forgiven filing fees up to $5,000 and required to collect significantly fewer notarized petition signatures than those who declined to stay within the limits.[14] Kansas reduced PAC contribution limits, and Florida enacted a ban on solicitation or acceptance of political donations during a legislative session.[15]

• 1990: Georgia adopted the state's first-ever system of political contribution limits. Minnesota sailed into uncharted waters by extending state public financing to candidates for Congress, which seems certain to be challenged in court on grounds of federal supremacy and preemption. Meanwhile, in Arkansas, the voters did what the legislature was reluctant to do. After campaign reform went nowhere during the session, proponents placed a measure on the ballot that tightened contribution and disclosure limits and created a new independent agency to oversee political finance. The voters passed the measure by a margin of 2-to-1. Two years earlier, voters approved an initiative enacting a sweeping government ethics law.

As in Arkansas, reform advocates in California have resorted to the ballot box in recent years in the face of a recalcitrant legislature. The end result, however, has been long on court fights and short on results. In June 1988, 53 percent of California voters approved Proposition 68, which created a system of public financing and contribution limits for state legislative candidates. During the same election, however, 58 percent of the voters approved Proposition 73, which provided contribution limits but expressly prohibited use of public funds in political campaigns.

After more than two years of regulatory and judicial maneuvering, a federal district court ruled in September 1990 that the contribution limits in Proposition 73 were unconstitutional. The judge stated that, because the limits were set on a per fiscal year instead of per election basis, they favored incumbents (who raise substantial money in the "off-years") over nonincumbents (who often do not decide to run until the year in which the election is held).[16]

Barely five weeks later, in November 1990, the California Supreme Court invalidated all provisions of Proposition 68 on the grounds that it was superseded by the regulatory system achieving the larger vote, Proposition 73.[17] The upshot was to leave the nation's largest state without any limits on political contributions. The hazards of dealing with a constitutionally fragile subject by means of public initiative became apparent.

Improper Influences

While the rising costs of campaigns have affected virtually every state, another catalyst for reform—corruption—continues to play a role. More than half a century has passed since Boston mayor James Michael Curley was reelected from a jail cell. But in many states and localities, money and politics interact in ways perceived by many as unsavory.

No empirical way exists to measure the extent to which campaign contributions are received in return for promises—explicit or tacit—of jobs, contracts, or policy changes. But the incentive is undoubtedly greater at the state and local levels than at the federal level, largely because the direct contracting of services—and the accompanying opportunities for chicanery and kickbacks—occurs in greater measure at the lower levels of government.

The past several years have brought forth several unhappy reminders of the truth of this axiom. In early 1990, state senator Joseph Montoya became the first California legislator convicted of a felony in a third of a century. Montoya was found guilty, as part of an FBI "sting" operation in Sacramento, of using his position to extort funds from lobbyists representing foreign medical schools. Ironically, Montoya was one of the chief sponsors of Proposition 73.

On the heels of the Montoya conviction came two other convictions of present and former California state legislators. Then came another FBI sting operation almost three thousand miles away in the South Carolina capital of Columbia. By the end of 1990, it had netted ten legislators, with five pleading guilty to bribery charges. And, in early 1991, a third sting operation caught several leading members of the Arizona legislature with their hands out.

The use of campaign contributions to gain preferential treatment is not limited to criminal elements. Respectable business owners and operators and other professionals engage in the practice as well. The amount of political money supplied by criminal elements, organized or otherwise, continues to be a subject of universal curiosity. But four decades after the Special Senate Committee to Investigate Organized Crime in Interstate Commerce—the so-called Kefauver Committee—found evidence of "contributions to the campaign funds of candidates . . . at various levels by organized criminals,"[18] the extent of such activity remains unknown. Some scholars have estimated that perhaps 15 percent of the money for state and local campaigns is derived from the underworld,[19] which would mean about $135.8 million contributed in 1988.

Even in the absence of criminal elements or clear malfeasance, in many states and localities, beneficiaries of government largesse customarily show gratitude by contributing. Sometimes, contributions are made to both parties as a hedge. Contributors hope to purchase good will and access, if not actual contracts, regardless of who is elected. In many places, systematic solicitation of those who benefit from the system occurs.

In New York, for example, Republican state comptroller Edward V. Regan was summoned in late 1988 before a commission investigating campaign contributors who received contracts from the comptroller's office. While Regan denied direct involvement in fund raising, the commission found that more than 90 percent of his political contributions over a five-year period came from firms doing business with the comptroller's office and that Regan aides had carefully monitored how much officials of these firms had donated.[20] Federal and local prosecutors expressed interest in the revelations, but—as of mid-1991—no charges had been filed, and indications were that prosecutors were not pursuing the matter actively.

Such behavior is hardly the exclusive province of a particular political party. The New York Commission on Governmental Integrity also criticized two Democrats, Gov. Mario Cuomo and state attorney general Robert Abrams, for fund-raising practices similar to those of Republican Regan.

A case in Illinois illustrates another variant of the often questionable links between campaign donations and governmental actions. Corporations with interests in two race track companies gave $100,000 to the state Republican party just twenty days after the Illinois Racing Board, which was controlled by Republicans, granted licenses to the race track firms. The board's decision followed an extensive inquiry into the firms' fitness to hold a license. The contributing corporations were controlled by a New Jersey resident who usually gave to Democratic party causes in his home state. While one of the corporations was fined for violating a prohibition of political contributions from liquor licensees, no other prosecutions ensued. In 1989, the Illinois legislature overrode the veto of Gov. James R. Thompson and voted to allow horse racing interests to contribute to political committees.

One of the few clear-cut cases of extortion or conspiracy to obtain campaign contributions involved Syracuse (N.Y.) mayor Lee Alexander, a Democrat who at one time chaired the U.S. Conference of Mayors. In January 1988, Alexander pleaded guilty to federal charges of racketeering and income tax evasion as well as extortion and conspiracy to obstruct a government investigation. He received a ten-year jail sentence and a $100,000 fine. Among the compensations Alexander required from government contractors, prosecutors said, were contributions to his campaign committee. Moreover, he used some of the money received from the kickbacks to provide financial and organizational support to national and local candidates.[21]

New legal ground was plowed in the 1990 conviction of former California state senator Paul Carpenter arising out of the Sacramento sting. The case is noteworthy because Carpenter was not accused of selling his vote or putting the money in his pocket. Instead he was convicted of selling access—his time, energy, and attention—in return for a $20,000 campaign contribution.[22]

But the line between legal contributions and illegal behavior on the part of elected officials frequently is hazy, making prosecution difficult. Perhaps the best-known local corruption case since the early 1970s involved Spiro T. Agnew, who was vice president in the Nixon administration. Routine investigations of corruption in Baltimore County—where Agnew had been county executive in the mid-1960s before going on to serve as governor of Maryland—led to his indictment on bribery, extortion, and tax fraud charges. Witnesses said that Agnew had pocketed more than $100,000 in payouts from several engineering firms that had been awarded county and state contracts.

According to these witnesses, Agnew sought to legitimize the transactions by claiming the money represented campaign contributions. Nonetheless, in October 1973, Agnew became the second man in U.S. history to resign from the vice presidency as part of a plea bargain. In return, he pleaded nolo contendere to just one count of tax evasion and avoided a jail sentence.[20] Ironically, Republican Agnew's successors as Baltimore county executive and Maryland governor—both Democrats—ultimately went to prison on corruption charges, again demonstrating that such behavior is by no means limited to a particular political party.

The Agnew case illustrates the benefits of detailed accounting of both campaign funds and a politician's sources of income. Disclosure laws make it difficult to claim, ex post facto, that ill-gotten personal gain was really meant to be a legal campaign contribution.

Granted, those caught in illegal acts are generally prosecuted for tax fraud, bribery, or extortion rather than for violations of an already flexible code of campaign finance. And old habits of laxity regarding campaign laws are likely to persist until candidates and their operatives and contributors are punished regularly, not selectively, for violations of the law. In the meantime, however, statutory disclosure brings at least some discipline to transactions involving money and elected public officials.

The State of State Laws

Disclosure requirements are based on the belief that the public has a right to know the sources of financial support candidates receive and the patterns of their expenditures. All fifty states have some disclosure requirements, and all except two call for both pre- and post-election reporting of contributions and expenditures. South Carolina and Wyoming mandate only post-election disclosure.[24]

In many states, however, the information is neither readily accessible nor compiled for the purpose of highlighting statewide trends in spending and contributions. As Sandra Singer, formerly of the National Conference of State Legislatures, noted, "Very few states actually compile this data.

Some review a small percentage of these reports randomly. Others simply place them in a file and forget them. Many states do not even have all of the reports collected in one place."[25] In Ohio, for example, disclosure reports for legislative candidates are collected and retained in the state's sixty-four counties instead of at the state capital. In contrast, for federal races, the Federal Election Commission places all information under one roof and publishes biennial analyses of the data.

Like federal law, state disclosure statutes usually require a breakdown of large contributions by amount and date as well as the name and address of the donor. These laws also generally require reporting of total spending, along with itemization of certain expenditures as to amount, date, and recipient of payment.

Where states differ markedly is the minimum amount at which reporting requirements kick in. Several states—Florida is a notable example—require itemization of all contributions, regardless of size. Most states have a threshold of $100 or less above which receipts must be itemized, as compared with the more than $200 under federal law for individual contributors. However, a handful of states have substantially higher thresholds for itemization of contributions; Kentucky sets the level at $300, and Maine, Mississippi, and Nevada at $500.[26]

Many states are not stringent about collecting information on donors. Federal law requires that political fund reports disclose occupation and principle place of business as well as name and address of contributors above the $200 threshold. Numerous states require the listing of only the name and address of the donor, making it difficult to determine whether the donor is part of a profession or constituency with current legislative or regulatory interests. New Jersey is but one state that now seeks only limited information about a candidate's contributors. In a report released in October 1990, the state's Ad Hoc Commission on Legislative Ethics and Campaign Finance wrote:

> The commission believes that more information must be required from individuals and organizations which make contributions, and that information must be readily available to the public. . . . The public does not now know whether a person contributes to a candidate because he simply agrees with the candidate's stand on current issues or because he is seeking to promote a particular issue favored by the members of his occupation or employer.[27]

Obtaining that information is even more difficult in the several states that allow so-called "conduit" contributions. In Ohio, employees of a large firm can make contributions through payroll deductions. These donations are then "bundled" and given in a lump sum to a candidate on a corporate check, so that the office seeker is well aware of his or her benefactor. The catch is that when the donations are disclosed, candidates are not required to make reference to the company writing the check. Instead, the money shows up as numerous small contributions. The reader of the disclosure form has no way of telling that the donors work for the same firm.

In several states, minor parties have been exempted from disclosing their contributors following a series of suits brought in the mid-1970s by the Socialist Workers party with the support of the American Civil Liberties Union.[28] The exemptions were based on the Supreme Court's *Buckley* decision, which said that case-by-case exemptions for minor parties are permissible if there is "reasonable probability that the compelled disclosure of party contributors' names will subject them to threats, harassment or reprisals from either government officials or private parties." [29]

Contribution Limits

Individuals. The states are closely divided on the question of restricting the amount an individual citizen can donate to a candidate, party, or political action committee. Of the fifty states, twenty-one allowed unlimited donations for individuals at the outset of 1991. Among the nation's most heavily populated states, the track record is uneven. California voters imposed contribution limits on individuals in 1988, but the courts ultimately threw out the structure of those restrictions as unconstitutional. The individual ceilings in the second most populous state, New York, have been criticized as overly lenient; a donor may give up to $50,000 to a statewide candidate. Florida and Michigan have individual limits, while Texas, Illinois, Pennsylvania, and Ohio do not.

Among the twenty-nine states that impose restrictions on individual contributors, the laws vary widely. Some limit the amount an individual may give to any one candidate, while others set a cap for total contributions to all candidates in an election year. Several states have a uniform contribution limit for candidates, while others use a multi-tiered structure with different restrictions for statewide, state legislative, and local candidates. Still other approaches exempt residential property use and travel expenses from counting against contribution limits. Federal and state law uniformly exempt volunteer services.

New York has perhaps the most complex system—with individual limits determined by multiplying a specified number of cents by the number of registered voters. New Jersey has a hybrid structure, with sources allowed to make unlimited donations to all races except the publicly funded governor's contest. In that election, they are restricted to $1,500 contributions per election.

Some generalizations can be made. Virtually all of the states with limits have caps in the $1,000 to $5,000 range for an individual contributor. Arizona has the lowest contribution limits with an indexed total in late 1991 of $610 per election cycle for the primary and general election combined. About half the states restrict gifts by individuals to political parties or PACs—either by setting ceilings on donations to those groups or placing aggregate limits on individual giving. The balance of the states with individual limits places them only on donations to candidates. Finally, to ensure accurate accounting, almost half the states bar cash contributions in excess of $100.

Committees, Corporations, and Unions. In the 1970s, Congress imposed strict limits on the amount that political parties and nonparty committees (PACs) can contribute. Numerous states followed suit in restricting PAC contributions. But state legislatures apparently are reluctant to regulate the activities of political parties.

While some in Congress fret that federal restrictions have weakened national political parties, two-thirds of the states place no limit on the level of help that state parties can provide to candidates. Several others impose very modest strictures. Florida, for example, until 1991 allowed state parties to play a financially unlimited role except for a ban on contributions to judicial candidates. Among the tightest rules are those in West Virginia, which limits party contributions to $1,000 per candidate each election.

All states now permit corporations and unions to form PACs—estimated at twelve thousand across the country—to solicit voluntary contributions from employees, stockholders, and members for donation to political campaigns. Industry and trade association PACs have proliferated in recent years in state capitals as well as in Washington, and they have been the subject of growing controversy at both levels. Half of the states have imposed limits on PAC donations. The bulk of these laws, however, apply only to contributions to candidates. Few states have placed limits on PAC giving to political parties.

Several states have experimented with the so-called aggregate ceilings now being promoted by Democratic leaders in Congress as a means of limiting federal PACs. In 1983, Montana became the first state to place such a ceiling on the total amount candidates for state legislative office could receive from all PACs—$600 for House candidates and $1,000 for Senate candidates. Wisconsin, which has an extensive public financing program, has aggregate PAC limits ranging from almost $500,000 for a gubernatorial candidate to just under $7,800 for a state assembly nominee. A 1986 campaign reform initiative enacted in Arizona placed a $50,000 aggregate ceiling on donations that a statewide candidate may accept from all political committees.

Legally distinct from PAC contributions are direct contributions from corporations and labor unions. While barred at the federal level, these types of donations are permitted in a number of states. Several states distinguish between the two—barring corporate contributions while permitting labor unions to donate directly to candidates.

Twenty states prohibit direct corporate contributions, eighteen place restrictions on the amount that corporations can donate, and the remaining twelve have no limits. In comparison, only nine states—Arizona, Connecticut, New Hampshire, North Carolina, North Dakota, Pennsylvania, Texas, Wisconsin, and Wyoming—prohibit labor union contributions to candidates.[30] However, twenty-one states limit labor union contributions in some way, while twenty have no restrictions.

In the past, in-kind contributions from corporations and unions—such as provision of office space, furniture, and transportation without charge—frequently never showed up on candidate disclosure forms. However, federal law and most state statutes now require that in-kind services and loans be treated the same as direct contributions for purposes of disclosure. Candidates must provide reasonable estimates of the fair market value of in-kind contributions, and that value must fall within the contribution limits for that jurisdiction.

Increasingly, states are seeking to restrict political money where it may pose a potential conflict-of-interest, such as in the case of corporations whose livelihood depends upon regulatory decisions by state officials. Half of the states have enacted outright prohibitions on donations by public utilities or other heavily regulated industries. Two such laws were passed in 1989. Georgia bars contributions from insurance companies and loan companies to candidates for insurance commissioner, while Indiana prohibits the State Lottery Commission from awarding a contract to anyone who has contributed to a statewide candidate during the preceding three years.

In the mid-1970s, several states sought to extend restrictions on corporate and union contributions to candidates to cover ballot initiative campaigns as well. But in 1978, the U.S. Supreme Court—in *First National Bank of Boston v. Bellotti*—ruled unconstitutional a Massachusetts law that prohibited corporations from spending money on ballot issues that did not pertain directly to their corporate interests. Subsequently, a Florida law and a Berkeley, California, ordinance restricting corporate spending or contributions on initiatives were struck down by the courts.[31] The result has been a geometric growth in the money spent on ballot initiatives—some $225 million in 1988. The insurance industry spent in excess of $70 million for or against five initiatives relating to automobile insurance rates on the November 1988 California ballot. Overall, $84 million was expended in that battle, making it the most expensive campaign in history with the exception of the race for the White House.

Bipartisan Election Commissions

Independent election commissions represent an attempt to isolate from political pressures the functions of receiving, auditing, tabulating, publicizing, and preserving the reports of campaign receipts and expenditures. These commissions have usually supplanted elected or appointed officials, such as secretaries of state, whose partisanship did not make them ideal administrators or enforcers of election law. Some commissions have strong powers, including the right to issue subpoenas, assess penalties, and file court actions. Others are limited to actions such as conducting administrative hearings and imposing fines.

In thirty states, independent authorities oversee some elements of campaign finance law (all of these states have commissions except Delaware and Montana, where a single officer is appointed). In the remaining twenty states, election law continues to be the province of the secretary of state—except for Utah, where such authority is vested with the lieutenant governor. Virtually all of the independent commissions are required by law to be bipartisan, if not nonpartisan; the remainder are structured so that major political parties likely will be represented. Perhaps the most unusual structure is in Massachusetts, where the board of the Office of Campaign and Political Finance consists of the secretary of state, the chairmen of the Democratic and Republican parties, and the dean of a law school located in the state—who is appointed by the governor. The four meet only to choose the director of the office.

In the other states with commissions, the authority to appoint members is given exclusively to the governor or divided between the governor and the state legislature. In several instances, the latter approach has run into problems in the courts. The latest was in Louisiana, where the state Supreme Court held in June 1989 that enforcement of campaign finance disclosure laws by the State Board of Ethics for Elected Officials violated the separation of powers in the state constitution. This mirrored the 1976 U.S. Supreme Court decision in *Buckley v. Valeo*, which struck down the original makeup of the Federal Election Commission in which Congress and the president shared appointive authority. Louisiana officials sought to correct their problem with an amendment to the state constitution, but it was rejected by the voters in October 1989.

Election commissions are responsible for receiving and auditing campaign contribution and expenditure reports, compiling data, writing and implementing regulations, and providing advisory opinions. While also empowered to conduct investigations, few commissions have the resources to initiate them. Because of a mounting paperwork burden combined with inadequate funding, these agencies generally rely on complaints filed by candidates and investigative newspaper reports to detect violations.

In a 1985 study of campaign finance regulation, Robert J. Huckshorn, a political scientist who also has been a Florida election commission member, found many ostensibly independent election commissions to be toothless tigers. Barely half of the commissions in existence at the time had the power to levy fines, Huckshorn said. And, among those that did, about three-quarters were "limited either by restrictive statutory provisions or self-imposed limits that cast their application of civil penalties into the nuisance mold of traffic tickets." [32]

Compounding the situation is that state election commissions, with the exception of Nebraska's, have only civil prosecutorial authority. They must refer possible criminal violations to the appropriate law enforcement official, which normally is an attorney general or district attorney, who is a partisan official with legal discretion as to whether to pursue the matter. Even if they have no political motivation, these officials are usually not as well informed as the commissions on issues relating to election law and are therefore less well equipped to deal with election law cases.

The obstacles faced by election commissions have been aggravated by across-the-board budgetary cutbacks in many states. Moreover, election commissions—which have been in existence for more than fifteen years in some states—have lost their novelty and glamour, and no longer enjoy the level of popular or legislative support they once did.

In addition to the disclosure of campaign finances, some thirty states require candidates or public officials to disclose personal finances. In some states, such as California, the same commission is responsible for enforcing both campaign and ethics laws. But definitions of ethics and conflict-of-interest remain elusive, and laws regulating them have been as difficult to enforce as campaign statutes. Efforts by independent commissions to interpret the gray areas in these laws often have caused antagonism among the state legislators who must comply with them. In turn, these legislators have sought to undercut administration of such laws by budget decreases, thereby adding to the already severe financial constraints faced by independent regulators.

Public Funding

Since 1973, twenty-six states have enacted programs of tax-assisted funding for political parties and candidate campaigns; twenty-two of these programs are currently in operation. The intention has been to reduce the fund-raising edge generally enjoyed by incumbents, lessen the advantages of wealthy candidates, provide an alternative to funding by interest groups, and provide an inducement for candidates to abide by voluntary spending limits—thereby slowing the growth of campaign expenditures.[33]

A quarter of the public financing programs in existence were adopted since the mid-1980s. However, the four most advanced state public financing programs—located in New Jersey, Michigan, Minnesota, and Wisconsin—had their inception in the 1970s, around the time of the Watergate scandal. New Jersey and Michigan pay substantial amounts of the costs incurred by gubernatorial candidates, while Minnesota and Wisconsin are the only two states that have significantly extended public financing to state legislative elections.[34]

Raising the Money

Of the twenty-two public financing programs in operation, nineteen raise money through their income tax systems. Twelve of these states use a tax checkoff system—the same method the federal government employs to collect funds for the Presidential Election Campaign Fund. Another eight use a tax surcharge, or add-on. One state, North Carolina, has both types of fund-raising mechanisms.

Tax Checkoffs. The checkoff procedure allows taxpayers to earmark a small portion of their tax payments, usually $1 for a single taxpayer and $2 for a joint return, for a special political fund. Accordingly, the states with this option are subsidizing the public financing system. The political funds are distributed to individual candidates, political parties, or both. In most states in which funds are allocated to parties, a taxpayer may designate the party he or she prefers. No additional cost is levied on the taxpayer because the full amount of the tax must be paid in any case.

Taxpayer participation in the tax checkoff systems varies by state. In 1988, the average participation rate in state programs was about 16 percent. But, like the federal checkoff, participation in the states reached a high in the late 1970s and early 1980s and has been declining steadily since. In New Jersey, the checkoff rate reached a high of 41.7 percent in 1980; by 1989, it had dropped to 32.3 percent. The experience is similar in other states with well-funded, highly visible public financing programs. In Michigan, participation in the checkoff was 28.3 percent in 1977; by 1988, it had dropped by half—to 14 percent. In Minnesota, the rate was 19.8 in 1977, 15.1 percent in 1987, but up slightly to 15.5 percent in 1989.

The uniform decline in taxpayer checkoff participation indicates that, while the general public may favor public financing in principle, overcoming a distrust of government subsidies to politicians is increasingly difficult. The consequence has been an apparent unwillingness by the taxpayers to provide the level of funding that will be needed to underwrite the costs of campaigns in the 1990s. To preserve public financing, state legislatures will increasingly be faced with a choice of raising the checkoff, as Minnesota has done (to $5), or making up the shortfall through general revenues, the course adopted in New Jersey.

Tax Add-ons. Unlike the checkoff, the add-on system requires a taxpayer to add to his or her tax liabilities to create a fund for distribution to candidates or political parties or both. Most states limit the add-on to one or two dollars. Because the participant is being asked to increase his or her tax liability, the rate of participation has been far lower than for checkoffs.

In the 1988 election year, the nine states for which figures were available showed an average participation rate of only 0.7 percent. When Montana switched from a checkoff to an add-on in the late 1970s, the participation rate plummeted from 16.4 the last year of the checkoff to 1.5 percent the first year of the add-on.

The political add-on also is facing increasing competition from other add-ons being placed on state tax forms for worthy causes ranging from environmental protection to child abuse prevention. In states with add-ons for both the political fund and other special funds, the amount designated for the political fund has declined. In California, for example, the number of taxpayers contributing to the political fund dropped by 31 percent when the number of special funds was increased from four to six in 1987.

Oregon has twice discontinued its tax provisions. First, from 1977 to 1980, it had a tax checkoff whose statutory authority expired in 1981, and the legislature did not renew it. Then, in 1987 and 1988, it had a tax add-on but failed to meet statutorily specified minimum receipt requirements of at least $50,000 collected in each of two consecutive years.

Add-on systems cannot be considered true public funding programs because they rely entirely on voluntary contributions that are collected through the tax system. However, they are designated as such because their proceeds are administered by state governments and often allotted on the basis of complicated statutory formulas.

How Funds Are Given Away

No state has adopted the disbursement format of the Presidential Election Campaign Fund, in which the federal checkoff fully funds both major party candidates during the general election. However, several states provide matching funds to candidates, just as the federal system does during the presidential prenomination period. Some states give funds directly to candidates, others channel the money through political parties, and yet others allocate the money to political parties while placing few restrictions on how they spend it. A few states provide for public financing of both primary and general elections, but such allotments are usually limited to the fall campaign.

Of the states that use the income tax system to raise money for public financing, ten allocate the money to political parties, six give it directly to candidates, and three—Minnesota, North Carolina, and Rhode Island—provide financing to both parties and candidates.

Disbursements to Political Parties. Besides Minnesota, North Carolina, and Rhode Island, ten other states—Alabama, Arizona, California, Idaho, Iowa, Kentucky, Maine, Ohio, Utah, and Virginia—provide funds to political parties, albeit with differing regulations on allocation and use of the money. Political parties in Rhode Island, for example, are limited to using the money for administrative purposes. In Ohio and Utah, the money collected by the state is divided equally between the state party and county party committees. In allocating the money to each county committee, the states use formulas in which the number of checkoff participants in a given county is divided by the number of participants statewide.

In eleven of the thirteen states with this type of system—Alabama, Arizona, California, Idaho, Iowa, Kentucky, Maine, Minnesota, Rhode Island, Utah, and Virginia—taxpayers may designate which political party will receive their money. Minnesota taxpayers are allowed to make such a designation, and the parties receive 10 percent of the funds. Moreover, the money that is distributed directly to candidates is in amounts proportionate to the number of checkoffs for each party.

In three of the states that permit a taxpayer to earmark a contribution, lawsuits have been filed challenging this option as unconstitutional and discriminatory. In all these instances, the program was upheld as constitutional, although courts in Minnesota and Rhode Island placed some restrictions on use of the funds.[35]

Behind these lawsuits lay an apparent fear that public money was being used to favor one political party over another. In 1980, in a majority of the states where parties received public subsidies, the Democrats were favored over the Republicans—in some cases by margins of 2-1 or better. The Democratic edge led some observers to express concern that "the stronger will get stronger and the weak will get weaker," resulting in one party dominating a state.

However, in two affected states—Iowa and Idaho—the amount collected by the Republicans surged ahead of the Democrats at the outset of the 1980s, reversing the trend present throughout the 1970s. In Minnesota, where the party checkoff favored Democrats by a ratio of almost 3-1 in 1978, the margin had been cut to 57-43 by 1988.

In a 1980 study of state public financing of campaigns, political scientist Ruth S. Jones concluded that "the relative advantages to majority and minority party organizations and candidates that may follow from different public finance policies are not immediately apparent."[36] While leaving the designation to the taxpayer seems inherently to favor the majority party in a state, Jones noted that challengers—usually from the minority party—will benefit more than incumbents from taxpayer-subsidized campaign funds, because challengers have a harder time raising money. In addition, public money made available to help party organizations rebuild or revitalize themselves is more essential to a fledging minority party than to its established majority counterpart.

Disbursements to Candidates. Along with Minnesota, North Carolina, and Rhode Island, six additional states—Hawaii, Massachusetts, Michigan, Montana, New Jersey, and Wisconsin—have operating programs to provide public financing directly to candidates. In New Jersey and Rhode Island, the aid is limited to the gubernatorial candidate. Michigan extends it to the candidates for lieutenant governor as well, while Massachusetts, North Carolina, and Montana have subsidies for other statewide office seekers. Only in Hawaii, Minnesota, and Wisconsin is public financing provided directly to state legislative nominees.

Hawaii's program is modest at best. Nonfederal candidates for many years were given a mere $50 per election ($100 per election year) in return for abiding by spending limits. In 1984, only two legislative candidates accepted the state's less than munificent offer, a number that rose to three in 1986 and five in 1988. In an action that applied only to the 1990 elections, the legislature raised the grant to $250 per election and $500 per election year, to see whether the increase would make the program more viable; it did as eighteen accepted the increased amounts. In comparison, state legislative candidates in Wisconsin were eligible for grants of $6,355 apiece in 1988 in return for accepting expenditure limits. About 63 percent of them did.

In Michigan, with expenditure limits of $1.5 million each for the primary and general election, a gubernatorial candidate can receive up to $990,000 in the primary and $1,125,000 in the general under 1989 revisions to the law. In the primary, public financing takes the form of matching grants, while state funds are provided outright to major party candidates in the general election. The most generous state program in the nation, New Jersey's, provides up to $1.4 million to primary candidates seeking nomination for governor along with $3.3 million to the two general election contenders—provided the candidates abide by spending limits. During the four elections in which the program has been in effect, thirty-eight gubernatorial candidates have participated; only two have declined to do so.

The first elections held under the New Jersey public financing program revealed a significant drawback to spending limits. When set extremely low, they give an advantage to well-known candidates. Low limits also reduce campaign flexibility, often preventing candidates from changing strategies and revising themes late in the campaigns. Recognizing this problem, the state's Election Law Enforcement Commission three times recommended that the expenditure limits be repealed. Responding to these concerns, the state legislature retained the limits but more than doubled them in time for the 1989 gubernatorial race: to $2.2 million for the primary, and $5 million for the general election.

To survive, public financing systems must come to be considered as the main alternative source of funding for political candidates. To achieve such status, they must be adequately funded to reflect current campaign costs while guaranteeing fair competition. The experience in states such as Wisconsin and Minnesota has shown that candidate participation will decline if funding levels drop below what aspirants for elective office regard as a minimum threshold.

Although critics have claimed that public financing has induced too many candidates to run for office, especially in New Jersey, the process has worked well in that state and in Michigan, where gubernatorial hopefuls must demonstrate public support by raising a set amount of private contributions. And while excessively low spending limits can cause public financing to work to the advantage of incumbents, evidence exists that public funding programs have provided significant benefits to challengers. In Wisconsin, challengers actually have received a greater proportion of public funding than incumbents in the last three elections.

Few incumbents want to do anything to increase their political vulnerability. Therefore, opposition to providing public financing to candidates remains strong in many states.

Implications of Public Funding

Although public subsidies in campaigns provoke many arguments, scant attention has been paid to the implications that the various state plans have for the political system in general and the two-party system in particular. Questions of fairness, cost, administration, and enforcement need to be asked, and assumptions need to be challenged before any decision is made to go ahead with subsidies. Public financing is not a panacea, and it will bring fundamental changes in the political structure and electoral processes.

Criteria. The main questions raised about public funding are who should receive the subsidy and how and when payment should be made. The goal of government subsidization is to help serious candidates. Any system must be flexible enough to permit viable challenges to those in power. It should not, however, support candidates who merely are seeking free publicity, and it should not attract so many candidates as to degrade the process. Accordingly, the most difficult policy problem is to clearly define major and minor parties and to distinguish between serious and frivolous candidates without doing violence to equality of opportunity or to "equal protection" under the federal or state constitutions. A certain number of signed petitions or small contributions indicating a base of support can be used to identify a legitimate candidate.

Although increasing competition in the electoral arena—a primary goal of public funding—is desirable, several questions must be raised about the impact of public funds on the political process. One is whether government funding can induce two-party competition in predominately one-party areas. Even with public funding, competition may be extremely hard to stimulate. Another consideration is whether public funding will strengthen the political parties and, if so, whether that is wanted. Still another question is whether government domination of the electoral process will follow government funding.

As the states establish systems of public financing, taxpayers will become concerned about the costs of underwriting the campaigns of large numbers of officials. In the United States, slightly more than 500,000 public officials are elected over a four-year cycle. Long ballots require candidates to spend money in the mere quest of visibility, and the long ballot and frequent elections often combine to produce voter fatigue and low turnout. In New Jersey statewide elections are held at least every six months because the gubernatorial and state legislative campaigns take place in odd-numbered years, and primary and general elections are held each year for these, as well as for presidential and congressional elections in even-numbered years. New Jersey, however, elects only one statewide public official—the governor—and lets him or her appoint the cabinet as well as other officials. As financial pressures mount, other states may give increasing consideration to reducing the number of elective offices, thus diminishing the amounts of money (whether public or private) needed to sustain the electoral system. Yet California added a statewide office—that of insurance commissioner—sought by candidates for the first time in 1990.

The Impact on the Parties. Although political parties traditionally have not provided much money to candidates, in many states they have eased fund-raising burdens by furnishing candidates with party workers to serve as campaign volunteers and by directing contributors to particular candidates. Public financing systems in which the subsidies are given directly to candidates probably make them even less dependent on political parties than they now are. Ready access to media has lessened the dependence of office seekers on party organizations. When government funding is made available—and it is particularly attractive to candidates in states where private contributions are limited—the need to identify with and rely upon a political party is further diminished.

Moreover, public financing could cause an erosion of philosophical loyalties in legislators once they are in office. Those who ignore the demands of the party's legislative leadership will be less fearful of being frozen out of reelection or denied adequate funding from party committees. To avoid splintering legislatures and to maintain party strength—considered a desirable goal by many political scientists—future public funding systems could channel the money for candidates through the parties, at least during the general election period.[37]

In a study of the operation and impact of the states' experience with income tax checkoffs to provide political campaign funds, researcher Jack L. Noragon found some hopeful signs.[38] He noted that the experiments in public financing so far have reinforced the theory that the machinery of government can be used to encourage the general public to participate financially in the electoral process. Noragon pointed out that some states have taken significant steps toward providing financing of gubernatorial campaigns by leveraging public funds with private seed money given in small amounts. And he observed: "About half a dozen states are revitalizing their state and party apparatuses, which holds out the hope that the election role of parties may be enhanced, thus balancing the 'cult of personality' that has become so apparent in today's election contests." [39]

The states that provide the tax checkoff or tax add-on money to the political parties, however, have designed their policies purposely to help strengthen the parties.

Beyond Public Financing: Broadening the Base

To the extent that campaigns are financed with public funds, the role of large contributors and special interests is reduced. As the dependency on private money is restricted, the opportunities for corruption and favoritism theoretically diminish.

Public financing is but one means of reducing the influence of financially powerful interests. Another is to replace a single large contribution with a multitude of small contributions from rank-and-file citizens. This can be encouraged by providing tax credits or tax deductions to taxpayers. By the mid-1980s, some eighteen states offered this kind of incentive. The 1986 Tax Reform Act, in which Congress repealed credits for political contributions, affected states that adjusted their tax structures to conform with the federal changes. By 1990, only seven states and the District of Columbia retained credits or deductions for political donations.[40]

While some support exists for restoring the federal tax credit to spur individual contributions, budgetary constraints are likely to restrain any such action. If a change were to be enacted, however, it might encourage similar action in state capitals. In the past, states with these incentives have tended to provide credits of up to $50 or deductions of $100 for political contributions. Credits provide greater incentive to donate, in that they directly reduce the amount of taxes paid. A deduction simply reduces the amount of income subject to taxation.

State governments have other means to provide direct or indirect assistance in shouldering the costs of campaigns. Instead of providing money, governments could supply services that would relieve parties and candidates of certain expenditures. Some state governments already provide indirect subsidies by assuming greater responsibility for voter registration, distributing voter information pamphlets, and underwriting election day activities.

Along this line, universal voter registration is perhaps the most important electoral activity for a state government to finance. Such a program would relieve political parties and candidates of having to pay for what is essentially a public function. It also would reduce dependence on special interest financing ("soft money") often used to pay for voter registration efforts. Furthermore, a state-run program would have a better chance of increasing persistently low voter participation in a nation whose population is highly mobile—and whose registration requirements from state to state are often notable for their complexity.

8 Reform on the National Agenda

Election reform was a popular issue of the 1970s, with two enactments in 1971 and one each in 1974, 1976, and 1979. A similar decade of reform had not been seen since the first years of the twentieth century, when a prohibition of corporate contributions and systems of disclosure were enacted.

In the Revenue Act of 1971 and the Federal Election Campaign Act (FECA) of 1971 and 1974, public funding of presidential campaigns was established. Since 1974, the main thrust of reform efforts has been to extend public funding to congressional campaigns. The 1980 elections, which brought Ronald Reagan the presidency and Republicans the control of the Senate, shocked the political finance reform movement. Following the 1986 congressional elections, however, when the Democrats regained control of the Senate, election reform was brought back to the national agenda.

Although serious problems arose in the public financing of presidential elections, reform efforts since the mid-1980s have focused on congressional campaigns. The escalating costs of elections imposed pressures on the process and provided opportunities for both major parties to posture and wrestle for political advantage.

Rising costs gave incumbents a leg up in retaining power and made challenges more difficult. Nevertheless, the time consumed in raising money was occupying more and more of the legislators' days. The search for cash in congressional campaigns—particularly in the House, which is subject to two-year election cycles—led to some of the same problems that afflicted presidential elections: independent expenditures and "soft money."

But reform gained political urgency when the hunt for money was linked with scandals surrounding the savings and loan (S&L) debacle, the Keating Five, and ethical lapses by House Speaker Jim Wright, D-Texas, and other members of Congress in both parties.

Despite sporadic but serious interest in reform, Congress in the late 1980s could not muster new laws as the two parties could not agree on how to regulate political action committees (PACs) or on whether to undertake public financing and expenditure limits.

The Search for Consensus

In two successive Congresses, in 1990 and 1991, both the Senate and House passed election reform bills. The bills suggested the most extensive changes in federal election law since 1974. In 1990, three factors prevented campaign finance reform bills from becoming law. One was the short time—only several months—before the 1990 elections. A second was partisanship: Both Democrats and Republicans perceived hidden motives behind each other's legislative proposals. The third was the longstanding dichotomy between the House and Senate on this issue. Although both were under Democratic control, the two houses were unable to resolve conflicting interests arising from their different approaches to reform.

In 1991, the time factor was less urgent because a year remained for resolving the differences in the dissimilar bills. In the second session of the 102d Congress, an attempt will be made to reconcile the two bills, but whether the Senate and House, Democrats and Republicans, Congress and the president, all agree sufficiently to produce new legislation will be a test of the sincerity of many partisan and bipartisan statements that election reform is desirable.

The issue of campaign finance reform was reopened on the Senate floor in December 1985. Democrat David L. Boren of Oklahoma and Republican Barry Goldwater of Arizona had introduced a bill to reduce the amount a PAC could donate to a candidate. Ironically, most Republicans, who were to embrace such a proposal later, worked to sidetrack this measure. At the time, the Republicans were in control of the Senate and were receiving a majority of donations from business and trade association PACs.

After regaining the majority in the Senate as a result of the 1986 election, the Democrats decided to make campaign finance reform a major issue. Led by Boren, their bill, S 2, provided direct public financing for Senate candidates who accepted spending limits. Also included were aggregate limits on the total amount of money a candidate could accept from all PACs, ranging in amounts depending on the population of the state.

A rancorous, on-and-off eight-month debate ensued, in which the Democrats sought without success to shut off a Republican filibuster against the bill. In an unsuccessful attempt to attract Republican support, Boren modified the legislation to provide public funding only to candidates whose opponents exceeded the prescribed spending limits. Eight cloture votes failed to close off debate or produce a bill.

Since 1987, Senate and House Democratic leaders have insisted on expenditure limits in congressional races similar to those in place for presidential campaigns, while Republicans have strongly objected. The issue has become the biggest single obstacle to achieving bipartisan reform.

Many Republicans see spending limits as giving further advantage to incumbents with widespread name recognition at a time when a majority of incumbents are Democrats. Some recent statistics back up the argument that spending limits could disadvantage challengers. For example, a study by the nonpartisan Committee for the Study of the American Electorate found that, of thirty-two winning Senate challengers between 1978 and 1988, only seven stayed within the spending limits proposed by Senate Democrats in 1990.[1] This conclusion reinforced that of an academic expert, Gary C. Jacobson, who demonstrated in a series of analyses that any campaign finance policy, such as public subsidies, that would increase spending for both incumbent and challenger would work to the benefit of the latter, thus making elections more competitive. In contrast, any policy that attempts to equalize the financial positions of candidates by limiting campaign contributions and spending would benefit incumbents, thus lessening electoral competition.[2]

A basic philosophical disagreement also lies behind the dispute. The Democrats insist that rising costs and the escalating money chase cannot be solved unless the total amount of money in campaigns is capped through expenditure limits. The Republicans counter that the chief problem is not the amounts of money, but its sources. They have focused on limiting certain kinds of money considered to be tainted (PAC contributions) and replacing it with other sources deemed more desirable (donations from in-state individuals and political party money).

The Republicans also oppose public financing, which they generally regard as an inappropriate use of tax dollars. This is a second major partisan difference between the Republicans and the Democrats, although all Democrats are by no means in favor of public financing. Budget constraints, meanwhile, make it difficult to enact legislation of benefit to politicians while educational, welfare, or other societal needs are not being met.

Political Finance Back on Legislative Agenda

Several factors converged to bring political finance reform to the forefront of the legislative agenda when the 101st Congress convened in January 1989. Bailout of the nation's savings and loan industry was going to cost several hundred billion dollars. Attention focused on the California-based Lincoln Savings and Loan. Lincoln's owner, Charles H. Keating, Jr., and his associates gave $1.3 million to political and semipolitical committees associated with five senators who met with federal regulators on Keating's behalf. The episode highlighted the role of "soft money" at the congressional level. No PAC contributions were involved.

Then, House members after the 1988 election began consideration of a substantial pay raise, in the hope of dealing with the issue almost two years before having to face the voters again. A firestorm of protest erupted, and the move was temporarily shelved. To make the pay raise more palatable, House leaders promised action on ethics and campaign reform measures.

House Task Force. House Speaker Wright, then the subject of an ethics investigation that ultimately would lead to his resignation, appointed a bipartisan task force on campaign reform in January 1989. House Democrats coalesced around two bills proposing campaign spending limits and aggregate ceilings on PAC donations. The chief difference between them was over public financing, reflecting divisions within the Democratic majority. One bill sought to achieve voluntary compliance with spending limits in return for discounts on postal rates and television ads; the other included public matching funds.

By the end of 1989, the cochairmen of the task force, Democrat Al Swift of Washington and Republican Guy Vander Jagt of Michigan, reached agreement on some secondary issues, including guaranteeing priority for political candidates in the purchase of broadcast time, reestablishing income tax credits for small donations, and doing away with leadership PACs. But, on the major issues—expenditure limits, public funding, PACs, and the role of parties—sharp partisan divisions remained. Republicans on the task force, however, came up with their own twenty-five-point program.[3]

Administration Proposal. In June 1989, President Bush offered a plan aimed largely at reducing the advantages of incumbency by doing away with most PACs and forcing candidates to "zero out" campaign treasuries after each election.[4] Incumbents routinely accumulate large war chests to scare away potential challengers. Not surprisingly, the proposal was strongly attacked by the Democrats.

Senate Campaign Finance Reform Panel. In the Senate, Boren reintroduced his 1987-1988 bill to provide public financing of Senate candidates only when an opponent exceeds spending limits. The Republicans, led by Mitch McConnell of Kentucky, countered with a proposed cut in PAC contribution limits, an increase in the amount that could be donated by an individual, and fewer restrictions on the money that political parties could give to candidates.

Just as ethics problems had placed pressure on House Democrats to act on campaign reform in 1989 (ethics controversies forced both Wright and Majority Whip Tony Coelho, D-Calif., from office), the Senate came under similar pressure in 1990 as a result of a decision by the Senate Ethics Committee to investigate the five senators involved in the Keating affair. To avoid a repeat of the 1987-1988 legislative battle over campaign financing, the two Senate leaders—Democrat George J. Mitchell of Maine and Republican Robert Dole of Kansas—named a panel of academic and legal experts to come up with possible solutions.

The panel's recommendations, released in early March, initially were hailed by both political parties as the basis for a possible compromise.[5] The panel proposed what became known as "flexible spending limits." Exempt from these limits would be relatively small contributions to Senate candidates from in-state residents, along with spending by political parties for research, voter registration drives, and get-out-the-vote efforts.

The panel sought a compromise between the Democrats' insistence on spending limits and Republican contentions that the chief problem is the sources of campaign money. While maintaining generous expenditure ceilings, the proposal favored political party contributions and individual donations from voting constituents over contributions from PACs and out-of-state individuals—both regarded as major sources of "special interest" money. In addition, the panel did not recommend direct public financing, an idea strongly opposed by the Republicans. Instead, it suggested reduced broadcast rates and postal discounts combined with income tax credits for in-state contributions as incentives for candidates to abide by spending limits.

The political opening created by the panel's report soon was lost amid political posturing; both Democrats and Republicans in the Senate were eager to be seen by voters as wearing the mantle of reform. Although differences also were evident within each party, the Democrats and the Republicans formulated separate bills as possible substitutes to one that had been reported out favorably by a Democratic-controlled Senate committee.

The Democratic-sponsored bill that the Senate passed in August 1990 would have provided vouchers to buy television time and discounted mail rates to candidates who comply with spending limits. The bill also would have made available direct public funding only to participating candidates whose opponents exceeded the spending limit in a particular state. The House Democratic bill included free television time and mail discounts. It did not, however, provide direct public funding for congressional candidates because some House Democrats were skeptical of the FEC's ability to administer such a program.

Another issue splitting the Democrats and Republicans was how to regulate PACs. In general, the Senate and House Democrats differ on reducing PAC contribution limits or prohibiting PAC contributions entirely, but both have favored aggregate ceilings on the total any candidate can accept from all PACs. Some Republicans have proposed reducing the current $5,000 per election limit that a PAC is allowed to give to a candidate, while some Democrats and Republicans want to ban PAC contributions completely. Proposals to reduce contribution limits seem aimed at the Democratic-leaning labor PACs and certain other membership PACs, which have tended to contribute the maximum allowed under law. Some have complained that the Democratic proposals for aggregate limits would enable candidates to accept large amounts of early "seed money" from well-endowed PACs, while the smaller ones may not be able to contribute at all if the large ones fill the candidate's aggregate limit early.

Two provisions would have faced almost certain judicial challenges if the 1990 Senate package had become law—the ban on PACs and the system of contingency public financing. The Senate bill contained a standby scheme for limiting PAC contributions to $1,000 in the event that the ban on PACs was found unconstitutional. (Besides corporate, trade association, and union PACs, the prohibition covered "nonconnected" or ideological or issue PACs.) During the Senate debate, contingency public funding was challenged as a coercive measure because it punishes a free-spending candidate by giving public money to his or her opponent.

The 1990 House bill, passed several days after the Senate legislation, emerged only after fierce in-fighting among House Democrats. Those from states likely to lose districts as a result of the 1990 decennial census feared that spending limits would harm their chances for political survival. To satisfy them, the spending limits were loosened for House candidates who won primary elections with less than two-thirds of the vote. Those complying with the limits were to be rewarded with broadcast and postal discounts.

In contrast to the Senate ban on PACs, the House-passed bill allowed candidates to accept an aggregate amount of PAC contributions equal to half of the spending limit. This clearly reflected House Democratic dependence on PACs. Almost 52 percent of the money received by the House Democratic majority during the 1988 campaign had come from PACs. The House legislation also gave favored treatment to those PACs that limited donations from their members to no more than $240 per year. Critics charged that this was simply a move to benefit labor and certain issue PACs, which rely largely on small contributions.

Soft Money Proposals. The experience of the 1988 presidential campaigns led to proposals to restrict soft money. The House bill would bar presidential candidates from raising soft money. The Senate proposal would place under the limits of federal law all contributions solicited by a national party committee on behalf of a state party organization, thereby curtailing the $100,000 gifts raised in 1988. Both bills also would sharply restrict the amount of money that a state party could spend on so-called generic campaigns (such as "Vote Democratic" or "Vote Republican" without mentioning federal candidates) in connection with a presidential race, including voter registration and get-out-the-vote drives.

But the Senate bill went further by placing strict spending limits on generic campaign activities by state and national party committees even when presidential and congressional candidates are not specifically mentioned. In the less stringent House approach, generic campaign efforts that made no mention of federal candidates were left outside the purview of federal law, even if a presidential or congressional candidate might realize some benefit.

Both bills would require disclosure of soft money receipts and expenditures. The FEC issued regulations, effective January 1, 1991, that required disclosure and set allocation formulas for generic spending on behalf of the party ticket, which may affect the election of federal candidates.[6]

Meanwhile, Senate Republicans wanted restrictions on other forms of soft money, specifically, nonparty money. They proposed to prohibit certain nonprofit organizations from activities on behalf of a particular candidate. This was aimed at organized labor as well as a number of other issue-oriented groups—such as environmental organizations—that tended to favor Democratic presidential and congressional candidates with various forms of assistance.

Independent Expenditures. In seeking to regulate another device used to skirt campaign spending limits—independent expenditures—the Democrats and Republicans have found more common ground. The reason is that they are nervous about becoming victims of the stridently negative advertising that often has characterized independent campaigns. Although *Buckley* and subsequent decisions found independent expenditures to be a protected form of free speech, both parties in Congress have looked for constitutional ways to discourage them.

The 1990 House-passed campaign bill would require any television advertisement underwritten by independent expenditures to contain a continuously displayed statement identifying the sponsor of the ad. The Senate bill proposed that any broadcaster selling air time to an independent campaign favoring one candidate would have to sell air time to the other candidate to allow him or her to respond immediately.

1991 Developments. The bills passed by the Senate and the House died when Congress adjourned for the 1990 elections. Many bills were introduced in the 102d Congress, and, in 1991, both chambers again passed bills.

The Senate bill was not markedly different from the one passed the year before. It featured a system of voluntary campaign expenditure limits. Candidates who agree to the limits would be eligible to receive lower postal rates, broadcast vouchers, and a broadcast rate discount. However, only those candidates whose opponents exceed the limits would be eligible for payments from the Senate Election Campaign Fund. A far-reaching provision of the bill prohibits PAC contributions to any Senate campaign.

Because this provision might be found unconstitutional, a fall-back position is included that would reduce PAC contribution limits from the current $5,000 per candidate per election to $1,000 and impose aggregate limits on the amounts candidates can receive from all PACs.

In the House, significant changes were made from the bill passed in 1990 as a result of the work of a new Task Force on Campaign Finance Reform. Chaired by Rep. Sam Gejdenson, D-Conn., the task force undertook extensive hearings and then introduced a comprehensive bill, HR 3750, that was forced to undergo some last-minute changes to garner enough support for passage on November 25, 1991.

Like the Senate-passed legislation, the House bill also provides for a voluntary system. Candidates who agree to the spending limits receive lower postal rates and direct public financing in the form of matching funds from a Make Democracy Work Fund. Additional payments would be available for candidates who have opponents that exceed a specified limit of financial activity and who are targets of independent expenditures. The bill permits PAC contributions as currently allowed, with an aggregate limit of $200,000 received from all PACs.

Both bills address problems of independent expenditures, bundling, and soft money. Neither bill specifies the means of paying for the benefits provided, which will require separate bills to achieve budget neutrality—offsetting costs of the legislation with corresponding cuts in order not to increase the budget deficit.

The Role of Reform Groups

The role of reform groups and the press has been significant in prodding Congress to reform the election law. Some 430 newspaper editorials—including those in the *New York Times* and the *Washington Post*—endorsed S 2, as did seventy-three organizations.[7] The most powerful of these, Common Cause, has made public financing the cornerstone of much of its rhetoric on the reform issue. Another organization heavily involved in election reform issues is the Ralph Nader-sponsored Public Citizen.

During the 1990 elections, Common Cause targeted thirteen House members for a lobbying campaign at the grass roots, placing ads in major newspapers of their constituencies with headlines such as "S&L Interests Gave Members of Congress Millions" and "Taxpayers Were Ripped Off for Billions . . . And Congress Has Done Nothing."[8] The ads revealed the amounts of PAC money particular members received in recent campaigns, suggesting to the casual reader they had been responsible for the S&L debacle. Fred Wertheimer, the president of Common Cause, claimed the targets represented a "cross-section" of House members, but study of the group suggested choices were more strategic. All thirteen were influential

Democrats who accepted considerable amounts of PAC money.

The House Democratic leadership responded angrily, vowing that Common Cause had overstepped its bounds and taken itself out of the debate on campaign reform.[9] Some observers claimed the ads exposed Common Cause as being hypocritical in the use of innuendo—a propaganda ploy they had denounced—and as willing as some candidates to engage in negative advertising.

While the reformers have not been able to muster enough media or public support to get meaningful reform enacted, they have been able to stop minimal, incremental change. Reform groups fear that minor change will enable legislators to claim reform has occurred and forestall major action for another five or ten years. Accordingly, reform groups seek comprehensive change, including public financing and spending limits, or none at all. This posture coincides with the strategy of some members of Congress who talk reform but seem to prefer exploiting the issue to crossing the reformers to achieve compromise.

A Pressing Issue

Campaign finance is a politician's issue. Along with redistricting, it is the lifeblood of most members of Congress. Though concerned about increasing amounts of time being spent raising funds, members have come to view election reform attempts as partisan maneuvers designed to exploit their party's strengths and their rivals' weaknesses. Those members with their ears to the ground, however, also have realized that the constant politician-bashing by reform groups, echoed by the media on campaign fund-raising ethics, has taken its toll. They felt compelled to stage at least a lively debate over the issue. Subsequently, each party made a dash for the popular high ground: Democrats by emphasizing the containment of campaign costs, Republicans by savaging PACs and nonparty soft money.

Both the Senate and House have seen a number of initiatives seeking to work out compromise. Several times in recent years Senator Mitchell, the Democratic majority leader, and Senator Dole, the Republican minority leader, have appointed joint Democratic-Republican committees, as well as the Senate Campaign Finance Reform Panel. Twice the House set up task forces, one appointed by Speaker Wright and one in 1991, the Task Force on Campaign Finance Reform, appointed from among members of the House Administration Committee by its newly elected chairman, Charlie Rose, D-N.C.[10]

Yet in 1990, when the Senate and House each passed a campaign finance reform bill, negotiations between the House and Senate to forge compromise legislation were never convened. Given the differences between the two houses—along with threats that President Bush would veto any bill calling for spending limits and public finance—action on the issue is uncertain in the near future. Nevertheless, both houses of Congress demonstrated in 1990 and again in 1991 their ability to pass campaign financing bills—something they had not done during the 1980s. Because both chambers had a Democratic majority, the bills that passed were not bipartisan but essentially Democratic bills with little, if any, Republican support.

Thus campaign finance reform remains a pressing issue for Congress. The leadership in both houses is braced for new rounds of debate. The dialogue was escalated early in 1991 when Bush, in his State of the Union address, again called for the abolition of PACs.[11] He later repeated his threat to veto any bill that included public financing or expenditure limitations.[12]

Dramatic changes in positions have not taken place, although new talk has been heard of each house going its own way. Common provisions relating to disclosure, the FEC, and soft money would appear, but a deeply fragmented federal election system would emerge in which campaigns for president, Senate, and House each would operate under different rules. It would hardly be a desirable public policy outcome to have, for example, some saying PACs are no good and some saying they are fine.

Despite gloomy predictions, the possibility of reform remains. A strong foundation was left by the congressional efforts of 1987-1991. Both the Senate and House have gone on record as favoring a number of policy changes that would be helpful: opening soft money to greater scrutiny, curbing the franking privilege (particularly in election years), and eliminating honoraria. A consensus appears to be present for requiring broadcast stations to cut political advertising costs. And House honoraria and the ability to convert campaign funds to personal use will be abolished in 1992. But working out differences between the Senate, the House, and the president will not be easy.

Momentum for a meaningful democratic reform of campaign financing has been generated and may be sustained by continuing investigations into the linkage between the savings and loan disaster and campaign contributions. Federal reform efforts will remain stymied, however, if toleration continues for the pursuit of reform hyperbole and partisan agendas at the expense of the public interest.

9 The Future of Reform

Nostalgia buffs may long for the days when candidates kissed babies; marched in torchlight parades; and passed out sponges, with their names printed on them, that expanded when dunked in water. But those days are gone and cannot be brought back. Even candidates for state legislature and city council now hire pollsters, direct mail consultants, and fund raisers, and these efforts pale in comparison with what occurs in a national-level or statewide campaign. A basic truth of campaigning today is that election services cost money—scarce money that never seems plentiful enough to candidates or parties.

The issue is not how to deprofessionalize politics, but how to pay for the essentials of modern campaigns in a manner that reduces the opportunities for corruption or the appearance of corruption while instilling public confidence in the system.

In 1979, amid complaints from state and local parties that public financing of presidential elections had cut them out of the process, Congress agreed to the seemingly modest step of allowing state and local party organizations to underwrite voter registration and get-out-the-vote drives, among several other functions, benefiting presidential candidates. What resulted was the controversial "soft money" provision that allowed parties to spend on behalf of George Bush and Michael S. Dukakis half again as much as the legislated spending limit during their 1988 campaigns. Widespread calls now are being heard to undo what was done more than a decade ago.

Given the pluralistic and dynamic nature of the American political system, political finance reform often does not work in the manner intended by its sponsors. While efforts should be made to improve the status quo, clearly no panaceas or simple solutions exist. As savvy political operatives and election lawyers find ways around existing laws to tap new sources of political money, the viability of these laws must constantly be reevaluated by their proponents.

Discussions over political finance reform touch many different aspects of campaigns, and as experience suggests, the targeted problem area is likely not to be the sole one influenced by any given reform. For example, public funding is generally seen to benefit the voting public as well as the candidate, but a new perspective is added when the question becomes raising taxes or diverting tax revenues from education or welfare or other needs. When debating the reform of political finance guidelines, the potential impact of political action committees (PACs) and political parties also needs to be considered. Some reforms involve the modification of campaign expenditure rules, with one of the most controversial being the establishment of spending ceilings. At first, setting expenditure limits seems a viable solution for keeping down mushrooming campaign costs, but the history of spending ceilings raises serious question as to their effectiveness. Spending limits are illusory.

Some suggestions for reform may be unique to the federal level. However, the states also provide lessons as "laboratories of reform," as fifty case studies of the short and long term effects of reform and of the status quo.

The Problem of Campaign Finance Reform

Reform works to change institutions and processes, sometimes in unforeseen ways. Election laws are used as instruments to achieve political goals. Laws that regulate relationships between candidates and political parties, and between citizens and politicians, and that affect the relative power of interest groups and political parties are bound to influence the entire political process and change the ways in which citizens, candidates, parties, and other groups participate and interact in elections.

How campaign financing is regulated affects numerous concerns that are central to the vitality of the democratic system of government, to the integrity of the election process and the levels of public confidence in it, to the robustness of public dialogue, and to the freedom to criticize and challenge effectively those in power. Election laws also affect the survival of the political parties, the durability of the two-party system, the participation by citizens in the political process, and the effectiveness of groups in a pluralistic society.

In every society in which free elections have been held, the problem of who pays the political bills and why has arisen. Reconciliation is needed between a theory of democratic government and a set of economic conditions—how to hold to the egalitarian assumption of "one person, one vote" (and "one dollar"?) in face of an unequal distribution of economic resources.

Compounding the problem is the operation of the constitutional and political system. The framers of the U.S. Constitution foresaw many of the problems that were to confront the new Republic and met them straight on. But, for the most part, they warned against the divisiveness and factionalism of political parties, as experienced in Europe, while at the same time requiring the election of officers of two of the three branches of government. Most state constitutions also failed to provide institutional means for bridging the gap between the citizen and the government, while they, too, were requiring the popular election of numerous public officials. The gap was closed by the advent of political parties.

The party system, however, has neither been accorded full constitutional or legal status nor been helped much financially by governments at the state and federal levels until recently. In any case, party power has deteriorated with the influence of television and the growth of a highly educated population that values the idea of political independence.

The problem of election reform may be stated in this way: How can political dialogue be improved, a more attentive and well-informed electorate be attracted, and citizens be encouraged to participate in the political process as workers, contributors, and voters, while financial inequalities among candidates and political parties are diminished, the dominance of big money is reduced, and opportunities for well-qualified persons to become candidates are opened up? How can democratic principles be applied to elections in an age of media politics, seemingly dominated by an atmosphere of dollar politics, in ways consonant with constitutional guarantees? The electoral process has become a classic case of conflict between the democratic theory of full public dialogue in free elections and the conditions of an economic marketplace.

If money is but one element in the equation of political power, it is the common denominator in the shaping of many of the factors comprising political power, because it buys what is not or cannot be volunteered. Giving money permits numbers of citizens to share the energies that must go into politics. Among affluent Americans, many find it easier to show their support for a candidate or their loyalty to a party by writing a check than to devote time by campaigning or doing political work. Most citizens have no special talent for politics, or will not give the time to learn about it, so money is a substitute, and at the same time a meaningful way to participate. While money can be considered a substitute for service, it somehow does not require as firm a commitment. One might give money to both parties but is less likely to give time to both parties. Money has an advantage over service, however, in that it is not loaded down with the idiosyncrasies of the giver.

In a sense, broadly based political power has been conceived to help equalize inequalities in economic resources. That promise is compromised if special interests get undue preferment from candidates and parties forced to depend on them because adequate funds are not otherwise available. Government funds thus become desirable alternative sources. But that promise also is compromised if special interests are unduly restricted in articulating their views. Limits and prohibitions, therefore, are public policies requiring constant evaluation to ensure significant avenues of expression are not being shut off.

In regulating money, certain guidelines should be followed:

- improve disclosure of political funds as the cornerstone of regulation, which is almost universally accepted;
- keep in check the most obvious concentrations of political power and the most dominant political influences;
- utilize government assistance where necessary, but with the least intrusion on the election and political processes that traditionally have been private sector activities;
- provide new or increased sources of political funds as alternatives to current "created dependencies" on large contributions and on PAC contributions;
- ease fund raising by enhancing private monies and private choice in part at government expense through income tax credits;
- provide that more monies be channeled through the political parties;
- retain as much flexibility in the system as possible, while seeking to avoid rigidifying processes unnecessarily; and
- ensure that policies do not chill citizen participation.

Disclosure: The Cornerstone of Reform

If several basic truths must be considered in designing a system of political finance regulation, at least one basic policy should be universal: comprehensive and timely disclosure. Both liberals and conservatives have deemed disclosure fundamental to the political system. The public has the right to know the sources from which candidates draw their money, as well as their expenditures, both before and after elections. The same principle applies to political action committees and political party committees.

Disclosure laws make it difficult for a political figure to claim, ex post facto, that an ill-gotten personal gain actually was meant to be a legal campaign contribution. In recent years, prosecutions of elected officials on corruption charges have relied increasingly on information filed in campaign reports.

To be fully effective, campaign disclosure by candidates must be accompanied by financial disclosure by officeholders, in which their personal holdings are declared as well as speaking fees and gifts from those who may be seeking to influence policy. Given the U.S. Supreme Court's decision that spending limits on independent expenditures are unconstitutional, disclosure is one of the few means by which to put a restraint on these often-negative campaigns. And disclosure should be required of state and local political committees that engage in soft money receipts and expenditures affecting campaigns for federal office.

Election Agencies

An election agency alone, no matter how strong its powers, cannot prevent candidates and officeholders from cutting corners. Ultimately, an aspirant for elective office must decide if his or her self-interest is best served by behaving in an ethical manner. The decision making is helped along by positive incentives, such as the availability of public funding, and negative incentives, such as the willingness of the public to throw out errant public servants.

An election agency, such as the Federal Election Commission, can play an important role in exacting punishment. If it pursues evidence of impropriety aggressively and is unafraid to bring charges when wrongdoing exists or is suspected, it will help the voting public to decide which officials are worthy of trust.

Just as too much money in the political system can be as harmful as too little, so can too much regulation by an election commission do as much damage as too little. If a paucity of regulation can shake public confidence in the system, an overabundance can stifle spontaneity on the campaign trail and result in an ill-informed public. The voters, to say nothing of the First Amendment, are hardly served when candidates begin to censor themselves for fear of running afoul of the mandates of an overzealous commission. Laws should not lead commissions to micromanage political campaigns.

To date, however, the major problem appears to be under-regulation, not over-regulation. While a bare majority of states now have established independent election commissions to oversee disclosure and enforce other campaign finance-related statutes, even the best of these agencies suffer from insufficient funding and inadequate enforcement powers. Some do not even have the resources to compile and analyze the campaign finance reports submitted by candidates. Such tabulations or summaries should be considered an integral part of an effective disclosure law.

In discussing the complexities of the Federal Election Campaign Act (FECA), Sen. Lee Metcalf, D-Mont., once wondered whether officeholders should not worry about serving time rather than constituents. His quip, seriously considered, suggests the contradictory nature of the reforms, the conflict between the goals their proponents sought to achieve and the statutory and procedural constraints their implementation has imposed on the democratic electoral process.

Election commissions are mainly an American innovation. Whether federal or state, they have multiple roles as judge, jury, administrator, prosecutor, enforcer, and magistrate. The potential for conflict among these roles is as clear as the tensions they invite, and it threatens good regulation unless the commissions tread cautiously. Enforcement of the law must not chill free speech or citizen participation. An expansive enforcement policy produces an unfortunate political climate. But a weak enforcement policy does not raise levels of confidence in the electoral process.

The power to interpret the law is essentially the power to make new law, and the commissions sit astride the political process, empowered to influence the outcome of elections. In these circumstances, legislatures have not been reluctant to restrain the agencies. Yet legislatures have a conflict of interest because their members enact the laws under which they themselves run for reelection and they fund the budgets of the agencies. Clearly no ideal can realistically be met.

Contribution Limits

In setting contribution limits, a balance must be struck between the need to reduce public perceptions of excessive campaign funds and the need for candidates to raise adequate funds to communicate with voters. Few have advocated a return to the era of the six-figure donor. The presence of $100,000 soft money contributions in the 1988 presidential election prompted criticism and negative public reaction. At the same time, setting contribution limits too low can have the effect of turning public officials into nonstop political fund raisers seeking to collect sufficient money in small lots. And low contribution limits may not produce enough money to fund challengers adequately.

The federal limits on individual and PAC contributions ($1,000 and $5,000, respectively) have not been raised since their adoption in 1974. But inflation has reduced the value of these amounts by almost two-thirds when considered in constant dollars. Therefore, once the decision is made to continue with contribution limits, they should be indexed with inflation and rounded to the next hundred dollars to ensure a constant effect in coming years.

Consideration also should be given to raising the federal limits. For example, if the individual contribution limit was increased to $2,500, it would merely catch up with the inflation rate since the law went into effect in 1975. And the overall contribution limit, now set at $25,000 per individual per year, could be repealed. These actions would make some needed additional funding available to underfinanced campaigns and would respect the values of diversity and increased participation. With a good disclosure system in place, undesirable sources would be publicized.

Despite the incumbent's advantage of having an established base of financial support, building and maintaining a donor list can be time consuming, especially if the incumbent is seeking a higher office. As a result, an excessively low contribution limit can adversely affect the attention incumbents give to the job to which they were elected. A higher contribution level also will help challengers to raise enough money to compete effectively.

Public Funding

Public funding is the one major element of campaign finance that offers positive instead of negative reinforcement. It provides an incentive for candidates who act in a preferred manner under conditions set forth by the government. In that sense, it is cost effective to the taxpayers, even though a successful system requires a significant outlay of public money. But the candidate as well as the voting public reap rewards. The candidate is not impelled to seek out undesirable sources of private funding, which helps to diminish the negative perception that such a money chase creates. The candidate can spend more time communicating with the public rather than trying to squeeze in campaigning between hours on the phone soliciting donors.

The public, in turn, gets not only more of the candidate's time, but also the likelihood of a more competitive campaign. In 1976, the Supreme Court decided in *Buckley v. Valeo* that spending limits are unconstitutional unless accepted voluntarily in return for an inducement such as public financing. As a result, if the government provides public financing or other incentives and the candidate opts into the system, he or she must limit the amount of campaign spending or personal resources to be utilized in the campaign. Advocates, therefore, argue that such a system can help to "level the playing field" by neutralizing the advantages of wealthy candidates or those with more campaign money.

This is not to suggest that public financing is universally embraced. From a fiscal standpoint, many feel that it is an inappropriate use of scarce government dollars in what has been traditionally a private sector activity. From a philosophical standpoint, others think that public financing places too much control over the elective process by those already in power and interested in staying there.

Despite these varying viewpoints, public financing of candidates and parties is slowly winning wider acceptance at all levels of government. It clearly has displaced a significant amount of private donations in U.S. presidential campaigns. For example, in 1988, public subsidies accounted for 36 percent of the $500 million spent. Were that money not available, presidential candidates and their parties would have been forced to do what congressional aspirants already are doing: pursue more money from special interests and other sources.

Although income tax checkoffs do not increase the taxpayer's liability, support for them has dropped sharply in recent years in several states as well as at the federal level. Polls sometimes show that while the voters support public funding in the abstract, many cannot overcome a general distrust of providing public funds to politicians when it comes time to exercising their opportunity as taxpayers to check off a dollar or so.

If the federal checkoff program is to continue as a source of public funding, lessons must be learned from the states' experiences with the program. First, the checkoff could be increased. This was done in Minnesota where the checkoff was raised to $5 during a period when checkoff participation fell by one-third. The participation rate showed some decline when the checkoff was raised, but the dollar receipts more than doubled.[1]

Second, Congress could utilize its own appropriations process as is currently done in New Jersey where money from the tax checkoff is directed to the general fund and the legislature then appropriates the money needed to implement public funding, in effect making up the difference between the amount collected by the checkoff and the cost of the program. The problem with relying on legislative appropriations is that what the legislature gives, it can take away. This was done in Florida where the legislature in 1986 appropriated $3 million for public funding, only to rescind the move several months later in the face of a tight state budget, and subsequently failed to appropriate the necessary funds for the 1990 elections.

The third consideration is the need to educate the public on the checkoff program. This was attempted by the Federal Election Commission in 1991 and in other years and also was tested in Wisconsin in 1987. Common Cause/Wisconsin administered an education program in four counties involving public service spots and brochures, with a resulting increase of 2 percent in those areas. A year later, that state's legislature voted to fund a statewide educational program, but the measure was vetoed by Gov. Tommy G. Thompson.[2]

Although the *Buckley* decision ruled out spending limits without public funding, some supporters of public funding would like to try a different approach. They advocate public funding floors instead of spending limit ceilings. This concept is favored by many of the mature democracies in Western Europe, where government subsidies are given to political parties with no limits on receiving and spending private contributions. The idea is that partial public funding, or a floor, gives candidates at least minimal access to the electorate and provides alternative funds so that candidates can reject private contributions with expressed or tacit obligations attached. At the same time, if this approach were used in the United States, the absence of spending limits would avoid the constitutional issues raised in the *Buckley* case. Some modifications, however, probably would be required to make such a system work in the United States, for in other countries subsidies are given not to candidates, but to political parties, based on their parliamentary strength, making for quite different systems.

Spending Limits

No issue has been as controversial as the establishment of limits on campaign expenditures. At the federal level, a partisan stalemate over imposing expenditure limits has held up efforts to amend the FECA for a decade. While spending limits can be shown to be illusory, ineffective, and damaging to competition, concern about high campaigns costs has led advocates to insist on their enactment. The problem with expenditure limits is that they reduce flexibility and rigidify the campaign process while inviting less accountable ways of spending, such as independent expenditures, issue campaigns related to the candidates' positions, and soft money. Moreover, to impose spending limits means restricting free speech. The First Amendment has no greater value than in the protection of political speech. Elections are improved by well-financed candidates able to wage competitive campaigns, not by stifling political dialogue.

Public funding and expenditure limits usually are assumed to be inextricably tied. While not intended, the presidential candidates operated in 1988 under the "floors without ceilings" approach, with so much soft money raised and spent beyond the expenditure limits. Dukakis's home state of Massachusetts has a floor-without-ceiling system that has operated with some success. In 1986, more than $865,000 was distributed by the state to candidates without forcing them to abide by spending limits. Candidates were given public funds as a financial "floor" on which to build a visible and viable campaign, but they were not limited in how much they could raise in private funds. The relatively modest investment of public funds nevertheless produced some significant results by weaning candidates from dependence on private contributions. The Democratic candidate for attorney general financed more than 13 percent of his campaign with public money; his Republican opponent underwrote almost a quarter of his campaign budget with public funds. And, while Democratic governor Dukakis financed only 4 percent of his campaign with public funds, they provided more than 30 percent of the money spent by Dukakis's Republican opponent.[3]

The establishment of spending ceilings has met with resistance in Congress and many state legislatures, where parties not in control of the legislature are reluctant to restrain campaign spending. Challengers may have to spend more than incumbents to gain the name recognition needed to compete effectively against better-known incumbents.

Proponents argue that ceilings hold down the rising costs of campaigns and prevent qualified candidates of modest means from being priced out of the electoral process. They say that contribution limits are not sufficient to do this; candidates will simply chase more contributions and continue spending. In practical terms, legislatures are reluctant to provide public dollars for campaigns with the sky the limit. They ask, "Why give public money and then leave the candidate free to seek as much private funding as desired?" Yet Massachusetts has shown the way.

And New Jersey provides state funds for nearly two-thirds of the cost of the gubernatorial campaigns, yet the state's Election Law Enforcement Commission has recommended three times that the expenditure ceilings be repealed. The recommendation was first made after the 1977 governorship race, in which the limits demonstrably curtailed the strategic options of the challenger in the closing days of the contest.

Many reasons exist for frustration with limits. Despite the actions of the New Jersey legislature to raise the spending ceilings significantly, both Democrats and Republicans found so many ways around them in the 1989 gubernatorial campaigns as to render them meaningless. Limitations of any kind—whether contribution or expenditure—develop leaks. But expenditure limits are the most problematic as was demonstrated by the Bush-Dukakis race of 1988 and the New Jersey experience. They lead to such hard-to-trace forms of political spending as soft money and independent expenditures.

Another frustrating effect associated with spending ceilings is that they tend to encourage more "negative campaigning" at a time when opinion polls reflect increasing public cynicism toward the political process. While voters often disdain such tactics in the abstract, negative campaigns persist because they have been shown to sway voter opinion in many instances. A candidate operating under spending ceilings is likely to "go negative" because that tactic is considered more cost effective than loftier forms of campaigning. A negative advertising barrage can quickly drive up an opponent's disapproval rating, thereby allowing the attacker to maximize the effect of a limited ability to use campaign cash.

A final problem with tying ceilings to the acceptance of public funds is what happens if all candidates do not accept the restrictions. In 1987, Minnesota adopted a provision to deal with this situation, thus allowing a candidate who accepts public funding to exceed the state's spending limits if his or her opponent qualifies but declines to accept public funding. As with Minnesota's recent attempt to impose state public funding of federal elections, it remains to be seen whether this approach ultimately will hold up under judicial scrutiny. Penalizing candidates for not accepting public money contains an element of coercion that may run counter to the intention of the *Buckley* decision.

If expenditure limits are adopted, the obvious question to be answered is: How much? If limits are to be established, legislators must set them high enough to ensure a full presentation and discussion of the issues, and to include provision for cost-of-living adjustments.

Political Action Committees

Seen in historical perspective, political action committees represent a system of political fund raising that developed, albeit unintentionally, from efforts to reform the political process. PACs represent an expression of issue politics that motivates many citizens these days. They represent an institutionalization of the solicitation process as they seek out large numbers of small contributors.

PACs have made several significant contributions to the political system. They increase participation in the political process. They allow more voices to be heard in determining who will be elected. PACs also allow individuals to increase the impact of their political activity given that they attain a sense of achievement that accompanies taking part in political activity with like-minded persons, instead of merely acting alone. Additionally, PACs are a mechanism for political fund raising that respects the manner in which society is structured. Occupation and interest groups, which PACs represent, have replaced the neighborhood wards or precincts as centers of political activity.

Individuals seem less willing to commit themselves to the broad agenda of political parties, gravitating instead toward single issues or clusters of issues represented by various PACs, allowing individuals to join with others who share their values and to undertake action to achieve the political goals they perceive as most important. Further, PACs serve as a safeguard against undue influence by the government or media by energetically promoting their competing claims and views, preventing the development of either a single official viewpoint or a monolithic media bias. As a result, PACs encourage the lively pluralism so highly valued and forcefully guaranteed by the framers of the Constitution. PACs also have made more money available for political campaigns, which helps ensure the transmission of candidates' views and positions, while encouraging the participation of individuals without wealth to run for office. Finally, PACs have contributed to greater accountability in political financing. By sanctioning the use of PACs, the laws governing them have replaced the undisclosed and questionable forms of secret money derived from sources PACs now represent.

Legislation designed to limit PACs further might cause more problems than it would solve. For example, because of continually rising campaign costs, alternative funding sources would have to be provided, but the budget restraints on Congress make it unlikely that compensatory legislation providing public funding will be enacted in the near future. The impact of lower contribution limits on certain groups would be greater than on others, causing more disparity and imbalance than now exists between business and labor PACs, and between liberal and conservative PACs.

At both the federal and state levels, proposals have been made to allow PACs with large memberships to contribute more than those with small memberships. The problem with this approach, besides adding unnecessary complexity to the regulatory system, is that it is not without political ramifications. Such a differentiation clearly favors labor unions, professional associations, and environmental groups, which comprise a majority of the large membership PACs. But it puts other PACs at a disadvantage.

Finally, introducing aggregate PAC limits might raise constitutional questions because they differ from both contribution and expenditure limits. Aggregate PAC limitations are in effect receipt limitations, and candidates would need to pick and choose among offered contributions to remain under the ceiling. Those PACs that would give early—likely larger PACs—would fill the candidate's limit and freeze out smaller PACs, which could then charge their constitutional right to give was being denied.

Political Parties

Strengthening the role of the political parties is one way to offset some of the influence of PACs. The parties once served a mediating role between policy makers and the organized groups and individuals who helped them achieve office and then sought to be heard. The revival of the Republican party in the 1980s demonstrated the vitality of parties. This is not to call for the return of the days of Tammany Hall and smoke-filled rooms, but for the development of modern parties based on democratic principles, open and welcoming, interested in issues, and seeking to accommodate conflicting interests.

Several proposals have been offered to help accomplish the goal of strengthening the parties. Although the political finance reforms of the early 1970s are by no means the sole, or even the major, cause of the decline of parties, FECA could be amended in ways that would strengthen the parties. Several proposals might be considered, including, first, the elimination of limits on party committee spending on behalf of candidates, or substantially increasing these limits. Second, elimination of limits on individual contributions to parties and on what parties may contribute to candidate committees, or else those limits should be substantially increased. Currently some candidates may receive hundreds of thousands of dollars in the aggregate from PACs, yet the law prevents parties from competing by providing candidates with similar large amounts.

Third, state and local party committees now are allowed to spend unlimited amounts on volunteer-oriented activities on behalf of candidates, such as registration and get-out-the-vote. Party building activities should be permitted without limitation.

Fourth, a separate tax credit should be established for small contributions to political parties. Also, party committee legal, accounting, and administrative expenses should be exempt from the law's definition of contribution or expenditure. While some would object on grounds that this opens the door to more soft money, its purposes in strengthening the parties are undeniable. Some advocates of political party renewal go so far as to suggest that all limits on contributions to parties should be eliminated as well as limitations on what parties can contribute to candidate committees.

Incumbents versus Challengers

Evidence exists that expenditure limits could place relatively unknown challengers at an even greater disadvantage at a time when races for the House and Senate are growing less competitive. While proponents of public funding argue that expenditure limits can help political challengers, opponents counter that a key feature of public funding—expenditure limits—serves to help incumbents. The public resources available to elected officeholders means that incumbents start their campaigns for reelection with a substantial head start in public recognition and acceptance. By limiting a challenger to spending no more than the incumbent, the insurgent is therefore placed at a substantial disadvantage. The lower the limit, the greater the disadvantage.

Analyzing campaign spending data, political scientist Gary C. Jacobson has shown that campaign spending does not have the same consequences for incumbents and challengers. His findings indicate that spending by challengers has more impact on election outcomes than spending by incumbents.[4] Simply being known and remembered by voters is a very important factor in electoral success. The incumbent, provided with the resources of office, already enjoys an advantage in name recognition. The dissemination of additional information about the incumbent during the campaign, therefore, may often be superfluous even though it helps reinforce voters' opinions. The challenger, meanwhile, not so well known to most voters, has everything to gain from an extensive and expensive effort to acquire more voter awareness.

Translated into financial terms, this means that because senators and representatives are generally better known, they usually need less money but are able to raise more. The challengers, while they may need more money, have difficulty getting it. But when they do, either through providing it to their own campaign out of their own pockets, or by attracting it, they become better known and are more likely to win. If the incumbent raises money to meet the threat, spending money helps him or her less per dollar than additional money spent by the challenger. In short, those votes that change as a result of campaign spending generally benefit challengers.

Jacobson concluded that any campaign finance policy, such as public financing, that would increase spending for both incumbent and challenger would work to the benefit of the latter, thus making elections more competitive. In the reverse, any policy that attempts to equalize the financial positions of candidates by limiting campaign spending would benefit incumbents, thus lessening electoral competition.[5] This analysis supports the principle of "floors without ceilings."

Conclusion

If voting is the most important individual act in politics, then financial participation may be the second most important. Those who would replace private financing with total government funding might succeed unwittingly in changing fundamental balances in the political system. Critics who minimize individual efforts ignore history: a system of free elections cannot survive without voluntarism. In whatever form or quantity elections draw upon government assistance, freely contributed money and services will be needed.

Limiting group political activity, therefore, should be approached slowly and carefully. A sense of balance and equilibrium between competing forces in society, in which government is expected to play a moderating but not a dominating role in their regulation, is difficult to achieve but should be sought.

The most significant events in the last several decades—the civil rights movement, the women's movement, the Vietnam peace movement, environmental issues, and political reform—all originated in the private sector, where the need for action was perceived and where the needed organizations were established to carry it out. Government reacted but did not initiate the activity, and government was part of the problem in each case. Hence, the continued existence of interest groups, which are aggregations of like-minded people whose political power is enhanced by combining forces, is important. Without groups, individuals in mass society are atomized and ineffectual.

Success in attracting individuals to charitable giving has not been a matter of accident or a spontaneous result of general good will toward organizations with good causes. Instead, it reflects a serious effort to educate the public in its responsibilities and to organize effective collection systems. Political responsibilities must be similarly learned.

The value of contributing small sums for political activity is neither taught in schools nor widely understood as an act of good citizenship, although voting is both honored and respected, at least in principle. The challenge is to associate contributing with voting as an act of good citizenship, to upgrade and dignify political giving, and to gain for the political financing of politics the public approval accorded voting.

The major changes in American political finance laws in the 1970s have not always resulted in systematic or consistent reform. One reason for this uneven progress is that various aspects of the problem have been dealt with separately and at different times by major actors in government—Congress, the president, the Federal Election Commission, and the Supreme Court.

What the Federal Election Campaign Act, its amendments, and many state laws have lacked has been a philosophy about regulation that is both constitutional and pragmatically designed to keep the election process open and flexible instead of rigid, exclusionary, and fragmented. The revision of federal and state laws following *Buckley v. Valeo* have not lead to the openness and flexibility a democratic and pluralistic society require.

Notes

1 *Money and Elections*

1. Public Law 93-443, 88 Stat. 1263 (codified in scattered sections of the *United States Code*).
2. These figures were developed by the Citizens' Research Foundation, Los Angeles.
3. The figures were derived from data collected and published by the Federal Election Commission, Washington, D.C.
4. George Skelton, "Legislators on the Take, Most in Survey Believe," *Los Angeles Times*, January 3, 1990.
5. Quoted in Louis M. Peck, "Campaign Financing," *Congressional Quarterly Issue Briefs*, no. 101-08, June 9, 1990, 3.
6. California Commission on Campaign Financing, *The New Gold Rush: Financing California's Legislative Campaigns: 1985 Report and Recommendations* (Los Angeles: Center for Responsive Government, 1985), 4.

2 *Pre-1972 Campaign Money*

1. Jasper B. Shannon, *Money and Politics* (New York: Random House, 1959), 14.
2. Louise Overacker, *Money in Elections* (New York: Macmillan, 1932), 102; and Robert E. Mutch, *Campaigns, Congress, and Courts: The Making of Federal Campaign Finance Law* (New York: Praeger Publishers, 1988), xvi.
3. Shannon, *Money and Politics*, 21.
4. Wilfred E. Binkley, *American Political Parties*, 4th ed. (New York: Alfred A. Knopf, 1962), 279.
5. Edwin P. Hoyt, Jr., *Jumbos and Jackasses: A Popular History of the American Political Wars* (Garden City, N.Y.: Doubleday and Co., 1960), 77.
6. Alexander Heard, *The Costs of Democracy* (Chapel Hill: University of North Carolina Press, 1960), 233.
7. Herbert E. Alexander, "Financing Presidential Elections" in *History of American Presidential Elections: 1789-1968*, vol. 4, ed. Arthur M. Schlesinger and Fred L. Israel (New York: Chelsea House, 1971), 3884.
8. Samuel Eliot Morison, *The Oxford History of the American People* (New York: Oxford University Press, 1965), 731.
9. Quoted in Shannon, *Money and Politics*, 26.
10. Eugene H. Roseboom, *A History of Presidential Elections* (New York: Macmillan, 1957), 242.
11. Shannon, *Money and Politics*, 27.
12. Robert H. Wiebe, *The Search for Order, 1877-1920* (New York: Hill and Wang, 1967), 182.

13. Hoyt, *Jumbos and Jackasses,* 189.
14. William Safire, *Safire's Political Dictionary* (New York: Random House, 1978), 220.
15. Roseboom, *A History of Presidential Elections,* 304.
16. Herbert Croly, *Marcus Alonzo Hanna* (New York: Macmillan, 1912), 425.
17. Shannon, *Money and Politics,* 33.
18. Croly, *Marcus Alonzo Hanna,* 220, 324-325.
19. Quoted in M. R. Werner, *Bryan* (New York: Harcourt, Brace and Co., 1929), 101.
20. Roseboom, *A History of Presidential Elections,* 316.
21. Quoted in Shannon, *Money and Politics,* 35.
22. Ibid.
23. Ibid.
24. Overacker, *Money in Elections,* 180.
25. Louise Overacker, *Presidential Campaign Funds* (Boston: Boston University Press, 1946), 29.
26. Shannon, *Money and Politics,* 54.
27. Overacker, *Presidential Campaign Funds,* 50.
28. Arthur M. Schlesinger, Jr., *The Politics of Upheaval: The Age of Roosevelt,* vol. 3 (Boston: Houghton Mifflin Co., 1960), 594-595.
29. Theodore H. White, *The Making of the President: 1968* (New York: Atheneum, 1969), 365.
30. Overacker, *Presidential Campaign Funds,* 49. On the early labor PACs, see Mutch, *Campaigns, Congress, and Courts,* 153-157.
31. Ben A. Franklin, "Inquiries into Nixon's Reelection Funds Turning Up a Pattern of High Pressure," *New York Times,* July 15, 1973.
32. Morton Mintz and Nick Kotz, "Automen Rejected Nixon Fund Bid," *Washington Post,* November 17, 1972.
33. Michael C. Jensen, "The Corporate Political Squeeze," *New York Times,* September 16, 1973.
34. Senate Select Committee on Presidential Campaign Activities, *Final Report of the Senate Select Committee on Presidential Campaign Activities,* 93d Cong., 2d sess., 1974, 470.
35. Ibid., 446-447.
36. James R. Polk, "Philippine Cash Surfaces," *Washington Star,* June 11, 1974; "Sugar Envoy Mum on Donation," June 12, 1974; and "Nixon Donation from Second Filipino Revealed," June 13, 1974.
37. Rowland Evans and Robert Novak, "Greek Gifts for President," *Washington Post,* July 20, 1972; and Seth Kantor, "Jaworski Eyes Probing Foreign '72 Gifts," *Washington Post,* January 25, 1974.
38. 18 U.S.C. at 613.
39. CRF Listing of: *Political Contributors of $10,000 or More in 1972* (Princeton, N.J.: Citizens' Research Foundation, 1975). For the motivations of the majority of contributors in 1972, see Roman B. Hedges, "Reasons for Political Involvement: A Study of Contributors to the 1972 Presidential Campaign," *Western Political Quarterly* 37:2 (June 1984): 257-271.

3 *The Drive for Reform*

1. Quoted in Jasper B. Shannon, *Money and Politics* (New York: Random House, 1959), 35.

2. This chapter is derived in part from Herbert E. Alexander, *Money in Politics* (Washington, D.C.: Public Affairs Press, 1972), 183-251. See also Louise Overacker, *Money in Elections* (New York: Macmillan, 1932), 107; Alexander Heard, *The Costs of Democracy* (Chapel Hill: University of North Carolina Press, 1960), 334-335; and David W. Adamany and George E. Agree, *Political Money: A Strategy for Campaign Financing in America* (Baltimore, Md.: Johns Hopkins University Press, 1975).
3. For a case study of the enactment of FECA and its 1974 amendments, see Robert E. Mutch, *Campaigns, Congress, and Courts: The Making of Federal Campaign Finance Law* (New York: Praeger Publishers, 1988).
4. On passage of the 1907-1911 laws, see Ibid., 1-16.
5. *Newberry v. United States*, 256 U.S. 232 (1921).
6. *United States v. Classic*, 313 U.S. 299 (1941).
7. *Congressional Quarterly Almanac*, vol. 21 (Washington, D.C.: Congressional Quarterly, 1966), 1552.
8. *Financing Presidential Campaigns: Report of the President's Commission on Campaign Costs* (Washington, D.C.: Government Printing Office, April 1962).
9. Robert A. Caro, *The Years of Lyndon Johnson: The Path to Power* (New York: Alfred A. Knopf, 1982), 577-578, 606-608.
10. Herbert E. Alexander, *Financing the 1968 Election* (Lexington, Mass.: Heath Lexington Books, 1971), 95.
11. Public Law 92-225.
12. Public Law 93-443.
13. Public Law 94-283.
14. Christopher Lydon, "President Urges Campaign Reform with Gift Limits," *New York Times*, March 9, 1974.
15. John Herbers, "Bill to Reform Campaign Funds Signed by Ford Despite Doubts," *New York Times*, October 16, 1974.
16. *Buckley v. Valeo*, 424 U.S. 1 (1976). See also Mutch, *Campaigns, Congress, and Courts*, Chapter 3.
17. Mutch, *Campaigns, Congress, and Courts*, Chapter 4. See also Paul T. David, "The Federal Election Commission: Origin and Early Activities," *National Civic Review* 65 (June 1976): 278-283.
18. *INS v. Chadha*, 462 U.S. (1983).
19. Public Law 96-187.
20. Institute of Politics, John F. Kennedy School of Government, Harvard University, *An Analysis of the Impact of the Federal Election Campaign Act, 1972-1978*, prepared for the House Administration Committee, 96th Cong., 1st sess., 1979.
21. Ibid., 17.
22. Common Cause, *Stalled from the Start: A Common Cause Study of the Federal Election Commission* (Washington, D.C.: Common Cause, 1980), iii-iv.

4 *Sources of Funds*

1. Alexander Heard, *The Costs of Democracy* (Chapel Hill: University of North Carolina Press, 1960), 68-74.
2. Frank J. Sorauf, *Money in American Elections* (Glenview, Ill.: Scott, Foresman and Co., 1988), 49-51.

3. Lynda Powell, "A Study of Financial Contributors in Congressional Elections" (Paper prepared for the annual meeting of the American Political Science Association, Washington, D.C., August 31-September 3, 1979), 10-11.
4. Federal Election Commission, "1990 Congressional Election Spending Drops to Low Point," press release, February 22, 1991, 1.
5. Herbert E. Alexander, *Financing the 1972 Election* (Lexington, Mass.: Lexington Books, 1976), 299-304.
6. E. J. Dionne, Jr., "Small Donors Gave Reagan Primary Aid," *New York Times*, July 2, 1980.
7. Herbert E. Alexander and Monica Bauer, *Financing the 1988 Election* (Boulder, Colo.: Westview Press, 1991), 21-24.
8. Sara Fritz and Dwight Morris, "House Members Spend Freely to Bolster Roles," *Los Angeles Times*, October 29, 1990.
9. Roger Craver, "Igniting a Political Revolution," *Fund Raising Management* (April 1989): 88-92.
10. Larry Makinson, *The Price of Admission: An Illustrated Atlas of Spending in the 1988 Congressional Elections* (Washington, D.C.: Center for Responsive Politics, July 1989), 23.
11. Charles Babcock, "Hill Fund Raising: Better Safe Than Sorry?" *Washington Post*, September 26, 1990.
12. Jill Abramson, "In the Art of Political Fund Raising, Lawmakers Arms Have Long Reach," *Wall Street Journal*, October 24, 1990.
13. Ibid.
14. "Now, It's Ollie the Fund-Raiser," *U.S. News and World Report*, September 26, 1988, 22.
15. Ronald Brownstein, *The Power and the Glitter* (New York: Pantheon Books, 1990), 348.
16. Ibid., 360.
17. Ibid., 352-357.
18. Ibid., 362-363.
19. Maureen Dowd, "Not on the Ballot This Election, But on the Line Nonetheless," *New York Times*, November 7, 1990.
20. "The Quayle Handicap," *Newsweek*, May 20, 1991, 23.
21. H. Richard Mayberry, Jr., and Kristine E. Heine, "Bundling Makes Strange Bedfellows," *Campaigns and Elections* (July 1986): 76-78.
22. Sara Fritz and Dwight Morris, "Political Money by the Bundle," *Los Angeles Times*, July 30, 1990.
23. Ibid.
24. Mayberry and Heine, "Bundling Makes Strange Bedfellows," 77.
25. Quoted in Ibid., 78.
26. Brooks Jackson, "GOP Panel's Bypass of Federal Aid Cap Totals $6.6 Million for Senatorial Races," *Wall Street Journal*, October 24, 1986.
27. Fritz and Morris, "Political Money by the Bundle."
28. Federal Election Commission, "FEC Releases 1990 Year-End Count," press release, January 11, 1991, 1.
29. Federal Election Commission, "PAC Activity Falls in 1990 Elections," press release, March 31, 1991, 1.
30. "The Top 100 PACs of 1989-90: They Gave 46.7 Percent of All PAC Gifts," *PACs and Lobbies*, April 17, 1991, 3.
31. "Have PACs Entered the 'Twilight Zone'?" *PACs and Lobbies*, April 3, 1991, 1, 3-5.

32. Federal Election Commission, "PAC Activity Falls in 1990 Elections," 10.
33. Theodore J. Eismeier and Philip A. Pollock III, "Political Action Committees: Varieties of Organization and Strategy" (Paper presented at the annual meeting of the Midwest Political Science Association, Chicago, April 21-23, 1983), 9.
34. Leadership PACs are analyzed at length in Ross K. Baker, *The New Fat Cats: Members of Congress as Political Benefactors* (New York: Priority Press Publications, 1989). Also see Richard L. Berke, "Incumbents Turn to Personal PACs," *New York Times*, June 16, 1989; and for a listing, see "PACs Affiliated with Members of Congress, January 1, 1987-December 31, 1989," *Campaign Practices Reports*, May 28, 1990, 4
35. Citizen Action, *Hidden Power: Campaign Contributions of Large Individual Donors* (Washington, D.C.: Citizen Action, July 1990), 10.
36. Ibid., 11-13.
37. *Federal Election Commission v. National Conservative Political Action Committee, et al.*, 1055 Ct. 1459, 1985.
38. Ibid.
39. Candice J. Nelson, "Loose Cannons: Independent Expenditures," in *Money, Elections, and Democracy: Reforming Congressional Campaign Finance*, ed. Margaret Latus Nugent and John R. Johannes (Boulder, Colo.: Westview Press, 1990), 48-49.
40. "Four Businessmen Indicted in Scheme to Help Cranston Win Reelection," *New York Times*, December 15, 1988.
41. Kenneth Reich, "Goland Gets Jail Term for Illegal Campaign Gift," *Los Angeles Times*, July 17, 1990.
42. Richard L. Berke, "Cranston Backer Guilty in Campaign Finance Case," *New York Times*, May 8, 1990.
43. "Four Businessmen Indicted in Scheme to Help Cranston Win Reelection."
44. Quoted in Gloria Borger, "The Dirty Big Secret of Campaign Finance," *U.S. News and World Report*, November 7, 1988, 29.
45. For a more extensive account of the Keating Five, see Alexander and Bauer, *Financing the 1988 Election*, 79-81.
46. Jack W. Germond and Jules Witcover, "Looking for a Smoking Gun on Campaign Funds," *National Journal*, December 2, 1989, 2956.
47. Statement of the Select Committee on Ethics following hearings involving Senators Cranston, DeConcini, Glenn, McCain, and Riegle, typescript, n.d., 1-6, plus 6 pp. of resolutions; and Phil Kuntz, "Cranston Case Ends on Floor with a Murky Plea Bargain," *Congressional Quarterly Weekly Report*, November 23, 1991, 3432-3438.
48. Ann DeVroy, "All the Ambassadorships Money Can Buy," *Washington Post National Weekly Edition*, July 24-30, 1989.
49. Jean Cobb and Jeffrey Denny, "The Fat-Cat Club: Membership Has Its Privileges," *Washington Post National Weekly Edition*, April 2-8, 1990.
50. Senate Select Committee on Presidential Campaign Activities, *Final Report of the Senate Select Committee on Presidential Campaign Activities*, 93d Cong., 2d sess., 1974, 904.
51. Quoted in Jack Nelson, "Reagan to Name More Political Ambassadors," *Los Angeles Times*, April 8, 1982.
52. Ibid.
53. Elaine Sciolino, "Friends as Ambassadors: How Many Is Too Many?" *New York Times*, November 7, 1989.

54. Reported by United Press International in *Trentonian*, November 22, 1974.
55. Alan Ehrenhalt, *Politics in America: The 100th Congress* (Washington, D.C.: Congressional Quarterly, 1987), 1616.
56. Jill Abramson, "In the Art of Political Fund Raising."
57. Michael Barone and Grant Ujifusa, *The Almanac of American Politics, 1990* (Washington, D.C.: National Journal, 1989), 1315.
58. Ruth S. Jones and Warren E. Miller, "Financing Campaigns: Macro Level Innovation and Micro Level Response," *Western Political Quarterly* 38:2 (June 1985): 203-205.
59. Ruth S. Jones, "Contributing as Participation," in *Money, Elections, and Democracy*, 40.

5 The Costs of Elections

1. Quoted in Jasper B. Shannon, *Money and Politics* (New York: Random House, 1959), 15.
2. Eugene H. Roseboom, *A History of Presidential Elections* (New York: Macmillan, 1957), 25.
3. Shannon, *Money and Politics*, 21.
4. Ibid., 23.
5. Jules Abels, *The Degeneration of Our Presidential Election: A History and Analysis of an American Institution in Trouble* (New York: Macmillan, 1968), 883.
6. Roseboom, *A History of Presidential Elections*, 121.
7. M. R. Werner, *Bryan* (New York: Harcourt, Brace and Co., 1929), 5.
8. Peter Baida, "The Legacy of Dollar Mark Hanna," *Forbes 400*, October 14, 1988.
9. Herbert E. Alexander and Monica Bauer, *Financing the 1988 Election* (Boulder, Colo.: Westview Press, 1991), 105.
10. For a brief history of the uses of radio and television broadcasting in political campaigns, see Herbert E. Alexander, "Financing Presidential Campaigns," in *History of American Presidential Elections 1789-1968*, ed. Arthur M. Schlesinger, Jr., and Fred L. Israel (New York: Chelsea House, 1971), 3873-3875. Other historical information in this chapter is drawn from the same source.
11. Charles R. Babcock, "Spending for 1990 Hill Races Fell," *Washington Post*, February 25, 1991.
12. Ibid.
13. Craig Endicott, "Philip Morris Unseats P&G as Top Advertising Spender," *Advertising Age*, September 28, 1988, 1.
14. Herbert E. Alexander and Brian A. Haggerty, "Misinformation on Media Money," *Public Opinion* 11:1 (May/June 1988): 5.
15. Louise Overacker, *Money in Elections* (New York: Macmillan, 1932), 28; and Frank J. Sorauf, *Money in American Elections* (Glenview, Ill.: Scott, Foresman and Co., 1988), 20.
16. Alexander and Haggerty, "Misinformation on Media Money," 5.
17. Alexander and Bauer, *Financing the 1988 Election*, 98.
18. Joseph E. Cantor and Kevin J. Coleman, "Expenditures for Campaign Services: A Survey of 1988 Congressional Candidates in Competitive Elections," in *CRS Report for Congress* (Washington, D.C.: Congressional Research Service, Library of Congress, September 12, 1990); and "Summary Data on 1988

Congressional Candidates' Expenditure Survey," addendum, November 8, 1990, 1-6.
19. Federal Communications Commission, "Mass Media Bureau Report on Political Programming Audit," September 7, 1990, 1-8.
20. Thomas B. Rosenthiel, "Candidates' Ad Rates Too High, FCC Says," *Los Angeles Times*, September 8, 1990.
21. Sara Fritz and Dwight Morris, "Burden of TV Election Ads Exaggerated, Study Finds," *Los Angeles Times*, March 18, 1991.
22. Cantor and Coleman, "Expenditures for Campaign Services," 28-29.
23. Fritz and Morris, "Burden of TV Election Ads Exaggerated, Study Finds."
24. Peter Bragdon, "Campaign Funds for Legal Fees. It's Legal, But Is It Proper?" *Congressional Quarterly Weekly Report*, November 18, 1989, 3191.
25. Ibid., 3190.
26. Ibid., 3191.
27. Stanley Kelley, Jr., *Political Campaigning: Problems in Creating an Informed Electorate* (Washington, D.C.: Brookings Institution, 1960), 5.
28. California Commission on Campaign Financing, *Money and Politics in the Golden State: Financing California's Local Elecions* (Los Angeles: Center for Responsive Government, 1989), 62.
29. Public Disclosure Commission, *Where the Money Goes: A Review of Campaign Vendors* (Olympia, Wash.: Public Disclosure Commission, June 1990), 19-20.
30. Sara Fritz and Dwight Morris, "Campaign Cash Takes a Detour," *Los Angeles Times*, October 28, 1990.
31. M. A. Farber and Ralph Blumenthal, "New York City Councilman's Fund Grows with His Political Influence," *New York Times*, May 21, 1991.
32. "Dems Complain GOP Challengers Use Funds for Living Expenses," *PACs and Lobbies*, August 15, 1990, 14.
33. Kevin Chaffee, *Saving for a Rainy Day: How Congress Turns Leftover Cash into 'Golden Parachutes'* (Washington, D.C.: Center for Public Integrity, 1991), 1-12.
34. Kenneth Reich, "The 64 Million Dollar Question," *Campaigns and Elections* 9:7 (March/April 1989): 15-21.
35. Ibid., 15.
36. Ibid.
37. Ibid.

6 Skirting the Limits in 1988

1. Richard L. Berke, "Spending Limit Up 14 Percent for Primaries," *New York Times*, February 6, 1988.
2. "Tax Checkoff, Presidential Primary Financing in Jeopardy as FEC, Treasury Prepare Stopgap Plan," *Campaign Practices Reports*, December 10, 1990, 2.
3. Federal Election Commission, "Presidential Fund-Income Tax Checkoff Status," press release, August 1990.
4. "Tax Checkoff, Presidential Primary Financing in Jeopardy as FEC, Treasury Prepare Stopgap Plan," 2.
5. Federal Election Commission, "FEC Announces Spending Limits for 1988 Presidential Race," press release, February 5, 1988, 1-2.
6. Richard L. Berke, "Election Unit Eases TV Ad Limit, Rejecting Advice of Own Counsel," *New York Times*, February 26, 1988.

7. L. Sandy Maisel, "Spending Patterns in Presidential Nominating Campaigns, 1976-1988" (Paper prepared for the annual meeting of the American Political Science Association, Washington, D.C., September 1-4, 1988), 21.
8. Anthony Corrado, "The Pre-Candidacy PAC Loophole," *Boston Globe*, May 6, 1990. Also see Anthony Corrado, *Creative Campaigning: PACs and the Presidential Selection Process* (Boulder, Colo.: Westview Press, 1992).
9. Corrado, "The Pre-Candidacy PAC Loophole."
10. Paul Houston, "Bush, Dukakis Got Record Big Gifts," *Los Angeles Times*, December 10, 1988. Not every contributor credited with donating $100,000 gave it all in soft money. Some contributed up to the legal limits of $20,000 in hard money to the national party committees. Others gave in varying combinations of hard and soft money totaling $100,000 and thus were credited with that amount. Still other gave directly to state party committees instead of routing the donations through the national parties.
11. Herbert E. Alexander and Brian A. Haggerty, *Financing the 1984 Election* (Lexington, Mass.: Lexington Books, 1987), 84-88.
12. Federal Election Commission, "Presidential Prenomination Campaigns" in *FEC Report on Financial Activity, 1987-1988, Final Report* (Washington, D.C.: Federal Election Commission, August 1989), Tables A6, A7, 9-10, and Appendix 1. The figures used in the text include 1989 expenditures through June 30, 1989.
13. Federal Election Commission, "FEC Approves Matching Funds for 1988 Presidential Candidates," press release, March 9, 1989.
14. Clyde Wilcox, "Financing the 1988 Prenomination Campaigns," unpublished manuscript, 20.
15. Ibid.
16. Democrats alleged that Bush not only exceeded the spending limit but also offset certain expenditures in the weeks before the Republican convention by charging them as "party-building" expenses or as official government expenses in his capacity as vice president. See "Democrats Claim Bush Exceeds Campaign Spending Limit," *PACs and Lobbies*, August 17, 1989, 11. Much of the textual formulation is based on Herbert E. Alexander, "The Price We Pay for Our Presidents," *Public Opinion* 11:6 (March/April 1989): 46-48.
17. Brian Sullam, "The Cash Campaign," *New Republic*, March 14, 1988, 9-13.
18. Maureen Dowd, "Hart, Conceding People Decided, Quits Again," *New York Times*, March 12, 1988.
19. Ibid.
20. Richard L. Berke, "Campaign Finances of '84 Haunt Hart in '88," *New York Times*, January 30, 1988.
21. Ibid.
22. Ibid.
23. David Lauter, "Panel Limits Hart in Using '88 Funds to Pay '84 Debts," *Los Angeles Times*, March 25, 1988.
24. Ibid.
25. Scott Shephard, "Cost of the Democratic Convention Will Reach at Least $22.4 Million," *Atlanta Constitution*, September 30, 1988.
26. Brooks Jackson, "Bush, Dukakis Presidential Campaigns Each Spent More Than $100 Million," *Wall Street Journal*, December 12, 1988.
27. For an extended analysis of soft money, see Herbert E. Alexander, *Strategies for Election Reform* (Washington, D.C.: Project for Comprehensive Campaign Reform, April 1989), 44-57.

28. Jackson, "Bush, Dukakis Presidential Campaigns Each Spent More Than $100 Million."
29. Larry Makinson, *The Price of Admission: Campaign Spending in the 1990 Elections* (Washington, D.C.: Center for Responsive Politics, September 1991), 8, 10.
30. Federal Election Commission, "1990 Congressional Candidates Post Spending Drop, Final FEC Report Shows," press release, December 10, 1991, 2; Common Cause, "Nearly Half of Senate Incumbents Seeking Election in 1990 Were Unopposed or Financially Unopposed; Senate Spending Increases for Incumbents, Decreases for Challengers, Common Cause Analysis Shows," press release, *Common Cause News*, February 28, 1991, 6; and Makinson, *The Price of Admission: Campaign Spending in the 1990 Elections*, 24, 37.
31. Mickey Edwards, "What 'Permanent Congress'?" *New York Times*, January 5, 1990.
32. Al Swift, "The 'Permanent Congress' Is a Myth," *Washington Post Weekly Edition*, June 26-July 2, 1989.
33. Larry Makinson, *The Price of Admission: An Illustrated Atlas of Spending in the 1988 Congressional Elections* (Washington, D.C.: Center for Responsive Politics, July 1989), 21.
34. Makinson, *The Price of Admission: Campaign Spending in the 1990 Elections*, 9.
35. Gary C. Jacobson, *Money in Congressional Elections* (New Haven, Conn.: Yale University Press, 1980), 48-49.
36. Makinson, *The Price of Admission: An Illustrated Atlas of Spending in the 1988 Congressional Elections*, 15.
37. Makinson, *The Price of Admission: Campaign Spending in the 1990 Elections*, 22.
38. Ibid., 35.
39. Ibid., 23.
40. Makinson, *The Price of Admission: An Illustrated Atlas of Spending in the 1988 Congressional Elections*, 21.
41. Federal Election Commission, "FEC Releases Summary of 1989-1990 Political Party Finances," press release, March 15, 1990, 1.
42. Ibid., 2.

7 State and Local Experience

1. *Buckley v. Valeo*, 424 U.S. 1 (1976).
2. Much of the information on state laws in this chapter is taken from National Clearinghouse on Election Administration, Federal Election Commission, *Campaign Finance Law 88* (Washington, D.C.: Federal Election Commission, 1988). Also used were Herbert E. Alexander, "Public Financing of State Elections" (Paper prepared for the State of the States Symposium, Eagleton Institute of Politics, Rutgers University, New Brunswick, New Jersey, December 1989); and Frederick M. Herrmann, *1990 Campaign Finance Update: Legislation and Litigation* (Los Angeles: Citizens' Research Foundation, 1990).
3. *The New Gold Rush: Financing California's Legislative Campaigns* (Los Angeles: Center for Responsive Government, 1987 update), 17.
4. *PAC Money in Maryland: November 19, 1986-August 26, 1990* (Annapolis, Md.: Common Cause/Maryland, September 6, 1990), 1.
5. *The New Gold Rush*, 15.

6. Herbert E. Alexander, *Financing the 1976 Election* (Washington, D.C.: CQ Press, 1979), 167; and Herbert E. Alexander and Brian A. Haggerty, *Financing the 1984 Election* (Lexington, Mass.: Lexington Books, 1987), 83.
7. The figures on the 1986 gubernatorial races were compiled by Thad L. Beyle, University of North Carolina, Chapel Hill.
8. Kent Jenkins, Jr., "$25 Million Race for Virginia Governor among Costliest," *Washington Post*, December 2, 1989.
9. Carol Matlack, "Elections You Can Afford," *National Journal*, June 24, 1989, 1633.
10. David Maraniss, "Texas, It Seems, Has Had Its Fill of Williams," *Washington Post*, October 27, 1990.
11. *The New Gold Rush*, 1.
12. Sandra Singer, "The Power of the Purse—It Costs to Run for Legislative Office!!" (Paper presented at the annual meeting of the Western Political Science Association, Salt Lake City, Utah, March 30-April 1, 1989), 5-6, 10.
13. Gary Moncrief, "The Increase in Campaign Expenditures in State Legislative Elections: A Comparison of Four Northwestern States" (Paper presented at the annual meeting of the American Political Science Association, San Francisco, California, August 30-September 2, 1990), 12.
14. Glen Craney, "Unusual New Spending Law Frustrates Candidates," *Congressional Quarterly Weekly Report*, June 17, 1989, 1497-1498. Also see "New Hampshire Sets $5,000 Fee for Candidates Who Fail to Accept Spending Limits," *Election Administration Reports*, June 26, 1989, 5.
15. This law was ruled unconstitutional a year later by the Florida Supreme Court, which said that it discriminated against nonincumbents who were not in a position to exchange legislative favors for political donations. See *State of Florida v. Jack P. Dodd*, No. 75,788, May 8, 1990. Similar laws, however, remain on the books in nine other states—including Connecticut, which adopted one during its 1990 legislative session.
16. Richard C. Paddock, "Judge Strikes Down Prop. 73 Funding Limits," *Los Angeles Times*, September 26, 1990; and *Service Employees International Union v. Fair Political Practices Commission*, U.S. District Court, Eastern District of California, No. CIV. S-89-433 LKK.
17. Philip Hager and Richard C. Paddock, "Proposition with Most Votes Would Nullify Rival One," *Los Angeles Times*, November 2, 1990; and *Taxpayers to Limit Campaign Spending v. Fair Political Practices Commission*, State of California Supreme Court, November 1, 1990, S012016.
18. Special Senate Committee to Investigate Organized Crime in Interstate Commerce, *Second Interim Report of the Special Senate Committee to Investigate Organized Crime in Interstate Commerce*, S Rept 82-141, 82d Cong., 1st sess., 1951, 1.
19. According to Alexander Heard, this estimate "embraces funds given in small towns and rural areas by individuals operating on the borders of the law who want a sympathetic sheriff and prosecutor, but who are not part of crime syndicates. The estimate applies chiefly to persons engaged in illegal gambling and racketeering. It does not extend, for example, to otherwise reputable businessmen who hope for understanding treatment from building inspectors and tax assessors." Alexander Heard, *The Costs of Democracy* (Chapel Hill: University of North Carolina Press, 1960), 164, 73n. Also see Harold Lasswell and Arnold A. Rogow, *Power, Corruption, and Rectitude* (Englewood Cliffs, N.J.: Prentice-Hall, 1963), 79-80; Donald R. Cressey, *Theft of the Nation: The*

Structure and Operations of Organized Crime in America (New York: Harper and Row, 1969), 253; and Herbert E. Alexander and Gerald E. Caiden, eds., *The Politics and Economics of Organized Crime* (Lexington, Mass.: Lexington Books, 1985).

20. Frank Lynn, "Regan Is Questioned on Fund Raising," *New York Times*, September 24, 1988.
21. Frank Lynn, "Ex-Syracuse Mayor's Schemes Cited," *New York Times*, February 7, 1988.
22. Daniel M. Weintraub and Richard C. Paddock, "Conviction Calls Capitol Practices into Doubt," *Los Angeles Times*, September 18, 1990.
23. *United States v. Spiro T. Agnew*, Crim. A. No. 73-0535, U.S. District Court, District of Maryland, October 10, 1973.
24. In 1988, Alabama voted to require preelection disclosure for the first time. In 1989, New Mexico closed a loophole in its law that allowed candidates to avoid listing those contributions received before January 1 of an election year or after election day.
25. Singer, "The Power of the Purse—It Costs to Run for Legislative Office!!" 2-3.
26. National Clearinghouse on Election Administration, Federal Election Commission, *Campaign Finance Law 90* (Washington, D.C.: Federal Election Commission, 1990).
27. *Findings and Recommendations of the Ad Hoc Commission on Legislative Ethics and Campaign Finance* (Trenton, N.J.: Ad Hoc Commission on Legislative Ethics and Campaign Finance, October 22, 1990), 18.
28. *Socialist Workers Party v. Jennings*, Civ. No. 74-1328 (D.D.C.)
29. *Buckley v. Valeo*, 424 U.S. at 68.
30. South Dakota permits contributions from unions if they are associations and not incorporated. Wisconsin permits use of corporate funds in referendums but not otherwise.
31. Karen J. Fling, "The States as Laboratories of Reform," in *Political Finance*, ed. Herbert E. Alexander (Beverly Hills: Sage Publications, 1979). See also the two Supreme Court cases: *First National Bank of Boston v. Bellotti*, 435 U.S. 765 (1978) and *Citizens against Rent Control v. City of Berkeley*, 454 U.S. 290 (1981).
32. Robert J. Huckshorn, "Who Gave It? Who Got It? The Enforcement of Campaign Laws in the States," *Journal of Politics* 47 (August 1985): 787.
33. Florida, Maryland, and Oklahoma have adopted public financing programs that are currently inoperative. The Maryland program has been stymied repeatedly by the unwillingness of the governor and legislature to provide funding, while Oklahoma's program encountered constitutional problems. Florida renewed a faltering program in 1991.
34. For more information on the programs in these four states, see Alexander, "Public Financing of State Elections."
35. James R. Klonski and Ann Aiken, "The Constitutional Law of Political Parties and the Emergent Dollar Checkoff" (unpublished manuscript, University of Oregon School of Law).
36. Ruth S. Jones, "State Public Campaign Finance: Implications for Partisan Politics," *American Journal of Political Science* 25 (May 1981): 342-361.
37. Extensive literature is available on party responsibility. See Gerald M. Pomper, ed., *Party Renewal in America: Theory and Practice* (New York: Praeger Publishers, 1980); Joel L. Fleishman, ed., *The Future of American Political Parties* (Englewood Cliffs, N.J.: Prentice-Hall, 1982); Austin Ranney, *Curing*

the *Mischief of Faction: Party Reform in America* (Berkeley: University of California Press, 1975); and Herbert E. Alexander, "The Impact Election Reform Legislation on the Political Party System" (Paper prepared for the annual meeting of the American Political Science Association, San Francisco, California, September 2-5, 1975). For earlier literature, see Herbert E. Alexander, *Responsibility in Party Finance* (Princeton, N.J.: Citizens' Research Foundation, 1963).

38. Jack L. Noragon, "Political Finance and Political Reform: The Experience with State Income Tax Checkoffs," *American Political Science Review* 75 (September 1981): 667-687.
39. Ibid., 686.
40. *Campaign Finance Law 90.*

8 *Reform on the National Agenda*

1. Louis M. Peck, "Campaign Financing," *Congressional Quarterly Issue Briefs*, no. 101-08, June 9, 1990, 3.
2. Gary C. Jacobson, *Money in Congressional Elections* (New Haven, Conn.: Yale University Press, 1980), 48-49.
3. "Campaign Reform," press release from the office of Rep. Guy Vander Jagt, R-Mich., cochair of the Bipartisan Task Force on Campaign Reform, September 22, 1989.
4. *Message from the President: Proposed Legislation—'Comprehensive Campaign Finance Reform Act of 1989,'* H. Doc. 101-96. 101st Cong., 1st sess., 1989.
5. U.S. Congress, Senate, Campaign Finance Reform Panel, *Campaign Finance Reform: A Report to the Majority and Minority Leader*, 101st Cong., 2d sess., 1990. The author of this book served as a member of the six-person panel.
6. The regulations are printed in the *Federal Register*, Vol. 55, No. 123, July 2, 1990, 26058-26073, under Federal Election Commission, "Methods of Allocation between Federal and Non-Federal Accounts: Payments, Reporting; Final Rule; Transmittal of Regulations of Congress."
7. See, for example, "Perfuming Money in the Senate," *New York Times*, June 9, 1987; and "The Tin Cup Club," *Washington Post*, July 6, 1987.
8. Tom Kenworthy, "Democrats Rip Common Cause," *Washington Post*, July 13, 1990.
9. Ibid.
10. "Senate Campaign Finance Rules Can Be Different, House Reform Task Force Chairman Says," *PACs and Lobbies*, March 6, 1991, 1, 5.
11. "Text of President Bush's State of the Union Message to the Nation," *New York Times*, January 30, 1991.
12. "Text of President Bush's Letter on Campaign Reform Legislation," *PACs and Lobbies*, June 5, 1991, 3.

9 *The Future of Reform*

1. Herbert E. Alexander, "Public Financing of State Election," (Paper presented at the State of the States Symposium, Eagleton Institute of Politics, Rutgers University, New Brunswick, N.J., December 1989), 50.
2. "Declining Public Participation in Tax Checkoff Threatens Presidential

Fund," *Campaign Practices Reports*, September 18, 1989, 5.

3. *Report of the Office of Campaign and Political Finance of the Commonwealth of Massachusetts, Boston, Mass.*, January 29, 1987, 10.
4. Gary C. Jacobson, "The Effects of Campaign Spending in Congressional Elections," *American Political Science Review* 72:2 (June 1978): 469.
5. Ibid.

Bibliography

Books

Adamany, David. *Campaign Finance in America.* N. Scituate, Mass.: Duxbury Press, 1972.

___. *Financing Politics: Recent Wisconsin Elections.* Madison: University of Wisconsin Press, 1969.

Adamany, David, and George E. Agree. *Political Money: A Strategy for Campaign Financing in America.* Baltimore, Md.: John Hopkins University Press, 1975

Alexander, Herbert E. *Financing the 1960 Election.* Princeton, N.J.: Citizens' Research Foundation, 1962.

___. *Financing the 1964 Election.* Princeton, N.J.: Citizens' Research Foundation, 1966.

___. *Financing the 1968 Election.* Lexington, Mass.: Heath Lexington Books, 1971.

___. *Financing the 1972 Election.* Lexington, Mass.: Lexington Books, 1976.

___. *Financing the 1976 Election.* Washington, D.C.: CQ Press, 1979.

___. *Financing the 1980 Election.* Lexington, Mass.: Lexington Books, 1983.

___. *Money in Politics.* Washington, D.C.: Public Affairs Press, 1972.

___. *Reform and Reality: The Financing of State and Local Campaigns.* New York: Twentieth Century Fund Press, 1991.

___, ed. *Campaign Money: Reform and Reality in the States.* New York: Free Press, 1976.

___, ed. *Comparative Political Finance in the 1980s.* Cambridge, England: Cambridge University Press, 1989.

___, ed. *Political Finance.* Beverly Hills: Sage Publications, 1979.

Alexander, Herbert E., and Monica Bauer. *Financing the 1988 Election.* Boulder, Colo.: Westview Press, 1991.

Alexander, Herbert E., and Mike Eberts. *Public Financing of State Elections: A Data Book on Tax-Assisted Funding of Political Parties and Candidates in Twenty States.* Los Angeles: Citizens' Research Foundation, 1986.

Alexander, Herbert E., and Brian A. Haggerty. *The Federal Election Campaign Act: After a Decade of Political Reform.* Los Angeles: Citizens' Research Foundation, 1981.

___. *Financing the 1984 Election.* Lexington, Mass.: Lexington Books, 1987.

___. *PACs and Parties: Relationships and Interrelationships.* Los Angeles: Citizens' Research Foundation, 1984.

___. *Political Reform in California: How Has It Worked?* Los Angeles: Citizens' Research Foundation, 1980.

Alexander, Herbert E., and Michael C. Walker. *Public Financing of Local*

Elections: A Data Book on Public Funding in Four Cities and Two Counties. Los Angeles: Citizens' Research Foundation, 1990.

Baker, Ross K. *The New Fat Cats: Members of Congress as Political Benefactors.* New York: Priority Press Publications, 1989.

Bishop, George F., Robert G. Meadow, and Marilyn Jackson-Beeck, eds. *The Presidential Debates: Media, Electoral, and Policy Perspectives.* New York: Praeger Publishers, 1979.

Bradshaw, Thornton, and David Vogel, eds. *Corporations and Their Critics.* New York: McGraw-Hill Book Co., 1981.

Bretton, Henry. *The Power of Money.* Albany: State University of New York Press, 1980.

Brownstein, Ronald. *The Power and the Glitter.* New York: Pantheon Books, 1990.

Crotty, William J. *Decision for the Democrats: Reforming Party Structure.* Baltimore, Md.: Johns Hopkins University Press, 1978.

———. *Party Reform.* New York: Longman, 1983.

———. *Paths to Political Reform.* Lexington, Mass.: D. C. Heath and Co., 1980.

———. *Political Reform and the American Experiment.* New York: Thomas Y. Crowell Co., 1977.

David, Paul, and David H. Everson. *The Presidential Election and Transition 1980-1981.* Carbondale, Ill.: Southern Illinois University Press, 1983.

Davis, James W. *Presidential Primaries: Road to the White House.* Westport, Conn.: Greenwood Press, 1980.

Dollar Politics. 3d ed. Washington, D.C.: Congressional Quarterly, 1982.

Domhoff, G. William. *Fat Cats and Democrats: The Role of the Big Rich in the Party of the Common Man.* Englewood Cliffs, N.J.: Prentice-Hall, 1972.

———. *The Power Elite and the State: How Policy Is Made in America.* New York: Adline de Gruyter, 1990.

Drew, Elizabeth. *Politics and Money: The New Road to Corruption.* New York: Macmillan, 1983.

Dunn, Delmer. *Financing Presidential Campaigns.* Washington, D.C.: Brookings Institution, 1972.

Eismeier, Thomas J., and Philip H. Pollock III. *Business, Money, and the Rise of Corporate PACs in American Elections.* Westport, Conn.: Quorum Books, 1988.

Etzioni, Amitai. *Capital Corruption: The New Attack on American Democracy.* New York: Harcourt Brace Jovanovich, 1984.

Ewing, Keith. *The Funding of Political Parties in Britain.* Cambridge, England: Cambridge University Press, 1987.

Fleishman, Joel L., ed. *The Future of American Political Parties.* Englewood Cliffs, N.J.: Prentice-Hall, 1982.

Fowler, Linda L., and Robert D. McClure. *Political Ambition: Who Decides to Run for Congress.* New Haven, Conn.: Yale University Press, 1989.

Godwin, R. Kenneth. *One Billion Dollars of Influence: The Direct Marketing of Politics.* Chatham, N.J.: Chatham House Publishers, 1988.

Goldenberg, Edie N., and Michael W. Traugott. *Campaigning for Congress.* Washington, D.C.: CQ Press, 1984.

Golembiewski, Robert T., and Aaron Wildavsky, eds. *The Costs of Federalism.* New Brunswick, N.J.: Transaction Books, 1984.

Graber, Doris A. *Mass Media and American Politics.* Washington, D.C.: CQ Press, 1980.

Handler, Edward, and John R. Mulkern. *Business in Politics.* Lexington, Mass.: D. C. Heath and Co., 1982.

Heard, Alexander. *The Costs of Democracy.* Chapel Hill: University of North Carolina Press, 1960.

Heath, Robert L., ed. *Strategic Issues Management.* San Francisco: Jossey-Bass Publishers, 1988.

Heidenheimer, Arnold J., ed. *Comparative Political Finance: The Financing of Party Organizations and Election Campaigns.* Lexington, Mass.: D. C. Heath and Co., 1970.

Heidenheimer, Arnold J., Michael Johnston, and Victor T. Levine, eds. *Political Corruption: A Handbook.* New Brunswick, N.J.: Transaction Books, 1989.

Jackson, Brooks. *Honest Graft: Big Money and the American Political Process.* Rev. ed. Washington, D.C.: Farragut Publishing Co., 1990.

Jacobson, Gary C. *Money in Congressional Elections.* New Haven, Conn.: Yale University Press, 1980.

———. *The Politics of Congressional Elections.* 2d ed. Boston: Little, Brown and Co., 1987.

Jacobson, Gary C., and Samuel Kernell. *Strategy and Choice in Congressional Elections.* New Haven, Conn.: Yale University Press, 1981.

Kay, James B., and Paul H. Rubin. *Congressmen, Constituents, and Contributors.* Boston: Martinus Nijhoff Publishing, 1982.

Magleby, David B., and Candice J. Nelson. *The Money Chase: Congressional Campaign Finance Reform.* Washington, D.C.: Brookings Institution, 1990.

Maisel, L. Sandy, ed. *Changing Campaign Techniques: Elections and Values in Contemporary Democracies.* Beverly Hills: Sage Publications, 1976.

———, ed. *The Parties Respond: Changes in the American Party System.* Boulder, Colo.: Westview Press, 1990.

Malbin, Michael J., ed. *Money and Politics in the United States: Financing Elections in the 1980s.* Chatham, N.J.: Chatham House Publishers and American Enterprise Institute for Public Policy Research, 1984.

———, ed. *Parties, Interest Groups, and Campaign Finance Laws.* Washington, D.C.: American Enterprise Institute for Public Policy Research, 1980.

McCarthy, Max. *Elections for Sale.* Boston: Houghton-Mifflin, 1972.

McKenna, George, and Stanley Feingold. *Taking Sides.* 7th ed. Guilford, Conn.: Dushkin Publishing Group, 1991.

Mutch, Robert E. *Campaigns, Congress, and Courts: The Making of Federal Campaign Finance Law.* New York: Praeger Publishers, 1988.

Newquest, Marilyn Fuller. *The Political Reform Act of 1974: A Case Study in California's Initiative Process.* Los Alamitos, Calif.: Hwong Publishing Co., 1981.

Nichols, David. *Financing Elections: The Politics of an American Ruling Class.* New York: New Viewpoints, A Division of Franklin Watts, 1974.

Nugent, Margaret Latus, and John R. Johannes, eds. *Money, Elections, and Democracy: Reforming Congressional Campaign Finance.* Boulder, Colo.: Westview Press, 1990.

Overacker, Louise. *Money in Elections.* New York: Macmillan, 1932.

Patterson, Thomas E. *The Mass Media Election.* New York: Praeger Publishers, 1980.

Patterson, Thomas E., and Robert D. McClure. *The Unseeing Eye.* New York: G. P. Putnam's Sons, 1976.

Peabody, Robert L., et al. *To Enact a Law: Congress and Campaign Financing.* New York: Praeger Publishers, 1972.

Pinto-Duschinsky, Michael. *British Political Finance 1830-1980.* Washington,

D.C.: American Enterprise Institue for Public Policy Research, 1981.
Polsby, Nelson W. *The Consequences of Party Reform*. Oxford, England: Oxford University Press, 1983.
Pomper, Gerald, ed. *The Election of 1988: Reports and Interpretations*. New York: Chatham House Publishers, 1989.
Ranney, Austin. *Channels of Power: The Impact of Television on American Politics*. New York: Basic Books, 1984.
——. *Curing the Mischiefs of Faction: Party Reform in America*. Berkeley: University of California Press, 1975.
Rose, Gary L., ed. *Controversial Issues in Presidential Selection*. Albany, N.Y.: State University of New York Press, 1991.
Sabato, Larry J. *Feeding Frenzy*. New York: Free Press, 1991.
——. *PAC Power: Inside the World of Political Action Committees*. New York: W. W. Norton and Co., 1984.
——. *The Party's Just Begun*. Glenville, Ill.: Scott, Foresman and Co., 1988.
——. *The Rise of Political Consultants: New Ways of Winning Elections*. New York: Basic Books, 1981.
Sanford, Terry. *A Danger of Democracy: The Presidential Nominating Process*. Boulder, Colo.: Westview Press, 1981.
Schwarz, Thomas J., and Alan G. Straus. *Federal Regulation of Campaign Finance and Political Activity*. Vol. 1 and 2. New York: Matthew Bender, 1982. Gross, Kenneth A. *Supplement, 1989-1990*. Los Angeles: Citizens' Research Foundation, 1990.
Shannon, Jasper B. *Money and Politics*. New York: Random House, 1959.
Sorauf, Frank J. *Money in American Elections*. Glenville, Ill.: Scott, Foresman and Co., 1988.
Stern, Philip M. *The Best Congress Money Can Buy*. New York: Pantheon Books, 1988.
Thayer, George. *Who Shakes the Money Tree? American Financing Practices from 1789 to the Present*. New York: Simon and Schuster, 1973.
Viguerie, Richard A. *The New Right: We're Ready to Lead*. Falls Church, Va.: Viguerie Co., 1981.

Reports and Articles

Adamany, David. "Money, Politics, and Democracy: A Review Essay." *American Political Science Review* 71:1 (March 1977).
——. "Political Finance in Transition." *Polity* 14 (Winter 1981).
Alexander, Herbert E. *The Case for PACs*. Washington, D.C.: Public Affairs Council, 1983.
——. "Communications and Politics: The Media and the Message." Part 1. *Law and Contemporary Problems* (Spring 1969).
——. "Financing Presidential Campaigns," in Arthur M. Schlesinger, Jr., and Fred L. Israel, eds., *History of American Presidential Elections 1789-1968*. Vol. 4. New York: Chelsea House Publishers (1971), 3869-3897.
——. "The High Cost of TV Campaigns." *Television Quarterly* 5:1 (Winter 1966).
——. "The Impact of the Federal Election Campaign Act on the 1976 Presidential Campaign: The Complexities of Compliance." *Emory Law Journal* 29:2 (Spring 1980).
——. "The Obey-Railsback Bill: Its Genesis and Early History." *Arizona Law Review* 22:2 (1980).
——. *Reform and Reality in Campaign Finance: The State and Local Experience*.

New York: Priority Press Publications, 1991.

———. *Soft Money and Campaign Financing.* Washington, D.C.: Public Affairs Council, 1985.

———. *Strategies for Election Reform.* Washington, D.C.: Project for Comprehensive Campaign Reform, April 1989.

———, ed. "Political Finance: Reform and Reality." *Annals of the American Academy of Political and Social Sciences* 425 (May 1976).

Alexander, Herbert E., and J. Paul Molloy. *Model State Statute: Politics, Elections, and Public Office.* Princeton, N.J.: Citizens' Research Foundation, 1974.

California Commission on Campaign Financing. *The New Gold Rush: Financing California's Legislative Campaigns: 1985 Report and Recommendations.* Los Angeles: Center for Responsive Government, 1985. 1987 update.

Cantor, Joseph E. *Campaign Financing in Federal Elections: A Guide to the Law and Its Operation.* Washington, D.C.: Congressional Research Service, Library of Congress, 1986.

———. *The Evolution of and Issues Surrounding Independent Expenditures in Election Campaigns.* Washington, D.C.: Congressional Research Service, Library of Congress, May 5, 1982.

———. *Political Action Committees: Their Evolution, Growth, and Implications for the Political System.* Washington, D.C.: Congressional Research Service, Library of Congress, November 6, 1981. April 30, 1984, and April 21, 1986, updates.

Center for Responsive Politics. *Open Secrets: The Dollar Power of PACs in Congress.* Washington, D.C.: Congressional Quarterly, 1990.

———. *Public Policy and Foundations: The Role of Politicians in Public Charities.* Washington, D.C.: Center for Responsive Politics, 1987.

Chaffee, Kevin. *Saving for a Rainy Day: How Congress Turns Leftover Cash into 'Golden Parachutes.'* Washington, D.C.: Center for Public Integrity, 1991.

Commission on National Elections. *Electing the President: A Program for Reform: Final Report.* Washington, D.C.: Center for Strategic and International Studies, Georgetown University, 1986.

A Common Cause Guide to Money, Power, and Politics in the 97th Congress. Washington, D.C.: Common Cause, 1981.

Council on Governmental Ethics Laws (COGEL). *A Model Law for Campaign Finance, Ethics, and Lobbying Regulation.* Lexington, Ky.: COGEL, July 1990.

———. *COGEL Blue Book: Campaign Finance: Ethics and Lobby Law.* 8th ed. Lexington, Ky.: COGEL, 1990.

Cutler, Lloyd N., Louis R. Cohen, Roger M. Witten. "Regulating Campaign Finance." *Annals of the American Academy of Political and Social Science* 486 (July 1986).

Electing Congress: The Financial Dilemma: Report of the Twentieth Century Fund Task Force on Financing Congressional Campaigns. New York: Twentieth Century Fund, 1970.

Federal Election Commission. *Combined Federal/State Disclosure Directory 1990.* Washington, D.C., 1990.

Financing a Better Election System: A Statement on National Policy by the Research and Policy Committee, Committee for Economic Development. New York, December 1968.

Financing Presidential Campaigns: Report of the President's Commission on Campaign Costs. Washington, D.C.: Government Printing Office, April 1962.

Grassmuck, George, ed. *Before Nomination: Our Primary Problems.* Washington, D.C.: American Enterprise Institute for Public Policy Research, 1985.

Green, Bruce A., ed. *Government Ethics Reform for the 1990s: The Collected Reports of the New York State Commission on Government Integrity.* New York: Fordham University Press, 1991.

Institute of Politics, John F. Kennedy School of Government, Harvard University. *An Analysis of the Impact of the Federal Election Campaign Act, 1972-1978.* Prepared for the House Administration Committee. 96th Cong., 1st sess., 1979.

Jackson, Brooks. *Broken Promise: Why the Federal Election Commission Failed.* New York: Priority Press Publications, 1990.

Kirby, James C., Jr. *Congress and the Public Trust: Report of the Association of the Bar of the City of New York Special Committee on Congressional Ethics.* New York: Atheneum, 1970.

Leonard, Dick. *Paying for Party Politics: The Case for Public Subsidies.* London: PEP, 1975.

Lowenstein, Daniel Hays. "On Campaign Finance Reform: The Root of All Evil Is Deeply Rooted." *Hofstra Law Review* 18:2 (Fall 1989).

Lydenberg, Stephen D. *Bankrolling Ballots Update 1980: The Role of Business in Financing Ballot Question Campaigns.* New York: Council on Economic Priorities, 1981.

Makinson, Larry. *The Price of Admission: An Illustrated Atlas of Spending in the 1988 Congressional Elections.* Washington, D.C.: Center for Responsive Politics, July 1989.

———. *The Price of Admission: Campaign Spending in the 1990 Elections.* Washington, D.C.: Center for Responsive Politics, September 1991.

Minow, Newton N., and Clifford M. Sloan. *For Great Debates: A New Plan for Future Presidential TV Debates.* New York: Priority Press Publications, 1987.

Money, Parties, and the Electoral Process: Report on Conference of California Committee for Party Renewal-Southern California. Los Angeles, October 8, 1983.

Moussalli, Stephanie D. "Campaign Finance Reform: The Case for Deregulation," in *The Madison Papers.* No. 5. Tallahassee, Fla.: James Madison Institute for Public Policy Studies, 1990.

National Clearinghouse on Election Administration, Federal Election Commission. *Campaign Finance Law 90.* Washington, D.C.: Federal Election Commission, 1990.

New York City Campaign Finance Board. *Dollars and Disclosure: Campaign Finance Reform in New York City.* New York: New York City Campaign Finance Board, September 1990.

The PAC Directory. Cambridge, Mass.: Ballinger Publishing Co., 1982.

Paying for Politics: The Report of the Commission upon the Financing of Political Parties. London: Hansard Society for Parliamentary Government, July 1981.

Peck, Louis M., "Campaign Financing," *Congressional Quarterly Issue Briefs*, no. 101-08, June 9, 1990.

Penniman, Howard R., and Ralph K. Winter, Jr. *Campaign Finance: Two Views of the Political and Constitutional Implications.* Washington, D.C.: American Enterprise Institute for Public Policy Research, 1971.

Pinto-Duschinsky, Michael. "Foreign Political Aid: The German Political Foundations and Their U.S. Counterparts." *International Affairs* 67, Vol. 1, 33-63. London: Royal Institute of International Affairs, 1991.

Project for Comprehensive Campaign Reform. *Executive Summary of the Study on Campaign Finance*. Washington, D.C.: Project for Comprehensive Campaign Reform, April 1989.

Ranney, Austin, ed. *The Past and Future of Presidential Debates*. Washington, D.C.: American Enterprise Institute for Public Policy Research, 1979.

Robinson, Donald L., ed. *Reforming American Government: The Bicentennial Papers of the Committee on the Constitutional System*. Boulder, Colo.: Westview Press, 1985.

Roeder, Edward. *PACs Americana*. Washington, D.C.: Sunshine Services Corp., 1982.

Sabato, Larry J. *Campaign Finance Reform Ideas: The Good, the Bad, and the Ugly*. Washington, D.C.: Project for Comprehensive Campaign Reform, April 1989.

———. *Paying for Elections: The Campaign Finance Thicket*. New York: Priority Press Publications, 1989.

Schwarz, Thomas J. *Public Financing of Elections: A Constitutional Division of the Wealth*. Chicago: American Bar Association, Special Committee on Election Reform, 1975.

Sorauf, Frank J. "Campaign Money and the Press." *Political Science Quarterly* 102:1 (Spring 1987).

Symposium on Campaign Financing Regulation. Tiburon, Calif.: American Bar Association, Special Committee on Election Reform, April 1975.

United States Senate. *Campaign Finance Reform: A Report to the Majority Leader and Minority Leader*. Washington, D.C.: Government Printing Office, March 6, 1990.

Voter's Time: Report of the Twentieth Century Fund Commission on Campaign Costs in the Electronic Era. New York: Twentieth Century Fund, 1969.

What Price PACs?: Report of the Twentieth Century Fund Task Force on Political Action Committees. New York: Twentieth Century Fund, 1984.

White, George H. *A Study of Access to Television for Political Candidates*. Cambridge, Mass.: Institute of Politics, John F. Kennedy School of Government, Harvard University, May 1978.

Wilcox, Clyde. *Financing Congressional Campaigns*. Washington, D.C.: American Political Science Association, 1988.

Winter, Ralph K., Jr., *Campaign Financing and Political Freedom*. Washington, D.C.: American Enterprise Institute for Public Policy Research, 1973.

Zelman, Walter A. *Twenty Who Gave $16 Million: A Study of Money and Politics in California 1975-1982*. Los Angeles: Common Cause, 1983.

Zuckerman, Edward, ed. *Almanac of Federal PACs*. Washington, D.C.: Amward Publications, 1990.

Index